"I consider it an honor and a mitz  Schwartz's work and all his endeavor health, the environment, and related is ~~~~ ~~~~~~~, especially to those of us who seek to lead a religiously observant lifestyle, in keeping with the precepts and goals of the Torah. May his efforts merit Divine blessing and success."—**Rabbi David Rosen**, Former Chief Rabbi of Ireland; President for Israel of the International Jewish Vegetarian Society

"Few books have ever been more timely or more needed than this one. Humankind stands on the brink of one of the greatest catastrophes in history and, once again, Richard Schwartz has rallied to the cause. Proving himself to be the true *tzadik* that he is, he addresses issues that will help humanity face a future too ghastly to contemplate if we do not immediately do something to curb the coming cataclysm. And it all starts at a very simple place . . . on our dinner plates!"—**Lionel Friedberg**, film producer, director, cinematographer, and writer of many documentaries, including *A Sacred Duty: Applying Jewish Values to Help Heal the World*

"I applaud Richard Schwartz's valiant efforts to raise the issue of a plant-based diet within the Jewish community. He taps into a millennia-old Jewish tradition supporting compassion toward animals, and does so at a time when all life on Earth depends on wise human action. He thoughtfully examines what type of food consumption fits with the ethics of kosher, which means appropriate. May God bless his holy efforts!"—**Rabbi Yonatan Neril**, Founder and Executive Director of the Interfaith Center for Sustainable Development and of Jewish Eco Seminars

"Once again Richard Schwartz has produced a thought-provoking book. It will be a very positive addition to our libraries. His writing is powerful in applying Jewish teachings to current critical issues. As always, Richard is not afraid to challenge us."—**Rabbi Michael M. Cohen**, Director of Development at the Friends of the Arava Institute for Environmental Studies

"This book is so crucial and urgently necessary! We once again owe deep gratitude to Professor Richard Schwartz for opening our minds and hearts to the essence of Jewish ethics!"—**Rabbi Dr. Shmuly Yanklowitz**, Founder and CEO of Shamayim v'Aretz: Jewish Animal Advocacy, and author or editor of over a dozen books of Judaica, including three on Jewish dietary teachings

"No one has been more creative, committed, and consistent than Richard Schwartz in arguing for a Judaism that can address in all its depth the world crises that all humanity and all the life-forms of our planet face today."
—**Rabbi Arthur Waskow**, director of The Shalom Center, author of *Down-to-Earth Judaism, Seasons of Our Joy*, and many other works on Jewish thought and action

"If you think Judaism consists of occasional visits to a synagogue or Temple where congregants perform rituals and recite prayers without feeling and attend mainly to socialize, then this book is a must read. Schwartz reminds us that the very essence of Judaism is to struggle to find what is right and to have the courage to do right, including speaking out against evil. Worship accompanied by indifference to evil, the prophets warned, is an abomination to God. Schwartz fulfills the best of Judaism by urging us to cry out against immorality, injustice, deceit, cruelty, and violence toward all living beings, rather than condone it with our silence. For, in condoning empty rituals and standing silent in the face of immoral deeds, we make a mockery of Judaism itself."—**Nina Natelson**, Director of Concern for Helping Animals in Israel (CHAI)

"I commend Dr. Schwartz for his integrity in reminding the Jewish community of its historic mission to serve as a light unto the nations. While most Jewish leaders are content to tell people what they want to hear, Dr. Schwartz, in his new book, speaks out in true prophetic spirit, courageously challenging our people to live up to the highest ideals of our heritage by acting as responsible stewards of our planet, speaking out for the voiceless, taking the side of the oppressed, and practicing kindness towards animals. Dr. Schwartz serves as a lightning rod to stimulate critically needed discussion about what it really means to be Jewish in more than just name alone, and how to live a Jewish life."—**Rabbi Barry Silver**, serving Congregation L'Dor Va-Dor in Boynton Beach, Florida, former State Representative, founder of the Palm Beach County Environmental Coalition and founder and leader of the Interfaith Justice League

"We are stewards of God's creation—how do we treat those with whom we share this world? Here is a passionate and compassionate guide to choosing what we eat and why."—**Rabbi David Wolpe**, rabbi at Sinai Temple in California and the author of many books on Jewish teachings

"This book by Prof. Richard Schwartz not only offers the reader a comprehensive research into Jewish teachings and their relevance to contemporary science and world affairs. It challenges the reader with an urgent cry out for action. For about forty years Schwartz has been a world authority on the deep linkage between Judaism and vegetarianism. Now he shows that a vegan revolution has been starting—in Israel and worldwide. But is it fast enough to save us from ecological catastrophe? And is the Jewish establishment assuming the role it should play within it? These are questions Schwartz addresses."—**Yossi Wolfson**, vegan and animal rights activist in Israel and coordinator of the Israeli Jewish Vegetarian Society in Jerusalem

"A timely, comprehensive, and much-needed contribution to our movement, Richard Schwartz's latest book presents an utterly compelling case for Jewish veganism, and more widely, for conscious consumption."—**Lara Balsam**, Director, UK-based Jewish Vegetarian Society

"Richard Schwartz has been a consistent, clear, compassionate voice for the planet. This book once again illustrates his wisdom, insight, and willingness to speak up. If the Jewish community takes this book to heart and makes the necessary changes, the world can follow. We can co-create a world that respects all life."—**Rae Sikora**, co-founder Plant Peace Daily, Institute for Humane Education, and Vegfund

"Reading the first edition of Richard Schwartz's book *Judaism and Vegetarianism* changed my life. It made me a vegetarian and an animal rights activist and led me to write and edit several books about these issues. I have worked with Richard now for decades in his tireless efforts to create a more compassionate, just, and environmentally sustainable world. Now, the vegan/vegetarian movement is the most important movement of our time, affecting the environment and our lives, and Richard's superb new book is an important continuation of his long-time efforts to elucidate this point."
—**Roberta Kalechofsky, PhD**, author or editor of many books, including *Jewish Vegetarianism, Rabbis and Vegetarianism*, and *Judaism and Animal Rights*; Founder and Director of Jews for Animal Rights

"When I consider Judaism and its highest ideals, I realize how consistent it is with veganism: being respectful and compassionate, protecting life and resources, guarding and increasing health, pursuing peace and justice, living by one's values. I have worked with Richard Schwartz for a long time and know him to be extraordinarily sincere, diligent, conscientious, respectful, caring, compassionate, intelligent, and deeply dedicated to Judaism, so much so that he is deserving of the Nobel Peace Prize. As with his previous books that have illuminated so many lives with their insight and wisdom, I likewise heartily recommend this book. Well-researched, well-written, well-thought-out, and absolutely vital for the continuation of life on our planet. Especially in this era of population explosion, overconsumption, globalization, and our climate crisis, this book needs to be read and shared."—**Dan Brook, PhD**, professor of sociology at San Jose State University and a board member of San Francisco Veg Society

"Richard Schwartz's new book is a clarion call, a shofar blast, to disturb the slumber of indifference and to align Judaism with its noblest values."
—**Jeffrey Spitz Cohan**, executive director of Jewish Veg, formerly Jewish Vegetarians of North America

"No one has done more than Richard Schwartz to advance the understanding of the relationship between Judaism, the environment, and respect for non-human animals. Like a modern-day prophet, Schwartz sees Jews straying from biblical edicts for Earth stewardship and prods us to embrace divinely ordained and inspired environmental action."—**David Krantz**, President and Chairperson at Aytzim: Ecological Judaism

"This pioneering book by Richard Schwartz, the world's greatest living authority on the teachings of Judaism on protecting animals and nature, provides nothing short of the revolution in our way of thinking and acting that is now required in efforts to avert a climate catastrophe and other environmental disasters. This compelling, magisterial book is a must read. Its message must be heeded. Our future depends on it."—**Lewis Regenstein**, author of "Commandments of Compassion: Jewish Teachings on Protecting the Planet and Its Creatures," *Replenish the Earth*, and other writings on Judaism and animals

VEGAN REVOLUTION

SAVING OUR WORLD, REVITALIZING JUDAISM

RICHARD H. SCHWARTZ, PhD

Lantern Publishing & Media ● Brooklyn, NY

2020
Lantern Publishing & Media
128 Second Place
Brooklyn, NY 11231
www.lanternpm.org

Printed in the United States of America

Quotations from the Tanakh are taken from "The Complete Tanakh
(Tanach)—Hebrew Bible: The Jewish Bible with a Modern English
Translation and Rashi's Commentary" https://www.chabad.org/
library/bible_cdo/aid/63255/jewish/The-Bible-with-Rashi.htm.

Library of Congress Cataloging-in-Publication Data

Names: Schwartz, Richard H., author.
Title: Vegan revolution : saving our world, revitalizing Judaism /
    Richard H. Schwartz, PhD.
Description: Brooklyn, NY : Lantern Publishing & Media, 2020. |
    Includes bibliographical references.
Identifiers: LCCN 2020022490 (print) | LCCN 2020022491 (ebook) |
    ISBN 9781590566275 (paperback) | ISBN 9781590566282 (ebook)
Subjects: LCSH: Veganism—Religious aspects—Judaism. | Jewish
    ethics.
Classification: LCC BM538.V42 S39 2020 (print) | LCC BM538.V42
    (ebook) | DDC 296.3/693—dc23
LC record available at https://lccn.loc.gov/2020022490
LC ebook record available at https://lccn.loc.gov/2020022491

To all the world's vegans, who are the vanguard of a movement that can help shift our imperiled planet onto a sustainable path and help revitalize Judaism and other religions; and

To my very devoted, supportive wife, Loretta, and our children and their spouses, our grandchildren, and our one great-grandson, with my hope that this book will help produce a more compassionate, just, peaceful, and environmentally sustainable world for them to enjoy; and

To my beloved sister, Muriel Gursky, who passed away as this book was being completed, as she approached her ninety-second birthday. May her memory continue to be a blessing. As Scottish poet Thomas Campbell expressed it: "To live in hearts we leave behind is not to die."

CONTENTS

PREFACE
About the Cover

Before this book was published, I showed some family members and advisors the cover design to see if they had suggestions for improvements. Although the response was very positive and sometimes extremely complimentary, several were puzzled about why the Hebrew capital letter *ayin* was on the front cover.

My short answer was that it looks like the *V* in the words *vegan* and *revolution* that compose the title of this book and adds a Hebrew touch to the cover, something very appropriate in a book that bases its arguments on fundamental Jewish values.

But there are several much deeper reasons. *Ayin* is not just a Hebrew letter; it is also a word that means "eye." This is very meaningful for my book because its major aim is to help Jews and others see the world and human activities from a new perspective—to see, recognize, and act on the knowledge that veganism is the diet and lifestyle most consistent with basic Jewish teachings on preserving our health, treating animals with compassion, protecting the environment, conserving natural resources, feeding hungry people, and pursuing peace; and that animal-based diets are contributing substantially to an epidemic of life-threatening diseases, climate change and other environmental threats, wasteful use of natural resources, widespread hunger, and other societal problems.

In addition, Judaism has many lessons on the importance of properly seeing situations and foreseeing the consequences of one's actions.

The Hebrew sages asked the question, "Who is wise?" One response was, "The person who foresees the consequences of his or her actions" (*Tamid* 32a). The failure to foresee the negative consequences of having animal-based diets and agriculture has led to the current epidemic of heart disease, cancer, and other life-threatening diseases, climate and other environmental threats, and other negative outcomes.

As I write this, many people have perished because our leaders did not have the vision to see and recognize that our continued massive abuse and consumption of animals could lead to the devastating coronavirus pandemic, ignoring the lessons learned from many previous pandemics, including SARS, MERS, Ebola, swine flu, and avian flu, that were caused by eating animals after raising them in close, unsanitary confinement. *A Vision of Vegetarianism and Peace* is the title of a collection of the vegetarian writings of Rabbi Abraham Isaac Hakohen Kook (Rav Kook), first chief rabbi of pre-state Israel, who believed that the Messianic period would be vegetarian.

The Hebrew words *nega* and *oneg* have the same letters, *nun, gimmel,* and *ayin. Nega* translates to "plague" and *oneg* to a "joyous event": quite different meanings. Why is this significant? For the word *nega,* the *ayin* comes at the end of the word, symbolically denoting that when we act before envisioning the possible consequences of our actions, the results can be very negative. By contrast, the word *oneg* has the *ayin* at the front of the word, symbolically suggesting that when one takes the time to envision the consequences of a potential action before acting, a positive result will be far more likely.

The Torah discusses a *nega,* a skin condition called *tzaarat* that afflicted many Israelites. The Jewish sages thought it was due to spiritual failings, one of which they considered to be *zarut ayin,* or "narrowness of vision." Narrow vision means not paying attention to the wider ramifications of one's actions. It is a decision-making process guided purely by the desire for immediate gratification, and not a larger plan to reach a positive goal.

Today, the world is, in effect, also suffering from narrowness of vision, as most people concentrate on immediate satisfactions, blocking them from seeing how horribly farmed animals are treated, how the planet is being threatened, and other negative effects of animal-based diets. This has resulted, as in biblical times, in a skin condition, but this time for the surface of the entire world, as deserts expand, forests are scorched, and oceans become increasingly polluted, heated, and acidified.

When the watchword of the Jewish faith, the *Sh'ma*, appears in the Torah in the Book of Deuteronomy, the *ayin* in the first word and the *daled* in the final word in the opening sentence are written larger, spelling the Hebrew word *aid*, which means "witness" in Hebrew. Jews are mandated to be God's witnesses, striving to make the world closer to God's desires, based on observations of unjust aspects of society. By coincidence, the word *aid* means to help in English, which describes the Jewish mission to help others.

Interestingly, this book's wonderful publisher has the name of Lantern. The purpose of a lantern is to shine a light into a dark area. That is also basically the purpose of this book, which aims to spotlight issues about animal-based diets and agriculture that most people seem to prefer to stay in the dark about.

There are additional interesting Jewish connections with the letter *ayin* and the importance of vision in the Jewish tradition.

The two letters *ayin* and *daled* also spell out the Hebrew word *ad*, which can mean "eternal." People always believed that humanity would exist eternally. Due to climate change causing a much warmer world, this is no longer assured. It is the purpose of this book to increase awareness of this major threat and the urgent need to take steps to prevent it.

FOREWORD

Rabbi David Rosen

The sages of the Midrash declare in relation to the laws of *kashrut* that the Commandments were given only to refine God's creatures. In keeping with this idea, both Maimonides and Nachmanides affirm that the purpose of the precepts of the Torah is to improve human character, instilling noble traits—above all, compassion.

Accordingly, even though Judaism permits the slaughter and consumption of certain animals and their products, it lays down extremely demanding conditions for such, which both the sages of the Talmud and later *rishonim* (commentators from the eleventh to fifteenth centuries) understood as having the purpose of minimizing animal pain and promoting compassion in consonance with the prohibition of *tza'ar ba'alei chayim* (causing needless cruelty to animals).

In more modern times, Rav Kook, first chief rabbi of pre-state Israel, expanded extensively on this theme,[1] highlighting a plant-based diet as the biblical ideal; that the consumption of animal products was a temporary concession; and envisioning the ideal society, the Messianic age, as one in which this understanding and compassion is manifest.

Indeed, compassion is portrayed by our sages as the defining Jewish character trait, so much so that they declare (*Beitzah* 32b) that it is compassion that proves whether or not one is an authentic descendent of the patriarch Abraham (thus questioning the provenance of one lacking in compassion). Moreover, compassion is at the heart of the key mitzvah

---

1   *Hazon Hatzimhonut Vehashalom*, ed. David HaCohen (Berlin: HaPeles, 1903).

to cleave to/emulate the Divine. Psalm 145:9 declares: "God's mercies are upon all His works" and thus we are told: "Just as He is compassionate and merciful, so you be compassionate and merciful" (*Shabbat* 133b; *Yerushalmi, Pe'ah* 3; *Sofrim* 3:17).

Accordingly, our sages declare that it is by showing compassion toward living creatures that we elicit God's compassion toward us (*Shabbat* 151b. See also *Sefer Hassidim*, 87).

The Talmud indicates that our sages urge us to go even beyond the letter of the law regarding compassion for animals, as reflected in the famous story of Rabbi Yehudah HaNasi, who received Divine punishment for refusing to protect a frightened calf that sought his refuge while being taken to slaughter (*Bava Metzia* 85a).

The tension between the Torah's permissive mandate to use animals and even take animal life for legitimate human needs versus our obligations to care for and be compassionate toward animal life has always raised the question in Jewish jurisprudence of determining what and when is a legitimate human need. Today, however, the questions in this regard are more dramatic than ever before.

There were surely many places and times in the past where the ability to find adequate sustenance from a plant-based diet would have been very difficult indeed. But today, the vast majority of us live in a world where we can obtain all necessary nutrients without needing to consume animal products.

However, the enormous problem and challenge in terms of *halachah* (Jewish law) and ethics for the overwhelming majority of Jews today is the fact that the consumption of animal products involves massive desecration of Jewish precepts and teachings.

It is not only the horrendous cruelty involved in conditions and production as never before that desecrates the above-mentioned prohibition against causing *tza'ar ba'alei chayim*; it is also the enormous waste of natural resources involved in modern factory farming that contravenes the prohibition of *bal tashchit* (against wastage). Judaism also understands the injunction in Deuteronomy 4:15, "You shall diligently guard your soul," to be a prohibition against doing anything that threatens our health. However, in order to survive the condition of factory farming and meet the public demand, animals are injected with hormones and antibiotics that are retained in the animal flesh and that pose a danger to human health (even beyond other health dangers involved in meat consumption).

Moreover, contemporary animal food production poses a very great threat to our environment (which humanity is charged in Genesis 2:15 to develop and protect), inordinately contributing to climate change (more than all the forms of transport in our world combined), imperiling human welfare and survival, which we are obliged to preserve and nurture. Indeed, Judaism's very affirmation that our world is a Divine Creation means that actions that lead to its degradation and destruction are in fact violations against the Creator.

There are those of our co-religionists who argue that these violations do not in themselves compromise the *kashrut* of products, as long as the actual slaughter and preparation are done in accordance with the letter of the law.

To begin with, one must respond that this is a dubious contention when the end result is perforce contingent upon known and willful transgressions. Moreover, the idea that one can consider a product kosher because the final fulfillment of the letter of the law is legitimate even when it is part and parcel of a major desecration of the spirit and purpose of *kashrut* makes a mockery of the precept. However, there is unquestionably an incontestable *halachic* violation in consuming these products today, as such consumption perforce encourages the continuation of the aforementioned violations and transgressions. This falls under the prohibition, "You shall not put a stumbling block in front of a blind person" (Leviticus 19:14), which Jewish sages understand to apply to any action which encourages others to violate religious prohibitions.

For all these reasons, the honest conclusion must be that *it is virtually impossible today to live in accordance with Jewish religious requirements if one is party to the consumption of animal products, especially in Western society; and that a contemporary dietary lifestyle that is consistent with* kashrut *in practice and in spirit must be a plant-based diet.*

I thus consider it an honor and a mitzvah to commend Professor Richard Schwartz's work and all his endeavors to bring this imperative to public attention, especially to those of us who seek to lead a religiously observant lifestyle in keeping with the precepts and goals of the Torah.

May his efforts merit Divine blessing and success, in keeping with the words of Psalm 90:17: "And may the pleasantness of the Lord our God be upon us and the work of our hands established for us; indeed may You establish the work of our hands."

Rabbi David Rosen *is former chief rabbi of Ireland and president for Israel of the International Jewish Vegetarian Society.*

INTRODUCTION
A Lifelong Journey

The time is short and the work is great. . . . We are not obligated to complete the task, but neither are we free to desist from doing all we can.

—*Pirkei Avot* 2:21

At the age of eighty-six, I find my attention increasingly focused on the future of those I love, the future of humanity, and the future of all of Earth's other inhabitants. Like many, I am deeply concerned about climate change, and I am distressed by humanity's refusal to confront this threat in meaningful ways. *Vegan Revolution* argues that, for practical and spiritual reasons, it is crucial that personally and collectively we shift toward a vegan diet. The book highlights my Jewish religion, but its principles apply to every religion and to every ethic that includes concern for others.

Writing this book has given me an opportunity to reflect on the long and circuitous journey I've taken to where I am today—a person of faith, a vegan, and someone living in Israel. Until January 1, 1978, I was a "meat and potatoes" person. My mother would be sure to prepare my then-favorite dish, pot roast, whenever I came to visit with my wife and children. It was a family tradition that I would be served a turkey "drumstick" every Thanksgiving. Yet, I now devote a major part of my time to writing, speaking, and teaching about the benefits of veganism and about related issues. What caused this major change?

In 1973, I created a course, "Mathematics and the Environment," at the College of Staten Island and taught it until 1999, when I retired from full-time teaching. The course was designed to show liberal-arts, non-science students, who were generally poorly prepared and poorly motivated in their study of mathematics but were required to take one mathematics course to meet a graduation requirement, that mathematics could be interesting, important, and fun. The course used basic mathematical concepts, including statistics, probability, sequences, and graph interpretation, to explore critical issues, such as climate change, pollution, resource scarcities, hunger, energy, population growth, the arms race, nutrition, and health.

While reviewing material related to world hunger for the course, I became aware of the tremendous waste of grain associated with the production of beef, at a time when hundreds of millions of people were chronically malnourished. Despite my own eating habits, I often led class discussions on the possibility of reducing meat consumption as a way to help lessen global hunger. After several semesters, I took my own advice and gave up eating red meat, while continuing to eat chicken and fish.

I then began to read about the many health benefits of vegetarianism and about the horrible conditions for animals raised on factory farms and how cruelly fishes were killed. I was more and more attracted to vegetarianism, and on January 1, 1978, I joined the London-based International Jewish Vegetarian Society. After becoming more aware of the negative effects of producing and eating dairy products and eggs, I became a vegan in 2000.

After becoming a vegetarian, I started to investigate connections between Judaism and vegetarianism. I did much background reading and attended a course, "Judaism and Vegetarianism," taught by Jonathan Wolf, founder and first president of Jewish Vegetarians of North America (JVNA), at Lincoln Square Synagogue in New York City in 1979. I became convinced that important Jewish mandates to preserve our health, treat animals compassionately, protect the environment, conserve natural resources, share with hungry people, and seek and pursue peace point to vegetarianism as the ideal diet for Jews (and everyone else), and weren't being heard. To get this message to a wider audience, I wrote *Judaism and Vegetarianism*, which was first published in 1982. Later editions came out in 1998 and 2001.

As I learned more and more about the shocking realities of the production and consumption of meat and other animal-sourced foods and their inconsistencies with fundamental Jewish values, I came to view vegetarianism and later veganism as not only important personal choices, but also as religious and societal imperatives, essential components in responding to many national and global problems.

I have always felt good about my decision to become vegetarian and then vegan. Putting principles and values into practice is far more valuable and rewarding than hours of preaching. When people ask me why I do not eat meat and other animal products, I welcome and use the opportunity to explain the many benefits of veganism. While my family was initially skeptical about my change of diet, they have grown ever more understanding and supportive. My wife is now also a vegan, as are one of our daughters and two grandsons, and a granddaughter is a vegetarian. I'm very thankful and pleased to say that they are happy, healthy, and energetic.

It has been a source of pleasure and pride that I've been able to contribute to the cause of Judaism and vegetarianism and veganism (veg*sm) in the course of my life. I became president of the Jewish Vegetarians of North America (now Jewish Veg), where I produced almost weekly email newsletters to keep Jewish vegetarians informed. I followed *Judaism and Vegetarianism* with another work, *Judaism and Global Survival*, and these works as well as hundreds of articles and two dozen podcasts are now available in their archives (JewishVeg.org/Schwartz). I remain president of the Society of Ethical and Religious Vegetarians (SERV), an interreligious group dedicated to spreading vegetarian and vegan messages in religious communities (www.SERV-online.org), and was for several years director of Veg Climate Alliance, a group dedicated to spreading awareness that a major shift to plant-based diets is essential to efforts to avert a climate catastrophe.

In recent years, I've been spending much time attempting to maximize awareness of the need to switch toward vegetarian, and preferably vegan, diets to reduce diseases and to help shift our imperiled planet onto a sustainable path. I've appeared on many radio and cable television programs, had many letters and op-ed articles published in a variety of publications, spoken frequently at conferences and meetings, given dozens of talks, and met with four Israeli chief rabbis and other religious leaders in Israel.

As I reflect on the above, I'm grateful that I have been able to be part of a movement that includes many compassionate, dedicated people who work tirelessly to raise awareness of the many benefits of veganism. Of course, much more needs to be done, and I hope to be able to devote much of any future time I will be blessed with to continuing the struggle.

THE MAKING OF A JEWISH ACTIVIST

I am a *ba'al t'shuvah*—"a Jew who has returned"—in that I started practicing Judaism late in life. I did not grow up in a religious family, and I did not receive a yeshiva education, as observant Jewish children generally do today. Most of my current Jewish learning comes not from formal education, but from extensive reading and conversations with Jews from many different backgrounds, plus Torah classes and lectures over the past few decades.

Like most Jewish children growing up in New York City during the 1940s, I went to a Talmud Torah school a couple of afternoons a week after public school in order to prepare for my bar mitzvah. But I was not particularly interested in Jewish teachings or societal issues.

One aspect of Judaism that did interest me in my early years was the wisdom teachings contained in a section of the *Mishnah* (part of the Talmud) called *Pirkei Avot*, the "Ethics of the Fathers." This tractate contains short, pithy sayings from the early Talmudic rabbis and scholars, providing a basic manual on how to be a good Jew. *Pirkei Avot* is still my favorite section of the *Mishnah*, and its teachings, especially the following, have helped guide me through life:

- You are not required to complete the task, but neither are you free to desist from doing all that you can. (2:21)
- Be of the disciples of Aaron [the brother of Moses]: love peace and pursue peace, love all people, and bring them closer to the Torah. (1:12)

- Who is rich? The person who rejoices in his or her portion. Who is wise? The person who learns from every other person. (4:1)

After graduating from high school in 1952, I was not sure what career to pursue. I finally decided to study civil engineering, mainly because that was the field my older brother had chosen. Because I didn't want to go to an out-of-town college, and because tuition was free at the city university, I attended the City College of New York. Since the campus was far from my home in Far Rockaway, I decided to take advantage of the option to take my pre-engineering courses for two years at Queens College, which was closer.

This decision was a major turning point in my life. Had I started at City College, I would have interacted primarily with engineering students, people interested mostly in mathematical, scientific, and technical concepts. At Queens College, I took liberal arts courses along with students who had a broader range of views and interests. Because I didn't drive at the time, I traveled in various carpools to and from the campus. This put me in contact with a wide variety of students, whose views ranged from very conservative to extremely radical. These conversations prompted me to investigate social justice issues, and I gradually came to see that I had an obligation to personally engage in the struggle against injustice. I began reading books like *The Grapes of Wrath* and viewing films like *Mr. Smith Goes to Washington*, which inspired me to try to learn more and to strive to improve society.

During this time, my involvement with Judaism diminished to practically nothing. I viewed the synagogues and Jewish groups as being primarily concerned with ritual for the sake of ritual. They didn't seem to be involved with the societal causes of the day and consequently seemed totally irrelevant to me. In fact, I was now so committed to working to end society's injustices that I seriously considered becoming an English major, in order to write and make others aware of what I was learning. I loved reading novels and non-fiction books about historical events and social issues. I yearned to learn more and to apply my knowledge in the struggle toward a more just, peaceful, humane, and environmentally sustainable world.

However, family members, fellow students, and college advisors all pointed out how well I was doing in my pre-engineering classes (I had the top grade-point average of all the students in the department), and stressed that I would have a much easier time making a living as an engineer than as a writer. I took their advice and remained in civil engineering, but my feelings about social issues were so strong that I seriously considered not being involved in the world of commerce and business.

Instead, I thought about moving to Israel after graduation to work on a kibbutz. I saw that system of communal living, cooperative efforts, and desire to serve one's community as a model of an ideal community most consistent with my views at that time. I even planned a trip to Israel immediately after graduating from City College, in order to further explore that possibility.

Then, in my final semester, something occurred that represented another major turning point in my life. Because I had the highest grade-point average in my civil engineering class, I was offered a position as an instructor in the Department of Civil Engineering at City College, starting in the spring semester of 1957. I saw this as a great opportunity and quickly accepted the position. This would enable me to help people, and I would stay out of the business world, which I then felt involved trying to advance one's career at the expense of others. As a college instructor, I would be able to apply and teach the many concepts I had learned in my studies. I would also be working with material that I had mastered and enjoyed.

I did go to Israel in the summer of 1957, and I spent some time working on a kibbutz. But my interest in living on a kibbutz was reduced by my great excitement at the prospect of teaching and the honor I felt at being chosen to be a member of City College's Civil Engineering Department, working side-by-side with teachers whom I admired.

I recall spending my last day in Israel excitedly preparing lecture notes for the course on "Strength of Materials" that I would be teaching shortly after my return. At the same time, I had a deep love for Israel, which I regarded as a modern-day miracle. Shortly after I returned to the United States, I gave a talk at a "cousin's club" meeting at which I extolled many aspects of life in Israel.

The next major change in my life came when I married Loretta Susskind, my partner of now over sixty years, in 1960. When I began dating Loretta, she was a social worker in Harlem. We shared an interest in addressing social ills and helping less fortunate people. Loretta came from a more religious family and background than I did. She had continued her Jewish studies beyond the pre-teen Talmud Torah classes and had graduated from Marshalia Hebrew High School. Loretta wanted to introduce Jewish rituals into our family life once we were married. So she presented me with some books on the Sabbath, the *mikveh* (Jewish ritual bath), and other Jewish practices.

I read these books somewhat reluctantly at first, but then with growing interest. I began to see that the Jewish worldview included my ideas about working for a better world. I now understood that the "task" from which *Pirkei Avot* says we are not free to desist is the ongoing process of improving the world. There was plenty of opportunity for a fulfilling spiritual, socially activist life within my own tradition! In fact, the whole saga of Jewish history involved a struggle to maintain the Jewish people and its ethical teachings in the face of oppression, anti-Semitism, hatred, and violence.

The more I read, the more I became interested in learning about all aspects of Judaism. In the process, I began to incorporate some Jewish practices into my own life. At first, I didn't attend synagogue services on Shabbat mornings, but would find a nice quiet place outdoors and read Jewish books on a wide variety of topics. Around this time, Loretta and I purchased a set of five wonderful anthologies: *A Treasury of Jewish Quotations, A Treasury of Jewish Poetry, A Treasury of Jewish Folklore, A Treasury of American Jewish Stories,* and *A Modern Treasury of Jewish Thought.*

As I read *A Modern Treasury of Jewish Thought,* I was thrilled to discover brilliant Jewish thinkers who wrote eloquently about applying Jewish values to the world. I was especially excited by the writings of Rabbi Abraham Joshua Heschel. I relished his radical analysis of Judaism and his challenging criticism of "religious behaviorism," which he defined as performing the *mitzvot* without any real devotion or any attempt to relate them to the realities of our society. And I loved how his words expressed his challenging ideas with a combination of poetic beauty and compelling power.

It was also very important to me that Rabbi Heschel was both a religious Jew and an activist. He marched with Dr. Martin Luther King, Jr., was an early advocate for the liberation of Soviet Jews, helped reform hateful Catholic teachings about Jews by meeting with the Pope and other Catholic leaders, and spoke out courageously against what he (and I) regarded as an illegal, unjust, and immoral war in Vietnam—despite disapproval of his views and activities from many Jewish leaders.

Through Rabbi Heschel, I recognized that my earlier rejection of Judaism was not because of any problems inherent in the religion itself; rather, it was because of what the practice of Judaism in the mid-twentieth century had become. As Heschel put it:

> Religion declined not because it was refuted, but because it became irrelevant, dull, oppressive, insipid. When faith is completely replaced by creed, worship by discipline, love by habit; when the crisis of today is ignored because of the splendor of the past; when faith becomes an heirloom rather than a living fountain; when religion speaks only in the name of authority rather than with the voice of compassion, its message becomes meaningless.[2]

I learned that Judaism supported all my social ideals and that it provides a structure for leading a meaningful and involved spiritual life—if only people would really practice it! I was inspired by Jews who had maintained their beliefs and practices in spite of rejection and perse-cution in many lands and historical periods.

Discovering Martin Buber's writings reinforced my emerging conviction that I was struggling against a distorted understanding of Judaism. I concluded that, in a sense, my religion had been "stolen," as I would much later devote a whole book to exploring. Back in the

---

2   Abraham Joshua Heschel, *God in Search of Man: A Philosophy of Judaism* (New York: Farrar, Straus and Giroux, 1955), 3.

1960s, many observant Jews around me seemed to be locked into ritual for its own sake, without seeing or applying the deeper values that could challenge an unjust status quo. People were reading in the Torah about Moses confronting Pharaoh, but few were confronting the oppressors of our own time.[3]

While teaching at City College, I studied for my master's degree in civil engineering. I was enjoying my teaching and interactions with students so much that I decided to make college teaching my career. However, I didn't want to seek a PhD, because it would involve doing research in a relatively narrow area. Back then, many engineering colleges were accepting professional engineering licenses in lieu of a PhD, so I decided to pursue that path instead. This involved getting some experience working in industry and passing several tests. My teaching experience and strong academic background made passing the tests a relatively easy matter, but I had to leave teaching for a while to get the required experience.

Before entering the engineering field, I decided to take care of my military obligations. At that time, the United States was in a major technological race against the Soviet Union. In 1958, the Soviets surprised the world by launching Sputnik I, the world's first artificial satellite. This was a wake-up call to the U.S. government, a warning that we were falling behind in technology. As a result, engineers were classified by the military into a special category called "Critical Skills."

The government's philosophy at the time was that everyone should get some basic training in order to be ready if the United States was attacked, but that people with special skills should not be taken away for long periods from the important work of improving the nation's technological abilities. Therefore, I only had to be in the U.S. Army for three months. Those few months in the army were the only substantial time in my adult life when I was not focused on studying for tests, preparing class lectures and other talks, researching and writing articles

---

3   Although, as the resources at the end of this book indicate, there are several active Jewish vegan, animal rights, environmental, and social justice organizations, far more needs to be done in the Jewish community to address current social issues.

and books, and dealing with other professional concerns. It was a valuable time for organizing my thoughts about social issues.

After leaving the army, I worked at an engineering company before seeking a position teaching civil engineering at a college. The only civil engineering department willing to hire me was at Rutgers University, but only if I also enrolled as a PhD candidate there. Seeing no other possibility that would enable me to resume teaching, I agreed. So I moved to New Brunswick, New Jersey, with my wife Loretta and our first child, Susan Esther.

I enjoyed my new teaching activities, and once again did well in my engineering studies. However, I had difficulty choosing a topic for my PhD thesis. Fortunately, I finally found a workable topic, "Analysis of Circular Plates on Elastic Foundations under Radially Symmetrical Loadings," which enabled me to use my mathematical skills as well as others. I also received National Science Foundation grants for two consecutive summers, which provided me with some income, enabling me to work full-time on the project. In 1967 I received my PhD in applied mechanics. This enabled me to continue my teaching career until my retirement from the College of Staten Island as a full professor in 1999.

In 1968, Loretta and I moved to Staten Island to be closer to Pratt Institute, where I served in the mechanical engineering department. By then, we had three children: Susan Esther, David Elliot, and Deborah Ann. In 1970, I learned there was an opening at Staten Island Community College (SICC). The college was only about five minutes by car from my house, which would make it easier to help out with the kids. The position had a better salary and benefits as well, so I decided to apply. I was accepted, but only as a substitute in the civil technology department for a professor who had left for a year to help set up Hostos Community College in the Bronx. I was told that the professor for whom I was substituting probably wouldn't come back. However, he did decide to return, and that put me in a very difficult position. I had given up a tenured position at Pratt Institute to be a substitute at SICC. Now it looked like I would have to leave. My efforts at finding another position were not panning out, and I was becoming increasingly desperate.

But, as the Chinese philosopher Lin Yutang says in his book *The Importance of Living,*[4] one does not know what is "good luck" or "bad luck" until the end of a sequence of events, because what appears to be a negative event often leads to a positive result and vice versa. In the Jewish tradition, there is a similar teaching. Joseph, who is sold into slavery by his brothers, ends up becoming an important official in Egypt and saves many people from famine, including those very same brothers who had betrayed him in the first place.

And so it turned out for me: my "bad luck" became my good fortune. During the difficult period when I was trying to find a new teaching position, I went to the director of an experimental department at SICC known as The Place, which offered a number of interdisciplinary courses. I asked about the possibility of teaching in their department. They had no opening at the time, but later, after I was teaching in the mathematics department, they asked me to teach a course on "The Impact of Science on Human Values and Problems."

At first, I hesitated. This topic was completely different from anything I had previously taught or even considered before. At the same time, it offered the possibility of applying my interest in social issues. I decided to accept the offer. That was another major turning point in my life, because teaching that course started me on the path of environmental and vegetarian/vegan activism that I still pursue today.

Through the study of essays, short stories, and plays, the students and I explored the implications of the rapid explosion of scientific and technological advances on society and its problems. This was right after the first Earth Day in April 1970, when there was widespread interest in environmental threats, so we devoted a lot of class time to environmental issues.

As my concern about the environment intensified, the original course was replaced by a new one called "Environmental Issues on Staten Island." I was a relatively new resident of Staten Island, so I had to rely on local resources to help me teach the course. I pored over old newspapers and reports, interviewed Staten Island environmentalists, invited guest speakers, and showed films and videos. We also went on field trips to places like Fresh Kills Landfill (then the world's largest garbage dump).

---

4   Lin Yutang, *The Importance of Living* (New York: William Morrow, 1998), 23.

We also visited different types of housing developments, sewage treatment plants, and natural areas. Instead of a final examination, the students were required to write a report and give an oral presentation about some current environmental issue impacting Staten Island.

Because this course was so different from anything I had previously taught, I devoted a great deal of my time, energy, and thinking to developing it. In the process, I became more active in responding to environmental issues, often writing letters to the editor and articles for publication in the *Staten Island Advance* about local, national, and global environmental and other societal concerns. I also spoke on these topics to various groups at the college and in the community.

After a number of years teaching "Environmental Issues on Staten Island," budgetary considerations led to an end of The Place. As a result, I was no longer able to offer the course. At first, this was a big disappointment. But I soon recognized that this "disaster" had, in fact, freed up a lot of time and energy that I could now devote to other activities. I was determined to continue educating people about environmental issues, and it dawned on me that perhaps I could teach a course that related mathematics to environmental and other global concerns. This led to the creation of my "Mathematics and the Environment" course discussed earlier. The course was well received. I found plenty of valuable material in the daily newspapers and weekly magazines, which I used to create mathematical problems. The annual *World Population Data Sheet* of the Population Reference Bureau and that organization's many demographic reports were also very valuable.

Analyzing the computer-generated graphs in a book entitled *The Limits to Growth,* we saw that the world would face severe future problems if global population and industrial production continued to accelerate. Once again, instead of a final exam, I required written and oral reports on environment-related topics, using the mathematics that students had learned in the course.

Designing this course resulted in my reading, thinking, and teaching about a wide variety of environmental crises. As I worked with the statistics related to these issues, my awareness grew of environmental threats and the urgent need to respond to them. During my first sabbatical, in the 1978–79 academic year, I wrote a course textbook called *Mathematics and Global Survival.* This book was updated and revised every few years to reflect changing conditions, and became the foundation for my later book *Judaism and Global Survival*, which is still in print today.

Throughout my academic career, my involvement in Judaism was also growing. After moving to Staten Island in 1968, my family immediately joined the local modern Orthodox synagogue, the Young Israel of Staten Island. I have met wonderful, generous, sincere, and deeply committed people in this congregation. I have found many members to be extremely charitable, kind, and deeply involved in learning and *davening* (praying).

Given these involvements and my personal friendships, as well as an awareness of my limitations and weaknesses, it has not been easy to criticize my community. But I came to see that criticism in the form of respectful dialogue is necessary for any religion to thrive and have a meaningful role in society. I have been deeply disturbed by the seeming lack of concern for universal issues among many of my religious Jewish brethren (as well as most other people). Within their own communities they are very caring and generous, but they often seem to have little interest in applying Jewish values to issues that affect the rest of humanity.

For this reason, I often went outside my immediate synagogue group to find support for my Jewish activism. Through my articles, talks, books, and letters to editors, I have been able to express my societal concerns, but I have often felt alienated from my local community in the process. How grateful I am to be living in the age of email, the Internet, and social media! The electronic age has enabled me to be in regular contact with many like-minded people around the world, express my ideas to a wider audience, and to reach beyond the limitations of my own community.

In the early 1970s, partly in an attempt to enhance my synagogue's involvement in social justice issues, I became co-editor of the synagogue's newsletter and frequently contributed articles. I was (and still am) searching for ways to demonstrate Judaism's meaning and relevance to the world. I sensed a great gap between the glorious Jewish teachings on social justice that I was learning about and the realities that I was seeing in my synagogue and Jewish community. Judaism teaches that God chose Jews to be His servants, a light unto the nations, and a holy people, descendants of the prophets, champions of social justice.

I saw great potential for applying the values I was reading about in Jewish texts to the real world around us. I wanted to help revitalize Judaism, to harness it to help save our imperiled planet. My reaction to the Judaism of the time is summed up in the following paragraph from one of my articles for the synagogue newsletter:

> It is generally not religious values that dominate in synagogues today, but rather materialistic, middle-class values. The problem is that far too few people (sometimes including myself) take God and religious teachings seriously enough. If we did, would we fail to protest against the destruction of the precious planet that God has given us as our home? Would we be so apathetic while millions of people die of hunger and its effects annually (when God has provided sufficient food for every person on Earth), and additional millions suffer from poverty and a lack of shelter, clean water, and other necessities, while hundreds of billions of dollars are spent creating newer and better ways to wage war? If a person took God and religious values seriously, he or she would be among the greatest critics of society, where religious values are generally given lip service, at best. She or he would be among the greatest champions of peace and justice.

Unfortunately, these editorials were like crying in the wilderness. Nobody appeared to be listening. I felt as if I were tilting at windmills. Recognizing that not enough was being done in the Jewish community in response to climate and other environmental threats, I next wrote *Who Stole My Religion? Revitalizing Judaism and Applying Jewish Values to Help Heal Our Imperiled Planet*, published in 2013 and 2016. The book argues that Jews should be doing far more to help shift our imperiled planet onto a sustainable path.

WHY THIS BOOK?

Climate change, which only came into focus for me (as it did for many others) in the 1990s, has obviously become the defining crisis of our time, and is the central reason for this book, which also draws on material from my previous three books. *Vegan Revolution* reflects forty years of growing consensus about the dire consequences of ignoring climate change, and the urgency of doing something about it now rather than wait another four decades to act. Indeed, given the outsized role that animal-based agriculture plays in greenhouse gas production, habitat loss, and food insecurity, the issue of veganism has never been more urgent.

Since becoming a vegan, I have seen interest in it expand as more and more people understand how a diet free of animal products is good for animals, health, and the planet. I have also been astonished and greatly gratified at the surge in vegan products available in stores, and am intrigued by the emergence of cellular or cultivated meat: this book reflects these realities, too. Nonetheless, as the name of this book suggests, veganism is still a revolutionary project, overturning our long-held preconceptions about our supposed dominion over animals and our rights to use them as we wish, as well as our need to reimagine our entire food system.

I write this "Introduction" in March 2020, as the world scrambles to confront the coronavirus COVID-19 pandemic. If nothing else, the pandemic is a wake-up call for us to sharply reduce, if not eliminate, the consumption of animals, or at least to end those practices in which animals are raised in dirty, cramped, stressed, disease-prone conditions. By the time the disease has run its course, or we have developed a vaccine, hundreds of thousands of people will have died, millions of people will have lost their jobs, trillions of dollars will have been spent or vanished in value, and many businesses and industries will have gone bankrupt. Is eating animals worth all of this devastation?

Vegan Revolution is also a culmination of my commitment to Judaism. In 2015, I spent two months in Israel on a speaking tour, during which I talked (and listened) to many about how Israel was grappling with the climate catastrophe. The following year, my wife and I moved to the country, where I have remained active in promoting veganism and related causes through letters to editors, articles, talks, and personal conversations. As someone who has celebrated the weddings of three grandchildren and become a great-grandfather after moving to Israel, I have a special interest in creating a decent, habitable world for future generations. I hope you will join me in this essential task.

I welcome comments, suggestions, questions, and constructive criticisms about the ideas I present in this book. You may contact me at <VeggieRich@gmail.com>.

1

WHY JEWS SHOULD BE VEGANS

There are several reasons why Jews should be vegans, all of which will be explored in this book.

The first is that veganism is the diet most consistent with basic Jewish teachings. Judaism emphasizes that people should carefully preserve their health and their lives. However, many scientific studies have linked animal-derived diets to a raised risk of heart disease, stroke, many forms of cancer, and other potentially fatal diseases. Judaism teaches that "[t]he land and the fullness thereof are the Lord's" (Psalm 24:1) and that we are to be God's partners and co-workers in preserving the world. However, modern intensive livestock agriculture contributes disproportionately to climate change, soil erosion and depletion, air and water pollution, overuse of chemical fertilizers and pesticides, the destruction of tropical rainforests and other habitats, desertification, and other environmental damage.

Judaism mandates *bal tashchit* (that we are not to waste or unnecessarily destroy anything of value, and that we are not to use more resources than are needed to accomplish a purpose). Nonetheless, animal agriculture requires us to squander grain, land, water, energy, and other resources. Judaism, furthermore, emphasizes that we are to assist the poor and share our bread with hungry people. However, 67 percent of the crops grown in the United States is fed to animals destined for slaughter, while an estimated nine million people worldwide die because of hunger and its effects each year.[1]

Judaism forbids *tza'ar ba'alei chayim*, inflicting unnecessary pain on animals. In spite of this, most farmed animals—including those raised

---

[1]   Brad Plumer, "How Much of the World's Cropland Is Actually Used to Grow Food?" *Vox*, December 16, 2014; Rebecca Lake, World Hunger Statistics: 23 Thought-Provoking Facts, n.d., https://www.creditdonkey.com/world-hunger-statistics.html.

for kosher consumers—are reared on factory farms, where they live in cramped, confined spaces and are often drugged, mutilated, and denied fresh air, sunlight, exercise, and any enjoyment of life before they are slaughtered and eaten. Finally, whereas Judaism stresses that we must seek and pursue peace and that violence results from unjust conditions, the wasteful depletion of vital resources by diets full of animal products sows hunger and poverty, which breed political instability and war.

In view of these important Jewish mandates, committed Jews (and others) should sharply reduce or eliminate their consumption of animal products.

One could say *dayenu* (it would be enough) after any of the preceding arguments because each constitutes a serious conflict between Jewish values and current practices that should impel Jews to switch to a plant-based diet. Combined, they make a compelling case for change.

Rabbi David Rosen reinforces the above arguments, stressing that eating meat and other animal-products is unjustifiable today.[2] (He has since become a vegan and has informed me that he would refer to veganism today rather than vegetarianism in the statements below.):

> [T]he current treatment of animals in the livestock trade definitely renders the consumption of meat as *halachically* unacceptable as the product of illegitimate means.
>
> Indeed a central precept regarding the relationship between humans and animals in *halacha* [Jewish law] is the prohibition against causing cruelty to animals, *tza'ar ba'alei chayim.* . . . Practices in the livestock trade today constitute a flagrant violation of this prohibition. I refer not only to the most obvious and outrageous of these, such as the production of veal and goose liver, but also to common practices in the livestock trade, such as hormonal treatment and massive drug dosing.
>
> Today not only are we able to enjoy a healthy balanced vegetarian diet as perhaps never before, and not only are there in fact the above-mentioned compelling *halachic* reasons for not

---

2   Rabbi David Rosen, "Vegetarianism: An Orthodox Jewish Perspective," in *Rabbis and Vegetarianism: An Evolving Tradition*, Roberta Kalechofsky, ed. (Marblehead, MA: Micah Publications, 1995), 53–60.

eating meat, but above all, if we strive for that which Judaism aspires to—namely the ennoblement of the spirit—then a vegetarian diet becomes a moral imperative . . . [an] authentic Jewish ethical dietary way of life for our time and for all times.

Rabbi Rosen has stressed that "products from animal sources on the market today are not *truly* kosher."[3]

Reinforcing Rabbi Rosen's message is Jerusalem-based Rabbi Nathan Lopes Cardozo in his book *Jewish Law as Rebellion: A Plea for Religious Authenticity and Halachic Courage*:

> Since when is the actual *shechita* [ritual slaughter] more important than the laws of *tza'ar ba'alei chayim* [the prohibition against causing harm to animals]? . . . Are not [mistreated farmed animals] as *treif* (non-kosher) as any other animal that is not slaughtered according to *Halacha* (Jewish law)? Can we hide behind the laws of *shechita* and look the other way when the laws of *tza'ar ba'alei chaim* are violated?
>
> In all honesty: How many of our *glatt* [strictly] kosher kitchens, including my own, are still truthfully kosher?[4]

I admire my fellow Jews who try to live according to the kashrut laws. But, I wonder, respectfully, how many can confidently answer "yes" to the above question, since it is hard to reconcile eating animals with the spirit and letter of these laws?

The third reason why Jews should be vegans is that scripture makes clear that veganism is the ideal Jewish diet. God's first dietary regimen, given in the very first chapter of the Torah, is strictly vegan: "And God said, 'Behold, I have given you every seed bearing herb, which is upon the surface of the entire earth, and every tree that has seed bearing fruit; it will be yours for food'" (Genesis 1:29). As indicated below, this is consistent with modern scientific findings that humans are closer to herbivorous

---

3   Rabbi Rosen emailed me this quote upon reviewing this section. He discusses all aspects of Jewish teachings on veganism in a video, found at https://www.youtube.com/watch?v=lsppkMyBufs.
4   Nathan Lopes Cardozo, *Jewish Law as Rebellion: A Plea for Religious Authenticity and Halachic Courage* (Jerusalem: Urim Publications, 2018), 405.

animals than to omnivorous or carnivorous animals, in terms of our hands, teeth, intestinal system, stomach acids, and other features.

God's original dietary plan represents a unique statement in humanity's spiritual history. It is a blueprint of a vegan world order. Yet many millions of people have read Genesis 1:29 without fully considering its meaning. Although most Jews eat meat today, the high ideal of God—the initial vegan dietary law—stands supreme in the Torah for Jews and the whole world to see: an ultimate goal toward which all people should strive.

According to Rav Kook, as well as other Jewish scholars, the Messianic period will also be vegan, based on Isaiah's prophecy (11:6–9): "And a wolf shall dwell with a lamb . . . and a lion, like cattle, shall eat straw. . . . They shall neither harm nor destroy in all my holy mount."

Rav Kook affirmed that the high moral level of the veganism practiced by the generations before Noah was a virtue of such great value it cannot be lost forever.[5] In the future ideal period, he believed, people and predatory animals would again not eat flesh.[6] Human lives would not be maintained at the expense of animals' lives.

In his booklet summarizing many of Rav Kook's vegetarian/vegan teachings, Joseph Green, a twentieth-century South African Jewish vegetarian writer, concludes that Jewish religious and ethical vegetarians are forerunners of the Messianic era. They are leading lives that make the coming of the Messiah more likely.[7]

Jewish tradition asserts that one way to speed the coming of the Messiah is to adopt the practices that will prevail in the Messianic time. For example, the Talmud teaches that if all Jews properly observed two consecutive Shabbats, the Messiah would immediately come (*Shabbat* 118b). This may mean symbolically that when all Jews have reached the level of fully observing Shabbat through devotion to God and compassion for people and animals, the conditions would be such that the Messianic period would have arrived.

---

5   Rabbi Alfred Cohen, "Vegetarianism from a Jewish Perspective," *Journal of Halacha and Contemporary Society* (Fall 1981), 45.
6   Rabbi J. H. Hertz, *The Pentateuch and Haftorahs* (London: Soncino Press, 1938), 5.
7   Joe Green, "Chalutzim of the Messiah: The Religious Vegetarian Concept as Expounded by Rabbi Kook" (1971 lecture in Johannesburg, South Africa), 1.

Hence, based on Rav Kook's teaching, if all Jews become vegans in the proper spirit, working to honor and preserve all of God's world, the spiritual conditions arguably will have been fulfilled for the Messianic period.

As was touched on above, and as I discuss more fully in chapters three through eight, animal-based diets have major negative effects on human health, animal welfare, environmental sustainability, resource conservation, hungry people, and prospects for peace. However, we humans are creatures of habit, resistant to changing our ways, even when negative consequences are clearly pointed out to us.

Human beings clearly aren't carnivores, as we need plant foods in order to thrive, but are we omnivores or herbivores? Actually both. People are omnivores in practice, with most eating from both the plant and animal kingdoms. However, physiologically/biologically we orient toward herbivorousness, as explained later. As I will discuss in chapter three, the differences between our eating habits and our natural conditions and inclinations are why so many people are suffering and dying from heart disease, cancer, and other life-threatening diseases.

Keeping Kosher

A more specific reason why Jews should be vegans stems from the many scandals that have rocked the kosher meat industry. Israel's 2017 annual State Comptroller Report cited widespread corruption and mismanagement in Israel's kosher certification process.[8] The first chapter blamed the local religious councils and the Israeli Chief Rabbinate for failing to create significant reforms in the system.

One of the report's major criticisms was that the vast majority of supervisors received money from the businesses they supervised, creating a conflict of interest and the potential for bribery. Another criticism raised was that supervisors were receiving pay for hours they did not work. Incredibly, a supervisor was reportedly paid for working

---

8   Jessica Steinberg, "Comptroller Slams Corrupt Kosher Supervision Process," *The Times of Israel*, May 16, 2017; also see Rabbi Aaron Leibowitz, "On the Ethics and Politics of Kosher Food Supervision," in *Kashrut and Food Ethics*, Rabbi Dr. Shmuly Yanklowitz, ed. (Boston, MA: Academic Studies Press, 2019).

twenty-seven hours a day! Still another area of concern was widespread reports of nepotism, with unqualified inspectors being appointed.

Rabbi Aaron Liebowitz, a Jerusalem council member who founded Private Supervision, an alternative supervisory agency that is more attentive to restaurants, praised the comptroller's report for spotlighting the "significant violations, failures, lies, and corruption" of the main kosher inspection system. He commented: "It's very sad to see how the rabbinate and some of the local religious councils brought kosher supervision in this country to levels of extreme violation and the absurd."[9]

Rabbi David Stav, chairman of Tzohar, an organization of Israeli Orthodox rabbis working to bridge the gaps between Israel's religious and secular populations, observed: "The *kashrut* system in this country is in a downward spiral" and needs to be privatized.[10] In a *Jerusalem Post* story, "Has the Religious Minority Taken over Israel?" Rabbi Stav is quoted as saying, "The reputation of the rabbinate supervision is very low. Most of the supervisors who give certification won't eat in the places they certify," and "that the [*kashrut* inspection] system is broken everybody knows. That it is corrupt everyone knows."[11]

Likewise, Rabbi Cardozo has asserted that he has doubts "about the kosher slaughtering of animals in America and here in Israel," because "the number of cows and chickens which have to be slaughtered every day is so enormous that I can't see how this will ever work *halachically*." He concludes: "I don't believe that any piece of meat today is *kasher l'mehadrin* (perfectly kosher). We should start educating people to no longer eat meat."[12]

Animal slaughter is not the only area of *kashrut* open to abuse. On November 1, 2017, the *Jerusalem Post* ran a story featuring a number of religious authorities, such as Rabbi Professor Daniel Sperber, president of Advanced Torah Studies at Bar-Ilan University, who likewise argued that modern meat production made it impossible to maintain *shechita*

---

9   Steinberg, *op cit.*
10   Quoted in *ibid.*
11   Quoted in Shoshanna Keats-Jaskoll, "Has the Religious Minority Taken over Israel?" *The Jerusalem Post*, June 30, 2017.
12   Quoted in David Israel, "Orthodox Rabbi Teaching Halakha Beyond the *Shulkhan Arukh*, Judaism Beyond the Commandments," *JewishPress.com*, May 25, 2016 (parentheses and italics in the original).

laws, or for *mashgichim* (supervisers) to do their job carefully. Indeed, Sabi Amar, a *shochet* (slaughterer), quit his job because of what he saw as the utter disregard of religious requirements in Jewish slaughterhouses. His response was blunt: "There is no kosher meat in this industry."[13]

After reading the article, Rabbi Cardozo emailed me:

> This is a most important article. In fact, totally shocking and the situation is much worse than I imagined. I thought that the chickens were at least a little better off.
>
> But that is clearly not true. It seems that any meat eating person seems to run the risk to eat *treifa* (non-kosher) and helps an industry which is violating the most basic Jewish religious values, and the rabbinate does not say a word.
>
> How can we stop this tragedy?

This concern was very dramatically reinforced when the *Jerusalem Post* reported on May 12, 2020, that the head of the Chief Rabbinate's Kashrut Division took bribes to declare foods kosher, starting eight years previously! One has to wonder how many of the kashrut inspectors he was supervising were also less than diligent and honest in carrying out their responsibilities.[14]

Lest this be considered only a problem for Israelis, in 2019, Roseman's Delicatessen, the main kosher eatery for Jews in Liverpool, England, was found to have been selling non-kosher meat and chicken.[15] The Liverpool Kashrut Commission wrote in a letter to residents that "serious breaches of kashrut have taken place at Roseman's Delicatessen." Rabbi Natan Fagelman, a member of the Liverpool Kashrut Commission, called on the deli's patrons not to use "all utensils that have ever been used to cook meat/poultry bought at Roseman's" and to discard all food bearing the Liverpool Kashrut Commission symbol. The *Jewish News* opined in an editorial: "Beyond the immediate cost and disruption to families, there

---

13 Quoted in Uri Bollag, "Thou Shalt Not Be Indifferent," *The Jerusalem Post*, November 1, 2017.
14 Jeremy Sharon, "Head of Chief Rabbinate Kashrut to Be Indicted for Bribery," *The Jerusalem Post*, May 12, 2020.
15 Marcy Oster, "Owner of Liverpool Deli Accused of Selling Non-Kosher Meat Found Dead," *The Jerusalem Post*, June 21, 2019.

must be a serious investigation into how non-kosher food was sold in good faith as kosher. It's truly scandalous."[16] In situations like the Liverpool case, Jews who are trying to observe the kosher laws and are being very careful to do everything possible to avoid violating them have suddenly found out that their dishes, silverware, and pots are not kosher. Needless to say, this is very frustrating to them.

A similar scandal occurred at a Jerusalem slaughterhouse, as reported in the *Jerusalem Post*: "Meat that in all likelihood was not kosher was used to make processed meat products." Making the situation even more scandalous was that "[t]he *kashrut* inspector at the plant knew of this situation but continued to allow the factory to operate in this manner while granting it a *kashrut* license and failing to report the situation to the Jerusalem Rabbinate or the Chief Rabbinate."[17]

Based on the above, as well as the other considerations in this chapter, it seems that the best way to keep kosher today is to be a vegan, or at least a vegetarian.[18]

Another reason for Jews to maintain a vegan diet, and a direct result of the immediately preceding one, is that it is much easier and even cheaper to maintain a kosher household on a vegan diet, which might attract new adherents to keeping kosher and eventually to other Jewish practices. A vegan need not be concerned with using separate dishes and other utensils for meat and dairy foods; waiting three or six hours, depending on their tradition, after eating meat before being permitted to eat dairy products; storing four sets of dishes, pots, and silverware (two sets for regular use and two for Passover use); and many other factors that the non-vegan who wishes to observe *kashrut* strictly must consider. In addition, a vegan is in no danger of eating blood, which is prohibited, or the flesh of a non-kosher animal. (For a more comprehensive discussion, see Appendix C.)

Some Jews today reject *kashrut* because of the higher costs involved for kosher foods. However, they could obtain proper (generally superior)

---

16 *Ibid.*
17 Jeremy Sharon, "'Kosher' and Non-Kosher Meat Products Made in Same Factory under Jerusalem Rabbinate Supervision," *The Jerusalem Post*, June 19, 2017.
18 Of course, the vast majority of *kashrut* inspectors are honest and dedicated people. But when human beings are involved, there is always the possibility of error and misjudgment.

nutrition at far lower costs with a balanced, kosher, vegan diet. Also, although religiously observant Jews try to be very careful about properly maintaining the laws of *kashrut*, mistakes can happen when they partake of meat and dairy products daily in their kitchens, year after year. Being vegan makes it far less likely that a Jew will violate the laws of *kashrut*.[19]

It's my belief that each of the above concerns should be enough to convince an omnivorous Jew to become a vegan or to at least sharply reduce their consumption of meat and other animal products. If you are a currently meat-eating religious Jew, I respectfully ask you to reconsider your dietary practice. If you are not ready to become a vegan now, you can take some intermediate positive steps, hopefully on your path to veganism. These include initially going vegetarian, eating meat only on Shabbat and holidays or only when eating out, eating smaller portions, stopping eating meat while continuing to consume dairy products, and giving up eating red meat. You will set an example and perhaps convince others to do the same, thus mitigating much suffering in the world today. The remainder of this book demonstrates how.

---

19   Any *kashrut* questions should be discussed with a trusted rabbinic authority.

2

THE VEGAN REVOLUTION

In the previous chapter, we discussed the problems associated with keeping kosher in Israel. This chapter showcases the extraordinary vitality of the vegan movement in that country, and around the world.

According to an article in the *Jerusalem Post* (see citation on next page) that focused on a large foodtech conference in Tel Aviv, Israel is leading a "meatless revolution—a culinary uprising that promises to transform the way humanity consumes its food." The article noted that "Israel has secured its place as an early and leading player in the fields of plant-based culinary innovation and cultured meat, grown in the laboratory from extracted animal cells."

The conference targeted professionals and suppliers from the food industry. Attendees munched on innovative food products, including "bleeding" vegan burgers and chickpea-based ice cream. Experts from the industry presented lectures on the future of meat and alternative proteins.

The chairwoman of Meatless Monday, Or Benjamin, told the reporter: "Everyone is here to learn what can be served instead of meat, fish, eggs and dairy to people who want to reduce their animal product consumption. . . . We believe that plant-based food is not only for vegans, but that everyone can benefit from moving to a more plant-based diet." She added: "With the growing range of plant-based solutions on offer, there is no longer any need to compromise on taste, enjoyment, or culinary interest when reducing meat consumption."

She continued: "There are both more and less processed products here, ranging from vegetables to burgers that simulate the experience of a beef hamburger, but they do so without the deforestation and without a lot of the resources that go into producing meat. This is a very exciting conference where the culinary scene meets the foodtech scene, and it is interesting to thousands of people visiting today."[1]

The conference showcased a startling reality about Israel's presence in the plant-based and cultured meat ecosystem. The market for meat substitutes in Israel and elsewhere is growing rapidly, and more than 350 high-tech firms are currently operating in Israel's agri-food sector, many of them having only begun in the last five years. Some companies, such as InnovoPro, are partnering with other Israeli companies to develop chickpea protein–based products—which include a chickpea-based milk substitute, an entirely plant-based egg, and two vegan ice cream flavors, which some customers believe is indistinguishable from creamy, dairy-based ice cream. Its founder and CEO, Taly Nechushtan, told the *Post*: "New raw materials need to be based on technology, and that's why Israel—the Start-Up Nation—is a magnet of foodtech."

Many of the visionaries working in this space not only sense the market possibilities in Israel and beyond, but are driven by a commitment to addressing global concerns. As Gil Harley, head of alternative protein export sales at Mixoy, another Israeli food start-up, said to the *Post*: "What we have invented is a plant-based raw material that serves as a substitute for livestock, while giving the same level of protein that is required." He added: "Our larger objective is to provide protein security. Because of the dry product's shelf life, it is a solution for emergency services, governments, local municipalities, armies and organizations tackling hunger in Third World countries. You can just ship it dry, mix it with water and you have your dishes. It's a dream, a 360-degrees vegan solution, that gives you the same nutritional value and makes the world a better place."[2]

Israel has (at 5 percent) the highest national percentage of vegans in the world, a number that has more than doubled since 2010, with an additional 8 percent calling themselves vegetarians. The Israel Defense Forces (IDF) provide vegan food, boots, belts, and hats to their soldiers, and the current IDF chief of staff, Aviv Kohavi, is a vegan. Israeli

---

1   Eytan Halon, "Major Meatless Meet-up Showcases Israeli Foodtech," *The Jerusalem Post*, February 20, 2020.
2   *Ibid.*

president Reuven Rivlin is a vegetarian, and the current prime minister, Benjamin Netanyahu, is sympathetic to animal rights and supports Meatless Mondays, which the Knesset (Parliament) practices.

Perhaps it's not surprising that InnovoPro should be using the chickpea for its products, since it's the major ingredient of the staples, hummus and falafel. Nor, given the many mandates against animal cruelty in the Hebrew scriptures, might it come as a shock to note that Israel has strong laws to protect their welfare, with an Animal Welfare Fund to provide education, information, and aid to animal welfare groups. Indeed, in 2003, the Israeli Supreme Court outlawed the production of *pâté de foie gras*, a "delicacy" obtained by force-feeding huge amounts of grain down the throats of ducks and geese to expand their livers. Sadly, in June 2020 the Israeli Chief Rabbinical Council declared imported foie gras to be glatt kosher.

Supermarkets are filled with vegan products; major metropolitan areas have many vegan restaurants; animal rights marches often take place in the country; and in June 2019 a Vegan Fest in Tel Aviv attracted 50,000 people.[3]

All of the factors discussed in chapter one form a background to the emergence of Israel as a center of the vegan revolution. However, it took Gary Yourofsky, a secular American Jew, to provide the impetus for the major shift to veganism in Israel.[4] His talk, called "Best Speech You Will Ever Hear," was initially presented at the Georgia Institute of Technology in 2010. It was very dramatic, hard-hitting, and challenging and had a great influence in moving people to vegan diets. When it was shown widely in Israel, with Hebrew subtitles, it went viral, was seen by an estimated million Israelis, and influenced many Israelis to become vegans. His challenging, transformative speech has been seen with subtitles in many languages, by millions of people worldwide. It can be seen on YouTube, and I strongly recommend it.

---

3   The facts in these paragraphs are sourced from: Ariel Dominique Hendelman, "Kosher Vegan: Bringing Two Values Together—Under God?" *The Jerusalem Post*, August 10, 2018; Rachel Frazin, "How Israel Became the Global Center of Veganism," *The Tower*, September 2016; and Daphne Rousseau, "Israel, the Promised Land for Vegans," *The Times of Israel*, October 22, 2014.
4   Gary Yourofsky, "Best Speech You Will Ever Hear—How Israel Was Taken by Storm," Gary-TV, http://www.gary-tv.com/garymain/about/about-the-israeli-campaign/.

AROUND THE WORLD

It is not only in Israel that there has been a shift toward veganism. Some indicators point to accelerating momentum worldwide. In December 2018, *The Economist* magazine predicted that the most popular topic of 2019 would be veganism, "the year that veganism goes mainstream."[5] *Forbes* likewise predicted that more people "would embrace a plant-based lifestyle" in 2019.[6] *The Economist* reported that interest in veganism was soaring, with a quarter of Americans ages twenty-five to thirty-four identifying as vegetarians or vegans. It noted that vegan food sales grew ten times faster than food sales overall from January to June 2018, and that many companies were investing heavily in plant-based food.[7]

New food companies, such as Beyond Meat and Impossible Foods, have experienced exponential growth, bringing out a range of plant-based meat products for retail, institutional, and service industries. When Beyond Meat debuted on the New York Stock Exchange in May 2019, its initial share offering of $25 rose to $155.20. (It surged again during April 2020's coronavirus pandemic.)[8] Meanwhile, Impossible Foods, according to Reuters, is available "at more than 7,000 restaurants worldwide, including White Castle, Qdoba and Red Castle, as well as Disney theme parks."[9] Furthermore, Burger King now offers the "Impossible Whopper," which uses Impossible Foods' plant-based patties, nationwide, having trialed it successfully around the United States.

Some school districts and hospitals are now serving plant-based meals. The largest U.S. grocer, Kroger, predicted that one of the five top food

---

5 Davide Banis, "Everything Is Ready to Make 2019 the 'Year of the Vegan.' Are You?" *Forbes*, December 31, 2018.
6 See Julie Cappiello, "2019 Will Be the 'Year of the Vegan,' Major News Outlets Report," Mercy For Animals, December 26, 2018, https://mercyforanimals. org/2019-year-vegan-mainstream-economist-forbes.
7 John Parker, "The Year of the Vegan," World in 2019, *The Economist*, https:// worldin2019.economist.com/theyearofthevegan.
8 Max Reyes, "Beyond Meat Stock Price Soars Amid Fear of a Coronavirus Beef and Pork Shortage," *Los Angeles Times*, April 25, 2020.
9 Angela Moon, "Exclusive: Impossible Foods Raises $300 Million with Investors Eager for a Bite of Meatless Burgers," *Reuters*, May 13, 2019.

trends in 2019 would be plant-based foods,[10] with Whole Foods naming vegan "meats" as a healthy food trend in 2019.[11] By way of confirmation of this momentum, an August 8, 2019, issue of the newsletter for *VegNews* magazine included the following headlines, reinforcing the message that a vegan revolution has begun: "Burger King Now Serves Vegan Whoppers"; "New Vegan Meat Line Coming to Whole Foods"; "Plant-Based Meat Is About to Become Cheaper"; "Subway to Debut 'Beyond Meat' Sub"; and "Just Mayo Back in Stock."

Progress toward veganism is not only indicated by the major increases in meat substitutes, but also by the substantial growth of activism by Jewish vegan groups. For example, Jewish Veg, formerly Jewish Vegetarians of North America, has made great progress since its new director, Jeffrey Spitz Cohan, converted it into a professional organization in 2012. The group has set up a board of directors, an advisory council, and a rabbinic council, and has taken major steps to spreading vegan messages based on Jewish values through wide use of social media and live presentations.

Among the group's recent accomplishments are setting up a website, organizing several vegan Birthright trips to Israel, arranging speaking tours of college campus Hillels by Israeli vegan activist Ori Shavit, creating several vegan-related videos, and initiating a vegan pledge campaign. They also led efforts that resulted in seventy rabbis signing a statement urging Jews to become vegans.

Another example of a U.S. organization actively promoting veganism is Shamayim v'Aretrz, meaning Heaven and Earth, so named because they want to symbolically bring Heaven down to Earth. Initiated and directed by Rabbi Dr. Shmuly Yanklowitz, Shamayim v'Aretrz holds an annual leadership retreat bringing together Jewish animal rights activists, sponsors a campus fellowship each year to train young Jewish vegan leaders, and engages synagogues in a Synagogue Vegan Challenge in order to have a deep impact within Jewish institutional life.

---

10   Sarrie Collins, "America's Largest Grocer Predicts Vegan Food Will Be Top Trend in 2019," Mercy For Animals, October 29, 2018, https://mercyforanimals.org/americas-largest-grocer-predicts-vegan-food.

11   Phil Lampert, "The Top 10 Food Trends for 2019, According to Whole Foods," *Forbes*, November 15, 2018.

VEGANISM IN THE UNITED KINGDOM

The United Kingdom and Europe have seen a similar amount of business activity, investment, and interest in veganism. In May 2019, the Netherlands-based vegan fast-food company Vivera brought its plant-based steaks to the U.K. supermarket chain Tesco, and in later months to dozens of supermarkets across the Netherlands and Belgium.[12] Each January since 2014, individuals in the United Kingdom and beyond have been invited to take a pledge to go vegan for that month—"Veganuary."[13] Participants receive daily recipes, tips, and information about how a vegan diet benefits the environment, animals, and people's health. According to Veganuary, 750,000 people from 192 countries have taken the pledge, with about half signing up for 2020. Hollywood stars like Joaquin Phoenix, Alicia Silverstone, and Mayim Bialik have publicly supported the cause. And on New Year's Eve, before the start of 2020, Natalie Portman urged her 5.9 million Instagram followers to take the pledge. "Fight climate chaos with your fork," she wrote.[14]

Veganuary's effect doesn't stop there. Come February 1, many participants decide to stay vegan; in 2018, 62 percent opted to keep avoiding animal products.[15] That year, Simon Winch, chief executive of Veganuary, said: "Right across the world, people are recognizing that each of us can truly make a difference to our health, to animals, and to the environment, and we can do it easily—and tastily—three times a day. Small changes that we make have a huge collective impact."[16]

One reason for the individuals maintaining a vegan diet might be due to the U.K. vegan charity Viva!, which has launched an app, called 30 Day Vegan, designed to help people continue their Veganuary challenge for an additional thirty days.[17] The app provides vegan recipes,

---

12   Cappiello, "2019 Will Be the 'Year of the Vegan.'"
13   Charlotte Pointing, "3 Million People Expected to Go Vegan in 2019, Survey Finds," Live Kindly, January 5, 2019, https://www.livekindly.co/nearly-3-million-people-vegan-2019-survey-finds/.
14   Alyson Krieger, "Pledging to Go Vegan, at Least for January," *The New York Times*, January 18, 2020.
15   Pointing, "3 Million People Expected."
16   *Ibid.*
17   Maria Chiorando, "'Interest in Veganism Is Soaring,' Says Charity Boss as She Launches App," *Plant Based News*, January 29, 2019. More information about this app can be found at 30dayvegan.org.uk.

comprehensive information about veganism, and answers to common questions about animal-free eating. Juliet Gellatley, founder and director of Viva!, notes: "The interest in veganism is soaring. The demand for plant-based alternatives is increasing and this is reflected in the availability of vegan products. Supermarkets and restaurants are rushing to provide delicious and accessible products for vegan consumers."[18]

The more people who take the pledge to go vegan, the more restaurants and food purveyors see opportunities to satisfy a growing market. In the United Kingdom, Pizza Hut launched a new jackfruit-topped vegan pizza; McDonald's debuted new vegan-friendly options in January 2018[19]; and Sainsbury's, Marks & Spencer, Iceland, Frankie & Benny's, and TGI Fridays also released vegan products that month. Here we can see the positive iterative effects across sectors of the economy when people shift their diet.

As in Israel, the United Kingdom has seen an exponential rise in those calling themselves vegan. Since 2006, England has seen an astonishing 360 percent rise, and veganism is one of the United Kingdom's fastest growing lifestyle movements. This shift is being driven by young people: 42 percent of vegans in the United Kingdom are between fifteen and thirty years old, compared to only 14 percent over age sixty-five. Social media is a major driver: countless blogs and social media sites enable vegans to share their ideas and opinions, provide advice, and raise questions. Many offer thoughtful video messages on YouTube. Among those sharing useful information and ideas are nutritionists, chefs, video bloggers, bodybuilders, environmentalists, and animal rights advocates. Some myths about veganism are promoted, but many more about veganism are shattered. As Charlotte Le Hardy observes: "Today, a new change is sweeping the nation, and indeed the planet. While it may not be new in itself, its increase as of late is unprecedented. It is one not of technology, but of values and morals."[20]

---

18 *Ibid.*

19 Quoted in David Bentley and Clare Youell, "Veganuary Sees Gregg's and McDonald's Launch New Veggie and Vegan Options," *EssexLive*, January 4, 2019.

20 Charlotte Marie Le Hardy, "Green for Go: The Rise in Veganism and Changes in Consumer Consciousness," Richtopia, n.d., https://richtopia.com/sustainable-development/veganism-revolution-changes-consumer-consciousness. The information in this paragraph comes from this article.

Jewish activists in the United Kingdom have both caught and accelerated the vegan momentum. In June 2019, the world's first Jewish vegan center opened at Finchley Road, headquarters of the Jewish Vegetarian Society (JVS).[21] Their leader, Lara Balsam, said about the opening:

> We are delighted to open the doors to the world's first Jewish vegan centre at just the right time, when community centres are in short supply, and when the production of animal products is crueler than ever.
>
> We hope to inspire the creation of many more such hubs around the world, servicing the ever-expanding demand for and interest in Jewish veganism.[22]

---

21 Liam Gulliver, "London Becomes First City to Open Vegan Jewish Center," *Plant Based News*, June 9, 2019.
22 *Ibid.*

3

HEALTH

Since maintaining a healthy and sound body is among the ways of God . . . ,
one must avoid that which harms the body and accustom oneself to that which
is helpful and helps the body become stronger.

—*Maimonides*[1]

As this book illustrates, there are many reasons to adopt a vegan diet. One of the most popular is concern for one's health.

This decision has particular resonance for Jews, since taking care of one's health is arguably the most important mitzvah. Of the 613 *mitzvot* (plural for mitzvah) in the Torah, 610 of them *must* be violated if considered potentially necessary to help save a life. For example, observing the Sabbath day is a major mitzvah; however, saving a life overrides prohibitions related to the holy day. The commandments were given to live by, not die by. The only exceptions are prohibitions against the "three cardinal sins": murder, idolatry, and sexual immorality. Furthermore, of the 613 *mitzvot*, only one includes the Hebrew word *meod*, very, and that relates to the mitzvah of safeguarding health. Jews are to be *very* diligent in taking care of their health (Deuteronomy 4:15). Finally, one can't properly carry out *mitzvot* if one is not in good health.

---

1   Maimonides, *Mishneh Torah, Hilchot Deuteronomy* 4:1, quoted in *Feasting and Fasting: The History and Ethics of Jewish Food*, Aaron Gross, Judy Meyers, and Jordan Rosenblum, eds. (New York: New York University Press, 2019), 334.

THE JEWISH APPROACH TO HEALTH

Contemporary Western medicine has generally focused on the treatment rather than the prevention of diseases. Medical schools teach that prescription drugs are the most powerful tools doctors have for combatting illness; diet and other lifestyle changes are seldom stressed as therapeutic tools. The generally accepted medical response to many diseases today is to prescribe medications first and perhaps recommend lifestyle changes later. Judaism's historic approach is fundamentally different from that of modern medicine. Although treating sick people is certainly a Torah obligation, Judaism puts a priority on prevention.

The foundation for the Jewish emphasis on preventive medicine can be found in the verse in the Torah where God is described as the *rofeh* (healer) of the Israelites:

> And He said, "If you hearken to the voice of the Lord, your God, and you do what is proper in His eyes, and you listen closely to His commandments and observe all His statutes, all the sicknesses that I have visited upon Egypt I will not visit upon you, for I, the Lord, heal you." (Exodus 15:26)

The great medieval scholar Rashi's commentary notes this verse means the following:

> I am the Lord, your healer, and I teach you the Torah and the commandments in order that you may be saved from these diseases—like a physician who says to a person: "Do not eat this thing lest it will bring you into danger from this illness."

What are the implications for modern medicine? Just as God's healing role in the above Torah verse is to prevent illness, so too a physician should emulate the Divine role by stressing disease prevention. For we are obligated to "to walk in all His [God's] ways" (Deuteronomy 11:22; *Sotah* 14a).

A story about the great philosopher Maimonides is instructive. During the period when Maimonides served as the royal physician to the Sultan of Egypt, the Sultan never became ill. One day, the Sultan approached his physician with a question:

> "How do I know that you are an expert physician, since during the period that you have been here, I have never been ill, and you have not had the opportunity to test your skills?"
>
> Maimonides replied: "In truth, the great and faithful physician is the Holy One, Blessed be He, as it is written, 'I am the Lord, your healer.' And this great and faithful physician was able to promise his people that because He is their Physician, He will be able to protect them from all the illnesses that were put on Egypt." Maimonides concluded: "Therefore, we learn that the ability of a physician to prevent illness is a greater proof of his skill than his ability to cure someone who is already ill."[2]

As this story shows, it would seem that physicians should put far greater emphasis on preventive medicine, advising their patients about dangers related to smoking, high-fat diets, and other lifestyle choices.

However, the Torah does not place the entire responsibility of maintaining good health on physicians. In fact, Jewish sages have averred that the major responsibility falls on the individual. To take care of one's health is a mitzvah, mandated in the words, "But beware and watch yourself very well" (Deuteronomy 4:9), and again, "You shall watch yourselves very well" (Deuteronomy 4:15).

Samson Raphael Hirsch, the outstanding nineteenth-century German rabbi, expands on the mitzvah of guarding our health:

> Limiting our presumption against our own body, God's word calls to us: "Do not commit suicide! Do not injure yourself! Do not ruin yourself! Do not weaken yourself! Preserve yourself!" You may not in any way weaken your health or shorten your life. Only if the body is healthy is it an efficient instrument for the spirit's activity. . . . Therefore you should avoid everything which might possibly injure your health. . . . And the law asks you to be

---

2   *Yalkut Lekach Tov, Shmot,* and *B'Shalach.*

even more circumspect in avoiding danger to life and limb than in the avoidance of other transgressions.[3]

Judaism regards life as the highest good, and we are obligated to protect it. An important Jewish principle is *pikuach nefesh*, the duty to preserve a human life. The Talmudic sages applied the principle "You shall observe My statutes and My ordinances, *which a man shall do and live by them*" (Leviticus 18:5 [my italics]) to all the laws of the Torah. Hence, as Rabbi Hirsch's statement indicates, Jews are to be more particular about matters concerning danger to health and life than about ritual matters.[4]

Biblical medicine is unique because of its many regulations for social hygiene. Of Judaism's 613 commandments, 213 are medically related.[5] Hygiene and prophylaxis became religious mandates designed for the preservation and well-being of the nation. To keep military camps clean, latrines were established outside their bounds, and soldiers were equipped with spades with which they were to dig holes and cover their excrement (Deuteronomy 23:13–15). Lepers and others who might spread serious diseases were excluded from the camp for specific quarantine periods (Leviticus 15:1–15; Numbers 5:1–4).

The rabbis also emphasized the importance of public measures to protect people's health. The Talmud indicates that no tannery, grave, or carcass may be placed within fifty ells of a human dwelling (*Baba Batra* 2:9), and rabbis stressed that streets and market areas be kept clean (*Yalkut Shimoni* 184). The sages declared it forbidden for a scholar to reside in a city that did not contain a public bath (*Sanhedrin* 17b).

Rabbinic literature also extended these hygiene teachings to individual behavior. The rabbis regarded the human body as a sanctuary (*Ta'anit* 11a, b). They gave much advice on types of food conducive to good health (*Chulin* 84a, *Berachot* 40a) and stressed the importance of regular nutritious meals (*Shabbat* 140b). They mandated that one must wash one's face, hands, and feet daily in honor of one's Creator (*Shabbat*

---

3   Rabbi Samson Raphael Hirsch, *Horeb*, Dayan Dr. I. Grunfeld, trans. (London: Soncino Press, 1962), Section 62, No. 428.
4   *Chulin* 9a, *Choshen Mishpat* 427, *Yoreh De'ah* 116.
5   Fred Rosner, *Medicine in the Bible and Talmud* (New York: Ktav Publishing House, 1995), 9.

50b), and also wash one's hands on specific occasions, including after rising from bed each morning and after using the toilet.[6]

THE MANY HEALTH BENEFITS OF VEGAN DIETS

There is much evidence that vegetarian diets (and even more so, vegan diets) have many health benefits and can reduce and in some cases reverse several life-threatening diseases.

The Academy of Nutrition and Dietetics, formerly known as the American Dietetic Association, a valuable, respected source for health and nutrition information, concludes that:

> Well-planned vegetarian diets are appropriate for individuals during all stages of the life cycle, . . . are associated with a lower risk of death from heart disease, . . . [result in] lower low-density lipoprotein cholesterol levels, lower blood pressure, and lower rates of hypertension and type 2 diabetes, . . . [and in] lower body mass index and lower overall cancer rates.[7]

Many different kinds of studies have shown that vegan diets have greater health benefits than animal-based diets. For instance, when Japanese people migrate to the United States and shift to the standard American diet, their rates of chronic degenerative diseases rise sharply.[8] Likewise, when the meat supply was sharply reduced for Denmark during World War I[9] and Norway during World War II,[10] the death rates due to diseases sharply decreased, only to return to pre-war levels after the conflicts ended and people returned to their animal-centered diets.

6   *Shulchan Oruch, Orach Chaim* 4:18.
7   W. J. Craig and A. R. Mangels, "Position of the American Dietetic Association: Vegetarian Diets," *Journal of the American Dietetic Association* 109, no. 7 (July 2009): 1266–82.
8   Katherine C. Harting, et al., "Mortality Outcomes for Chinese and Japanese Immigrants in the USA and Countries of Origin (Hong Kong, Japan): A Comparative Analysis Using National Mortality Records from 2003 to 2011," *British Medical Journal* (October 28, 2016), doi:10.1136/bmjopen-2016-012201.
9   Cited in Nathaniel Altman, *Eating for Life* (Wheaton, IL: Theosophical Publishing House, 1977), 22.
10 Cited in John A. Scharffenberg, *Problems with Meat* (Santa Barbara, CA: Wadsworth, 1977), 28.

The China-Cornell-Oxford study,[11] the largest study of its kind in history and dubbed by the *New York Times* as "the *Grand Prix* of epidemiology," investigated the health and mortality conditions for 6,500 people in sixty-five Chinese communities, in each of which the diet conditions were relatively uniform. The researchers concluded that the more animal protein and fat in the diet the greater the risk for serious diseases. Other epidemiological studies have reached similar conclusions.[12]

Countries like China and Japan that have shifted toward animal-concentrated diets in recent years have seen a sharp uptick in potentially fatal diseases.[13] By contrast, Finland has sharply reduced its meat consumption and made other positive lifestyle changes, resulting in an 80 percent decrease in heart disease.[14]

Dr. Dean Ornish, clinical professor of medicine at the University of California, San Francisco, carried out a study with patients who had severe heart problems. Twenty-eight patients went on a mainly vegan diet, along with making other positive lifestyle changes. Twenty served as a control group, adopting the diet recommended by the U.S. medical establishment, involving up to 30 percent fat and permitting chicken without the skin and fish. Both groups were randomly chosen. After one year, almost everyone on the vegan diet saw sharp decreases in coronary blockages and a complete or nearly complete disappearance of chest pains, whereas none of the people in the control group saw an improvement, and some experienced greater heart problems. Other doctors have found comparable results from similar studies. Initially, insurance companies would not reimburse people who were treated using Dr. Ornish's approach. However, some have recognized that this form of treatment is far less expensive and more permanent and now reimburse for it.[15]

---

11   For more on the China study, visit https://nutritionstudies.org/the-china-study/.
12   See Thomas Colin Campbell, "A Plant-based Diet and Animal Protein: Questioning Dietary Fat and Considering Animal Protein as the Main Cause of Heart Disease," *Journal of Geriatric Cardiology* 14, no. 5 (May 2017): 331–37.
13   Asian Science Newsroom, "Cardiovascular Disease on the Rise in Asia, Particularly in Japan," *Asian Scientist*, July 24, 2015.
14   Emily Willingham, "Finland's Bold Push to Change the Heart Disease of a Nation," *Knowable Magazine*, March 7, 2018.
15   For more on Dr. Ornish's work, visit https://www.ornish.com/proven-program/nutrition/ or read *Dr. Dean Ornish's Program for Reversing Heart Disease* (New York: Random House, 1990).

Based on a comprehensive review of studies such as those listed above, Robert M. Kradjian, MD, a breast cancer surgeon for thirty years, concluded that the main cause of breast cancer is animal-concentrated diets.[16] He argued that prevention, not early detection, is the best defense against the disease.

These and many other studies help explain why former chief rabbi of Ireland David Rosen has said: "As it is *halachically* prohibited to harm oneself and as healthy, nutritious vegetarian alternatives are easily available, meat consumption has become halachically unjustifiable."[17]

Herbivorous Humans (and Other Reasons for Veganism)

So, why might it be the case that a meat-and-dairy-intensive diet might prove detrimental? One reason may be that, on the whole, the human body is not optimally designed to eat animal products. Our small and large intestines, like those of primates, are up to four times longer in proportion to height than those of omnivores. Because of the length of the intestines, meat passes very slowly through the system. Indeed, it takes up to four days, during which the disease-causing products of decaying meat are in constant contact with the digestive organs.

Our saliva is alkaline, like that of our closest ape ancestors; it contains ptyalin to digest carbohydrates. Carnivores and omnivores have acidic saliva, and their stomach acids are up to twenty times stronger than those of human beings. Moreover, omnivores have proportionally larger kidneys and livers than humans; they need these larger organs in order to handle the greater amount of nitrogenous waste of a flesh-based diet. Unlike omnivorous animals, humans do not have claws that can rip flesh. Our nails are rounded, which suggests that we are not constituted to prey upon animals. Instead, we have hands for picking fruits, vegetables, leaves, flowers, seeds, etc. Nor do we possess long, hard, dagger-like teeth for biting into flesh. Our so-called canine teeth are not truly canine like

---

16   See Robert M. Kradjian, MD, *Save Yourself from Breast Cancer: Life Choices That Can Help You Reduce the Odds* (New York: Berkley Publishing Group, 1994).

17   Rabbi David Rosen, "Vegetarianism: An Orthodox Jewish Perspective," in *Rabbis and Vegetarianism: An Evolving Tradition*, Roberta Kalechofsky, ed. (Marblehead, MA: Micah Publications, 1995), 54.

those of lions, tigers, bears, and other carnivorous and omnivorous animals.[18]

A further reason why we continue to eat animal products is the prevalent erroneous belief that abundant amounts of protein and calcium are needed for proper nutrition. Indeed, probably the most common question that vegetarians and vegans get asked is, "How do you get enough protein?" The assumption that humans need a lot of protein came about largely as a consequence of the fact that much of the initial protein research was based on experiments with rats. Whereas a female rat's milk has almost 50 percent of its calories in protein, a human mother's milk, ideal for a human infant who will double his or her birth weight in about six months, has only 6 percent of its calories in protein.[19] Many plant foods (such as nuts, seeds, legumes, beans, and spinach) and even some fruits (including melons) have far more than 6 percent, and positive health effects besides.

It's also commonly believed that consuming large amounts of calcium, especially in the form of dairy products, is the best way to stave off osteoporosis. However, the countries that consume the most dairy products, including the United States, Israel, and Scandinavian countries, have the highest percentages of people with osteoporosis.[20] Most East Asians are lactose intolerant and therefore consume fewer dairy products, resulting in less calcium in their diets. Yet they are afflicted far less by osteoporosis, although this is changing as their diets shift to greater consumption of dairy products. Several plant foods, including green, leafy vegetables and soybeans, are good sources of calcium.[21]

---

18 Michael Bluejay, "Vegetarian Guide: Humans Are Natural Plant-eaters, According to the Best Evidence: Our Bodies," June 2002, updated December 2015, https://michaelbluejay.com/veg/.
19 John McDougall, *The McDougall Plan* (La Vergne, TN: Ingram Book Company, 1983), 101.
20 *Ibid.*, 68. For more on milk and osteoporosis, visit Cleveland Clinic, "Can Drinking Too Much Milk Make Your Bones More Brittle?" November 10, 2014, https://health.clevelandclinic.org/can-drinking-too-much-milk-make-your-bones-more-brittle/.
21 Extensive information and research about the health benefits of plant-based, animal-free diets can be found on the website of Michael Greger, MD, at https://nutritionfacts.org/.

Is Chicken Healthy?

Most people are aware of the negative effects to their health of eating red meat.[22] However, many believe chicken to be a suitable alternative and that dairy products and eggs have positive health benefits.

Many chickens are raised in intensive confinement systems around the world. In order to promote rapid growth and to prevent the spread of infections, the chickens' feed is routinely loaded with antibiotics. Scientists are sounding the alarm that this nontherapeutic use of antibiotics (as much as 80 percent in animal agriculture) is leading to the evolution of antibiotic-resistant strains of bacteria, which may make it much harder for doctors in the future to treat people for everyday infections, the curing of which we currently take for granted.[23] Indeed, scientists are warning that antibiotic-resistant diseases could lead to 10 million deaths each year by 2050.[24]

Chickens are also like us in that they are susceptible to bugs: in the case of chicken meat, these are salmonella, campylobacter, and other germs and bacteria. Some reports show harmful bacteria in as many as 97 percent of sampled chickens.[25] Indeed, *E. coli*, infamous for causing bouts of diarrhea, is a concern, because "broiler" chickens (birds raised for their flesh, not their eggs) often end up contaminated with feces due to the extremely congested and unhygienic sheds in which they're raised. Traces of fecal matter may remain even after the birds are rinsed following slaughter. The result of *E. coli* contamination could end with the bird acquiring a urinary tract infection, pneumonia, or respiratory illness.

Even if the chicken meat is thoroughly cleaned and cooked to remove infections, its consumption presents health consequences. Although

---

22   The material in this section is largely taken from, "What Are the Side Effects of Eating Chicken?" *New Vision*, February 28, 2017, https://www.newvision.co.ug/new_vision/news/1447382/effects-eating-chicken.

23   Michael J. Martin, et al., "Antibiotics Overuse in Animal Agriculture: A Call to Action for Health Care Providers," *American Journal of Public Health* 105, no. 12 (December 2015): 2409–10.

24   World Health Organization: Interagency Coordination Group on Antimicrobial Resistance, "No Time to Wait: Securing the Future from Drug-Resistant Infections," April 2019, https://www.who.int/antimicrobial-resistance/interagency-coordination-group/IACG_final_summary_EN.pdf.

25   Beth Hoffman, "Report Finds Harmful Bacteria on 97% of Chicken," *Forbes*, December 19, 2013.

chicken is healthier for you than cold cuts and fatty red meats, it does have several negative outcomes. Chicken has high levels of cholesterol. Indeed, a 3.5-ounce chicken contains about 85 mg of cholesterol, almost as much as beef sirloin, which has about 89 mg.[26] When measured in terms of calories rather than weight, chicken is actually higher in cholesterol than beef. This raises the risks for heart disease and stroke. If the chicken meat is deep fried, especially if it is cooked in animal fat or reused oil, it contains trans fats and high levels of saturated fats. Furthermore, as the China study illustrated, the high protein content of chicken enhances the risks for cancer and osteoporosis.

DAIRY PRODUCTS

In the case of dairy products,[27] the industry spends considerable effort attempting to convince people that milk is nature's ideal food. Actually, in the case of cow's milk they are correct, but only for calves, not humans, since cow's milk was designed for them. For humans, it's a very different story, as there are many negative effects from consuming milk and other dairy products.

A major twenty-year study in Sweden found that women who consumed more than three glasses of milk daily had almost twice the mortality rates of women who consumed less than one glass each day. Also, those who consumed high amounts of milk had more fractures, especially those of the hip, contrary to the milk industry's arguments that high consumption of milk strengthens bones.[28]

Many peer-reviewed studies have shown that milk consumption boosts risks for prostate cancer, ovarian cancer, diabetes, multiple

---

26 Healthline, "Cholesterol Control: Chicken vs. Beef," n.d., https://www.healthline.com/health/high-cholesterol/chicken-vs-beef#1.

27 Much of the material in this section comes from: Thomas Campbell, MD, "12 Frightening Facts About Milk," *CNS*, October 31, 2014, updated on November 1, 2018, https://nutritionstudies.org/12-frightening-facts-milk/. See also, Michael Greger, "Nutrition Facts: Dairy," n.d., https://nutritionfacts.org/topics/dairy/.

28 Karl Michaëlsson, et al., "Milk Intake and Risk of Mortality and Fractures in Women and Men: Cohort Studies," *British Medical Journal* 349 (2014), doi.org/10.1136/bmj.g6015.

sclerosis, high cholesterol levels, acne, constipation, and ear infections. Milk is also perhaps the most common self-reported food allergen.[29]

It is noteworthy that humans are the only species that consumes milk from another species and beyond the weaning period. These choices may represent significant reasons for these negative outcomes and may explain why about 65 percent of the world's populations has some degree of lactose intolerance.[30] Indeed, although this is not widely known, the majority of Jews, especially Ashkenazi Jews, are lactose intolerant.[31]

Fortunately, the momentum behind veganism and allergenic reactions to animal milks have led to the creation of many plant-based substitutes for cow's milk, including rice, almond, soy, oat, and coconut milk (many fortified with extra calcium and vitamin D), as well as vegan cheeses and ice creams. These now make it entirely unnecessary to consume products that are both unnatural and harmful to people and animals.

EATING EGGS

The egg industry also tries to convince people that eggs are a healthy food choice.[32] However, there are reasons to be skeptical. About 80 percent of the calories in eggs are from fat, much of which is saturated, and eggs are a very concentrated source of cholesterol, with about 200 mg in an average size egg, more than double the amount in a Big Mac! This augments the potential for heart disease and other cardiological problems, colorectal cancer, prostate cancer, rectal cancer, and diabetes.

---

29 Physicians Committee for Responsible Medicine, "Health Concerns about Dairy," n.d., https://www.pcrm.org/good-nutrition/nutrition-information/health-concerns-about-dairy.
30 U.S. National Library of Medicine, "Lactose Intolerance," n.d., https://ghr.nlm.nih.gov/condition/lactose-intolerance.
31 Josie Glausiusz, "Jewish Genetics: 75 Percent of Jews Are Lactose Intolerant and 11 Other Facts," *Haaretz*, July 8, 2015.
32 Much of the material in this section comes from: *Health Concerns with Eggs: Eggs Can Be Hazardous to Your Health*, a report by Physicians Committee for Responsible Medicine, https://www.pcrm.org/good-nutrition/nutrition-information/health-concerns-with-eggs. Additional negative effects of eating eggs are in Michael Greger, MD, "Eggs and Nutrition: the Latest Research," https://nutritionfacts.org/topics/eggs/. See also, Francisco Lopez-Jimenez, "Eggs: Are They Good or Bad for My Cholesterol?" Mayo Clinic, n.d., https://www.mayoclinic.org/diseases-conditions/high-blood-cholesterol/expert-answers/cholesterol/faq-20058468.

In his November 1, 2010, editorial entitled "It's the Cholesterol, Stupid!" in the *American Journal of Cardiology*, William Clifford Roberts, MD, a former long-time editor of the publication, asserted that the only true risk factor for coronary heart disease was cholesterol. We humans make our own cholesterol, usually to an adequate level. It is reckless to believe that adding more cholesterol to our diet would be health-affirming.[33]

The egg industry, like other animal-oriented industries, tries to hoodwink people through false or misleading studies. This is not a random decision. Between 2010 and 2019, 60 percent of studies on eggs were funded by the industry, and 49 percent of them arrived at conclusions that did not match the results of the research.[34] One example used to deceive involves measuring cholesterol levels many hours after a meal during which eggs are eaten, when the spike in cholesterol level immediately after a meal has decreased.[35]

A final word is worth mentioning about another aspect of public health, connected to our feeding of nontherapeutic antibiotics to farmed animals, and that is zoonotic diseases. About two-thirds of the major pandemic diseases that have affected humankind have their origins in wild animals (thus the term, *zoonotic*). This is likely true of the 2019–2020 COVID-19, as it is of Ebola, HIV, SARS, MERS, avian flu, and swine flu.[36] Whether we are moving into habitat and converting it into grazing land or feedstock; whether we're farming and eating wild or exotic animals; or whether we're confining domesticated animals in intensive systems, we're providing the means by which viruses can find a home in human bodies. Scientists believe that zoonotic spread will broaden with climate change as temperatures rise and people move in great numbers.[37] Given our continued and accelerating destruction of animal habitat *and* our turning of that habitat into a confined space, we're only reinforcing

33   William Clifford Roberts, "It's the Cholesterol Stupid!" *American Journal of Cardiology* 106, no. 9 (November 2010): 1364–66.
34   Tim Newman, "Eggs and Cholesterol: Is Industry-Funded Research Misleading?" *Medical News Today*, December 18, 2019, https://www.medicalnewstoday.com/articles/327333.
35   Michael Greger, MD, "How the Egg Board Designs Misleading Egg Studies," n.d., https://nutritionfacts.org/video/how-the-egg-board-designs-misleading-studies/.
36   Joshua Emerson Smith, "HIV, Ebola, SARS and now COVID-19: Why Some Scientists Fear Deadly Outbreaks Are on the Rise," *Los Angeles Times*, April 6, 2020.
37   Science Daily, "Changing Climate May Affect Animal-to-Human Disease Transfer," May 1, 2019, https://www.sciencedaily.com/releases/2019/05/190501114619.htm.

the possibilities that COVID-19 will only be the start of more frequent, and perhaps more deadly, pandemics in the future.[38]

Now, as someone who trained as a scientist and was a long-time consumer of meat, I am skeptical about any claims (and would expect you to be also) without seeing the evidence. You should feel free to conduct rigorous research, question the sources, and ensure that there is neither a financial nor economic reason why a study affirms a particular perspective. You should also have regular medical checkups, including blood tests, to assure that you are obtaining all necessary nutrients—no matter what diet you are eating—as well as getting enough exercise, sleep, and social interactions, and reducing stress. I would urge everyone, including vegans, to avoid excessive consumption of sugar, salt, oils, and refined foods because of their negative effects.[39]

All that said, it seems to me that the preponderance of evidence and the numerous *halachic* rules prohibiting dangerous activities should be extended by rabbis to include a very strong recommendation that Jews eliminate the consumption of meat and other animal-sourced foods, or at least reduce them to a minimal level. Such an extension by leading rabbinic authorities of our time, with proper awareness-raising, would save many lives and improve the health, sense of well-being, and life expectancy of Jews.

38   See Ichiko Sugiyama, "Are the Risks of Zoonotic Diseases Rising in the Anthropocene Due to Climate Change?" EGU Blogs, March 16, 2020, https://blogs.egu.eu/divisions/cl/2020/03/16/corona/.
39   In all cases, consult a medical doctor before changing your diet.

4

THE TREATMENT OF ANIMALS

There are probably no creatures that require more the protective Divine word against the presumption of people than the animals, which like people have sensations and instincts, but whose body and powers are nevertheless subservient to humans. In relation to them people so easily forget that injured animal muscle twitches just like human muscle, . . . that the animal being is just as sensitive to cuts, blows, and beatings as humans. Thus people become the torturer of the animal soul.

—*Rabbi Samson Raphael Hirsch*[1]

It is a source of pride to me that Judaism contains many authoritative teachings on the proper treatment of animals. If Jews applied these teachings, I believe, we would be in the vanguard of the struggle against humanity's widespread cruelty to other creatures.

Jews are mandated to be *rachmanim b'nei rachmanim*, compassionate children of compassionate ancestors (*Beitzah* 32b), emulating a compassionate God. God is referred to in daily Jewish prayers as *Ha-rachaman* (the compassionate One) and as *Av harachamim* (Father of compassion). Since Judaism teaches that human beings, uniquely created in God's image (Genesis 1:27; 5:1), are to imitate God's positive attributes, we should surely strive to be exemplars of compassion.

The Talmud states that one who is not compassionate cannot truly be of the seed of Abraham, our patriarch (*Bezah* 32b). It also avers that Heaven grants compassion to those who are compassionate to others, and withholds it from those who are not (*Shabbat* 151b).

---

1   Rabbi Samson Raphael Hirsch, *Horeb*, Dayan Dr. I. Grunfeld, trans. (London: Soncino Press, 1962), Vol. 2, 203 (Section 60, No. 415).

In the *Baruch Sheh'amar* prayer, recited daily in the morning (*Shacharit*) services, Jews proclaim: "Blessed is the One [meaning God] Who has compassion on the earth; blessed is the One Who has compassion on the creatures." Hence, in imitating God, we should also exhibit concern and compassion toward our Earth's environment and all of God's creatures.

The *Ashrei* prayer (Psalm 145), recited three times in the Jewish daily prayers, declares that "[t]he Lord is good to all, and His mercies are on all His works" (verse 9). According to Rabbi David Sears, author of *The Vision of Eden: Animal Welfare and Vegetarianism in Jewish Law and Mysticism*, this verse is "the touchstone of the rabbinic attitude toward animal welfare, appearing in a number of contexts in Torah literature." Referring to the Talmudic teaching that we are to emulate God's ways, Sears observes: "Compassion for all creatures, including animals, is not only God's business; it is a virtue that we too must emulate. Moreover, compassion must not be viewed as an isolated phenomenon, one of a number of religious duties in the Judaic conception of the Divine service. It is central to our entire approach to life."[2] In the spirit of the above teachings and writing of our capacity to imitate God's compassion and other positive attributes, the Chofetz Chaim, a Jewish sage of the late nineteenth and early twentieth centuries, stated:

> The existence of the entire world depends on this virtue. . . . Hence, whoever follows in this path will bear the Divine image on his person; while whoever refrains from exercising this virtue and questions himself, "Why should I do good to others?" removes himself completely from God, the Blessed One.[3]

According to Judaism, animals are part of God's creation and people have special responsibilities to them. The Jewish tradition clearly indicates that we are forbidden to be cruel to animals and that we are to treat them with compassion. These concepts are summarized in the Hebrew phrase *tza'ar ba'alei chayim*, the Torah mandate not to cause "pain

---

2   David Sears, *The Vision of Eden: Animal Welfare and Vegetarianism in Jewish Law and Mysticism*, 2nd edition (Create Space, 2014), 19.
3   Chofetz Chaim, *Ahavath Chesed: The Love of Kindness as Required by God* (Jerusalem/New York: Feldheim, 1967), 82.

to a living creature." Perhaps the Jewish attitude toward animals is best summarized by the statement in Proverbs 12:10: "A righteous man has regard for the desire of his beast." In Judaism, one who is cruel to animals cannot be regarded as a righteous individual.

There are many Torah laws involving compassion to animals. An ox is not to be muzzled when threshing in a field of corn (Deuteronomy 25:4). It would be less than compassionate to prevent the ox from stealing an occasional bite of the fruits of his labor. A farmer should not plow with an ox and an ass together, so that the weaker animal would not suffer pain in trying to keep up with the stronger one (Deuteronomy 22:10). Animals, like people, are to be allowed to rest on the Sabbath day (Exodus 20:10; Deuteronomy 5:12–14). The importance of the latter verse is indicated by its inclusion in the Ten Commandments and its recitation as part of *kiddush* (sanctification ceremony using wine or grape juice) on Sabbath mornings.

Many Jewish heroes were chosen because they showed kindness to animals. Moses and King David were considered worthy to be leaders because of their tender care of animals when they were shepherds (*Exodus Rabbah* 2:2). Rebecca was judged suitable to be Isaac's wife because of her kindness in providing water to the ten thirsty camels of Eliezer, Abraham's servant, who had just crossed a desert (Genesis 24:20).

Psalms 104 and 148 show God's close identification with the animals of the field, creatures of the sea, and birds of the air. Sea animals and birds receive the same blessing as people—"Be fruitful and multiply" (Genesis.1:22)—while the important Hebrew expression *nefesh chaya* ("living soul") is applied in Genesis (1:21, 1:24) to people and animals alike. Animals are initially given a vegan diet in the garden of Eden, similar to that of people (Genesis 1:29–30).

Although the Torah indicates that people are to "rule over the fish of the sea and over the fowl of the heaven and over the animals and over all the earth and over all the creeping things that creep upon the earth" (Genesis 1:26), the sages have interpreted dominion as responsible stewardship and stressed that the rights and privileges of animals are not to be neglected or overlooked. Animals, they note, are also God's creatures, possessing sensitivity and the capacity for feeling pain; hence they must be protected and treated with compassion and justice.

The Jewish scriptures indicate that God made treaties and covenants with animals, just as with humans:

> And I, behold I am setting up My covenant with you and with your seed after you. And with every living creature that is with you, among the fowl, among the cattle, and among all the beasts of the earth with you, of all those who came out of the ark, of all the living creatures of the earth. (Genesis 9:9–10)

> And I will make a covenant for them on that day with the beasts of the field and with the fowl of the sky and the creeping things of the earth; and the bow, the sword, and war I will break of the earth, and I will let them lie down safely. (Hosea 2:20)

Ecclesiastes discusses the kinship between people and animals. Both are described as sharing the common fate of mortality:

> For there is a happening for the children of men, and there is a happening for the beasts—and they have one happening—like the death of this one is the death of that one, and all have one spirit, and the superiority of man over beast is nought, for all is vanity. All go to one place; all came from the dust, and all return to the dust. Who knows that the spirit of the children of men is that which ascends on high and the spirit of the beast is that which descends below to the earth? (Ecclesiastes 3:19–21)

God considers animals, as well as people, when He admonishes Jonah: "Now should I not take pity on Nineveh, the great city, in which there are many more than one hundred twenty thousand people . . . and many beasts as well?" (Jonah 4:11). The Psalms indicate God's concern for animals, for, as discussed above, "God's mercies are upon all His works" (Psalm 145:9). They portray God as "satisfying the desire of every living creature" (Psalm 145:16); "He gives the animal its food, to the young ravens which call out" (Psalm 147:9); and, in general, "You save both man and beast, O Lord" (Psalm 36:7).

God is depicted as giving animals the attributes necessary for survival in their environment. For example, camels possess short tails so they won't become ensnared when feeding upon thorns; oxen have long tails that can be swung to keep away gnats when they are feeding on the plains; the feelers of locusts are flexible so they won't be blinded by their feelers breaking against trees.

Based on the angel of God's reproachful question to Balaam, "Why have you beaten your she-donkey?" (Numbers 22:32), the Talmud argues that animals are to be treated humanely. Based on Deuteronomy 11:15, "And I will give grass in your field for your livestock and you will eat and be sated," the Talmud concludes that Jews should feed their animals before they themselves eat.

A WORLD OF PAIN

Unfortunately, the conditions under which animals are raised for food today are quite different from any that the Torah would condone, or would even be recognized by the sages of the past. Modern animal agriculture primarily involves placing animals in dense numbers in huge facilities that seek maximum profits by treating animals as industrial units rather than sentient creatures.[4]

Cattle and Veal

The suffering of cows begins almost from the moment they're born.[5] They are commonly dehorned, castrated, and branded with hot irons, without any painkillers. When workers drag calves shortly after birth from their

---

4   For a glimpse at some of the conditions for animals in human confinement around the world, visit We Animals Media, https://weanimalsmedia.org/.

5   Abuses of farmed animals are described in detail in *Diet for a New America: How Your Food Choices Affect Your Health, Happiness and the Future of Life on Earth*, 25th Anniversary Edition (Kindle, 2012) by John Robbins, and *The Food Revolution: How Your Diet Can Help Save Your Life and Our World* by John Robbins, 10th Anniversary Edition (San Francisco, CA: RedWheel/Weiser, 2011); *Old McDonald's Factory Farm* by C. David Coats (New York: Continuum, 1989); and *Eating Animals* by Jonathan Safran Foer (New York: Little, Brown, 2009), as well as in many other books listed in the bibliography. Many videos of undercover investigations also show the horrors of factory farming. For the context of this work, see *The Ghosts in Our Machine*, directed by Liz Marshall (Toronto: Ghosts Media, 2013).

mothers, they throw them on the ground to punch holes in their ears through which to put name tags.

Whereas calves, like human infants, would nurse for nearly a year if there were no human intervention, it is usual practice to separate mother and calf, which is traumatic to both, very early. In the veal industry, male calves are torn from their mothers within days, if not hours, after birth. Those calves are raised in narrow stalls that prohibit movement so that the flesh is kept soft, and they are unable to suckle—an intense desire for a newborn. Lest you imagine this is a mere byproduct of the beef and dairy industries, "veal" is inherent, because cows only provide milk after being impregnated and giving birth, and many female calves and nearly all the male calves are considered surplus. Those cattle that are bred for beef are generally slaughtered between one and five years of age, a fraction of their natural lifespan.

Dairy Cows

Today's modern milk factories raise cows for maximum milk production at minimum cost, resulting in much cruelty to the cows.[6] For cows to produce milk they must lactate, which means they must give birth. In order to ensure there is no downtime between pregnancies, farmers artificially inseminate each cow annually so that the mother cow will constantly produce milk for human consumption. She lives with an unnaturally enlarged and sensitive udder and is milked up to three times a day.

Although the dairy industry would have you believe that its cows are content, today's factory-bred cows have to be fed tranquilizers to reduce their anxiety. As soon as their milk production wanes to an unprofitable level, after only about five years, they are culled and sent to slaughter to produce hamburgers. Broken down by a lifetime of "sweat shop" service to the food industry, they are still biologically young; the domestic cow's natural life span is about twenty-five years.

---

6   Much valuable information about the widespread mistreatment of dairy cows is in *Farm Animal Welfare: Cows*, a report from MSPCA Angell, https://www.mspca.org/animal_protection/farm-animal-welfare-cows/. For more on industrial farming, see Philip Lymbery, *Farmageddon: The True Cost of Cheap Meat* (London: Bloomsbury, 2014).

The following story by Dr. Michael Klaper, the author of several books, including *Vegan Nutrition: Pure and Simple* and *Pregnancy, Children, and the Vegan*, dramatically illustrates the cruelty of the dairy industry:

> The very saddest sound in all my memory was burned into my awareness at age five on my uncle's dairy farm in Wisconsin. A cow had given birth to a beautiful male calf. The mother was allowed to nurse her calf but for a single night. On the second day after birth, my uncle took the calf from the mother and placed him in the veal pen in the barn—only ten yards away, in plain view of the mother. The mother cow could see her infant, smell him, hear him, but could not touch him, comfort him, or nurse him. The heartrending bellows that she poured forth—minute after minute, hour after hour, for five long days—were excruciating to listen to. They are the most poignant and painful auditory memories I carry in my brain. Since that age, whenever I hear anyone postulate that animals cannot feel emotions, I need only to replay that torturous sound in my memory of that mother cow crying her bovine heart out to her infant. Mother's love knows no species barriers, and I believe that all people who are vegans in their hearts and souls know that to be true.[7]

Egg-laying Hens

There is no less cruelty in the egg industry.[8] Most "layer" hens (hens bred to lay eggs) live their lives confined inside rows of stacked wire cages, with five hens generally squeezed into each eighteen-by-twenty-inch cage. Overcrowding is so severe that a hen cannot fully stretch even one wing. As a result of these very unnatural conditions, the birds are driven to pecking at each other, which harms and sometimes kills their fellow cellmates, thus reducing the producers' profits. To avoid this, the lighting

---

7   Vegan Peace Initiative, "Choose Life Over Death, Kindness Over Killing," n.d., http://www.veganpeace.com/veganism/compassion.htm.
8   Much information about the mistreatment of egg-laying hens can be found in Jaya Bhumitra, "Costco's Egg Supply: Cruelty Cracked Wide Open," Mercy For Animals, n.d., https://mercyforanimals.org/cruelty-in-costcos-egg-supply-cracked-wide. For a full view of the lives and deaths of poultry in today's factory farms, see Karen Davis, *For the Birds: From Exploitation to Liberation* (Brooklyn, NY: Lantern, 2019).

is kept very dim (chickens are diurnal and not as active in low light), and the chickens are "debeaked." Debeaking is a very painful, often debilitating procedure that involves cutting off much of the hen's beak with a hot knife while her head is held by hand or in a vise. There is neither anesthesia nor painkillers. This is the industry's callous strategy to maximize profit at the expense of providing its animals with adequate space, exercise, fresh air, and other essentials of life. Because male chicks have no value to the egg industry and, unlike "broilers," have not been bred to grow fat, fast, they are discarded within hours of birth. Each day in the United States, hatchery workers stuff over half a million live male chicks into plastic bags where they die of suffocation, or they feed them into macerators to be ground up alive.

Broilers

Chickens raised for slaughter spend their shortened lives in long, windowless, crowded sheds, unable to see sunlight, breathe fresh air, or get any exercise. When the tiny chicks arrive, there is plenty of room, but they have progressively less and less of it as they grow. The shed quickly becomes too crowded for the birds to move properly; just prior to slaughter, the area that each chicken occupies—about half a square foot on average—is barely enough to move. Overcrowding and stress mark the lives of these chickens, and they are generally slaughtered when only about six weeks old. By contrast, a normal chicken's lifespan is eight to ten years.

The chickens are made to grow so fast that they frequently cannot even walk without pain. Air suffused with ammonia causes severe skin and throat irritation, blindness, and fatal respiratory problems. Abuse from factory farm workers is also rampant. Video footage taken by the animal welfare group Mercy For Animals shows workers stabbing chickens with spiked clubs, stomping birds to death, and ripping limbs from live chickens. In his April 14, 2003, article in *The New Yorker,* Michael Specter describes his first visit to a chicken farm:

> I was almost knocked to the ground by the overpowering smell
> of feces and ammonia. My eyes burned and so did my lungs,
> and I could neither see nor breathe. . . . There must have been

thirty-thousand chickens sitting silently on the floor in front of
me. They didn't move, didn't cluck. They were almost like statues
of chickens, living in nearly total darkness, and they would spend
every minute of their six-week lives that way.[9]

Confronting the Hypocrisy of the Meat on Our Tables

In 1964, just two years following the publication of *Silent Spring* by
Rachel Carson, the book that helped launch the modern environmental
movement, a Quaker humanist of Jewish origin named Ruth Harrison
was among the first thinkers to sound the alarm on a growing moral
threat: factory farming. In her seminal book, *Animal Machines*, to which
Carson contributed the foreword, Harrison wrote:

> How far have we the right to take our domination of the animal
> world? Have we the right to rob them of all pleasure in life simply
> to make more money more quickly out of their carcasses? Have
> we the right to treat living creatures solely as food converting
> machines? At what point do we acknowledge cruelty?[10] . . .
>
> Farm animals have always been exploited by man in that
> he rears them specifically for food. But until recently they were
> individuals, allowed their birthright of green fields, sunlight, and
> fresh air; they were allowed to forage, to exercise, to watch the
> world go by, in fact to live. Even at its worst . . . the animal had
> some enjoyment in life before it died. Today the exploitation has
> been taken to a degree that involves not only the elimination
> of all enjoyment, the frustration of all natural instincts, but its
> replacement with acute discomfort, boredom, and the actual
> denial of health. It has been taken to a degree where the animal
> is not allowed to live before it dies.[11]

---

9   Quoted in Leah Garces, "Why We Haven't Seen Inside a Broiler Chicken Factory Farm
    in a Decade," *Food Factory News*, January 24, 2013. For a visit inside an intensive chicken
    farm, see Nicholas Kristof, "Abusing Chickens We Eat," *The New York Times*, December
    3, 2014.
10 Ruth Harrison, *Animal Machines* (London: Vincent Street, 1964), 12.
11 *Ibid.*, 3.

Since the publication of Harrison's influential book, many more thinkers of conscience have questioned the morality of so much of the food on our tables. In 1971, John Harris challenged readers to overcome their lack of sensitivity:

> Every year millions of animals are born and bred for the sole purpose of satisfying those who like the taste of meat. Their lives vary in length from a few weeks to a few years; most live a fraction of the time they would in more natural conditions. They die in slaughterhouses where, if the tranquilizers have their effect, they know only a few moments of the awful fear of death before they are stunned and their throats cut. This is what all meat-eaters actively support, for there would be no batteries, no sweatboxes, no need to castrate male animals or artificially inseminate females, no cattle markets and no slaughterhouses if there was no one insensitive enough to buy their products.[12]

By the late 1980s, author C. David Coats described the cycle of misery that results from our addiction to meat, laying bare the pretense of "old McDonald's *factory* farm":

> Aren't humans amazing? They kill wildlife—birds, deer, all kinds of cats, coyotes, beavers, groundhogs, mice and foxes by the million in order to protect their domestic animals and their feed.
>
> Then they kill domestic animals by the billion and eat them. This in turn kills people by the million, because eating all those animals leads to degenerative—and fatal—health conditions like heart disease, stroke, kidney disease, and cancer. So then humans spend billions of dollars torturing and killing millions more animals to look for cures for these diseases.
>
> Elsewhere, millions of other human beings are being killed by hunger and malnutrition because food they could eat is being used to fatten domestic animals.

---

12 John Harris, "Killing for Food," in *Animals, Men, and Morals: An Inquiry into the Maltreatment of Non-humans.* S. R. Godlovitch and John Harris, eds. (New York: Taplinger Publishing Co., 1972), 98.

Meanwhile, few people recognize the absurdity of humans, who kill so easily and violently, and once a year send out cards praying for "Peace on Earth."[13]

Can such a diet—and all that flows from it—truly be considered kosher? By the 1990s, Rabbi Aryeh Carmell, a twentieth-century Torah scholar living in Jerusalem, had ventured an opinion: "It seems doubtful from all that has been said whether the Torah would sanction factory farming, which treats animals as machines, with apparent insensitivity to their natural needs and instincts. This is a matter for decision by halachic authorities."[14] For Rabbi David Rosen, the decision would soon become plain: "The current treatment of animals in the livestock trade definitely renders the consumption of meat as *halachically* unacceptable as the product of illegitimate means."[15] Rosen makes clear that he is not referring only to the production of veal and goose liver, "the most obvious and outrageous" examples of animal mistreatment, but also to common practices in the livestock trade, such as massive drug dosing and hormonal treatment.[16]

We have already discussed the mismanagement of some kosher venues in Israel and the United Kingdom. In addition, the kosher meat inspection industry tends to focus only on the actual moment of slaughter, and the packing and preparation of the meat afterward. Very little, if any, attention is paid to how the animals are treated *before* slaughter. One has to wonder if this can be reconciled with *kashrut*, because *kashrut* is designed to be humane. But how can it be humane if most kosher meat, dairy, and eggs come from the same abominable factory farm conditions as does non-kosher food?

Shouldn't we—whether we're Jewish or not; whether we keep kosher or not—be concerned, indeed alarmed, about the ways that meat and other animal products are produced? As Harrison observed, in the past,

---

13   C. David Coats, *Old McDonald's Factory Farm* (New York: Continuum, 1989), preface.
14   Rabbi Aryeh Carmell, *Masterplan: Judaism—Its Programs, Meanings, Goals* (New York/Jerusalem: Feldheim, 1992), 69.
15   Rabbi David Rosen, "Vegetarianism: An Orthodox Jewish Perspective," in *Rabbis and Vegetarianism: An Evolving Tradition*, Roberta Kalechofsky, ed. (Marblehead, MA: Micah Publications, 1995), 53.
16   *Ibid.*, 54.

farmed animals ran free in pastures or open country, grazed on grass, and were slaughtered only for special occasions, such as when Abraham slaughtered a calf for his angelic guests. Chickens were hatched naturally under mother hens and Jews generally ate them only on Shabbat and holidays—and then only after the birds had a life of freedom to scratch, peck, and live as a chicken was created to live. There was nothing remotely resembling the year-round factory farm conditions under which food animals are raised today. And those farms that practice these forms of husbandry are vanishingly rare, as industrialized farming consolidates and globalizes throughout the world—even in Israel.[17]

Therefore, although the Torah does permit eating meat, generally considered by the Jewish sages as a concession to human weakness, the conditions under which animals are raised today do not remotely resemble those for the flocks of our ancestors. So, just as the rabbis widely agree that humans and nonhumans differ in fundamental ways, one need not believe that human beings and animals have the same value to protest against the extremely brutal treatment that animals are subjected to today.

In summary, in view of the horrible conditions under which almost all animals are raised today, Jews who eat meat are in effect supporting a system contrary to basic Jewish principles and obligations. They should seriously consider becoming vegans, and, if they find this diet and lifestyle too difficult for them, they should at least strive to be as vegan as possible. Being an advocate for improved conditions for animals is not a rejection of Judaism, but an attempt to apply Judaism's splendid teachings. It is essential that these messages become widely known and practiced in order to end the horrendous realities within which so many animals currently exist, very much contrary to basic Jewish values, and to show the applicability of Judaism's eternal values to some of today's critical issues.

---

17 For an overview of the globalization of factory farming in select countries around the world, see the publications of Brighter Green, https://brightergreen.org/publications/. For an examination of intensive animal agriculture, see Joyce D'Silva and John Webster, eds., *The Meat Crisis: Developing More Sustainable Production and Consumption* (London: Earthscan, 2010).

5

THE CLIMATE CATASTROPHE

In the hour when the Blessed Holy One created the first human being, God took him and let him pass before all the trees of the Garden of Eden and said to him: "See my works, how fine and excellent they are! All that I have created, for you have I created them. Think upon this and do not despoil and destroy My world. For if you destroy it, there is no one to set it right after you."

—*Ecclesiastes Rabbah* 7:28

In ancient times, Jews may have wondered about the significance of this *midrash* (rabbinic teaching). How could it be possible to destroy the world that God had created? Did humans have such power? Today, we know that it is not only possible, but probable. This chapter demonstrates that a dietary shift away from the planet-heating effects of animal agriculture may be the single most significant change we can make to stop the destruction.

HOW SERIOUS ARE CLIMATE THREATS?

The greatest threat to humanity today is climate change, even more so than the 2020 global coronavirus pandemic and other zoonotic diseases that I talk about later in this chapter. Our human civilization is set on a path that could lead to a possibly uninhabitable planet by the end of the century—or one so torn asunder by climate disaster and its social, political, economic, and health consequences that few of us would want to inhabit it.

Is this alarmism or an outrageous exaggeration, given how many in the past predicted an end to the world? Not according to scholars worldwide, including some 97 percent of climate scientists, and virtually all peer-reviewed papers (thousands of them) on the issue in respected scientific journals. They convincingly argue that global warming and the resulting climate change we see today are the product of our own activities (we cannot blame it on natural cycles—not this time) and pose an existential threat to humanity.[1]

The leaders of the 195 nations who attended the December 2015 Paris Climate Change conference, including Israel and the United States, agreed that immediate steps must be taken to avert a climate catastrophe, and almost all the nations pledged to reduce their greenhouse gas emissions.[2] Although this was an important step forward, climate experts believe that even if all the pledges are kept (they are not binding), the measures would still be insufficient to prevent severe climate disruption later this century.

Indeed, in October 2018, when the UN's Intergovernmental Panel on Climate Change (the IPCC) released its much anticipated update on the science (the fruit of ninety-one climate experts from forty countries reviewing thousands of the latest climate-related studies and reports), the authors warned that the world has until 2030 to make "rapid, far-reaching and unprecedented changes in all aspects of society" if we are to have a reasonable chance of limiting global warming to 1.5°C above pre-industrial levels and averting the climate disasters that are likely to follow if we don't.[3]

A year later, the urgency of the IPCC's report was echoed when over 11,000 scientists signed on to a paper in the journal *BioScience* declaring

---

1 NASA, "Science Consensus: Earth's Climate Is Warming. State of the Planet Report," n.d. https://climate.nasa.gov/scientific-consensus/. For a grim overview of the realities, see David Wallace-Wells, *The Uninhabitable Earth* (New York: Crown, 2019) and Dale Jamieson, *Reason in a Dark Time: Why the Struggle against Climate Change Failed—and What It Means for Our Future* (Oxford, UK: Oxford University Press, 2014).

2 UN, "UN Climate Change Conference Paris 2015, Sustainable Development Goals Report," n.d., https://www.un.org/sustainabledevelopment/cop21/.

3 IPCC, "Summary for Policymakers of IPCC Special Report on Global Warming of 1.5°C Approved by Governments," October 8, 2018, www.ipcc.ch/2018/10/08/summary-for-policymakers-of-ipcc-special-report-on-global-warming-of-1-5c-approved-by-governments/.

that "the climate crisis has arrived and is accelerating faster than most scientists expected."[4] "It is more severe than anticipated," they warned, "threatening natural ecosystems and the fate of humanity."[5]

"We declare, with more than 11,000 scientist signatories from around the world, clearly and unequivocally, that planet Earth is facing a climate emergency," the paper began. "To secure a sustainable future," it continued, "we must change how we live. [This] entails major transformations in the ways our global society functions and interacts with natural ecosystems."[6] The scientists' prescription for humanity included leaving fossil fuels in the ground, ending population growth, and halting forest destruction—and massively reducing the amount of meat produced and eaten.[7]

A UN report on November 26, 2019, was also extremely alarming.[8] It pointed out that, despite many nations' pledges to reduce them, greenhouse gases are still rising perilously, growing an average of 1.5 percent annually in the past ten years. The report asserted that countries need to make their emissions-reductions goals *five times* greater in order to limit warming to 1.5°C—the threshold scientists believe is a dangerous line to cross for global warming. Even if *all* the countries involved in the Paris Agreement brought emissions down to the levels they initially pledged to meet, the report noted, the world would still be on track for 3.2°C warming since the start of the Industrial Revolution, three times the present rise. That's 5.76°F, a scenario that would dramatically augment the severity of current wildfires, hurricanes, heat waves, and droughts. Since many of the world's biggest greenhouse gas emitters are not on track to meet their climate reduction pledges, the final warming number could be substantially greater even than this.[9]

---

4   William J. Ripple, et al., "World Scientists' Warning of a Climate Emergency," *BioScience* 70, no. 1 (January 2020): 8–12, academic.oup.com/bioscience/article/70/1/8/5610806.
5   Michael Slazek, "Climate Emergency Declared by 11,000 Scientists Worldwide Who Warn of 'Catastrophic Threat' to Humanity," *ABC News Australia*, November 9, 2019.
6   Damian Carrington, "Climate Crisis: 11,000 Scientists Warn of 'Untold Suffering,'" *The Guardian*, November 5, 2019.
7   *Ibid.*
8   Somini Sengupta, "'Bleak' U.N. Report on a Planet in Peril Looms Over New Climate Talks," *The New York Times*, November 26, 2019; and Tierstein Zoya, "Paris Agreement Targets Need to Be 5 Times Stronger to Actually Work," *Grist*, November 26, 2019.
9   Fiona Harvey and Jennifer Rankin, "Paris Climate Deal: World Not on Track to Meet Goal Amid Continuous Emissions," *The Guardian*, December 4, 2019.

How Climate Change Makes Violence, Terrorism, and War More Likely

Another profound implication of climate change has been analyzed by the Pentagon, U.S. intelligence agencies, and other nations' military organizations, for obvious reasons. The reality is that climate change will escalate the potential for instability, terrorism, and war by reducing access to food and clean water, and causing tens of millions of desperate refugees to flee from droughts, wildfire, floods, storms, and other disasters wrought by climate change.[10]

Compelling evidence exists that major droughts caused or worsened by climate change helped spark recent civil wars in Darfur[11] and Syria.[12] Syria experienced a very severe drought between 2006 and 2011, which led to widespread crop failures, resulting in many farmers leaving their land for the cities at a time when many refugees fleeing the violence in Iraq were pouring into Syria. The instability caused frustration, tension, and anger, which eventually exploded into a civil war that was exploited by jihadists and fanatics, including ISIS.

The negative effects of climate change in Darfur and Syria are especially frightening when one considers that drought and desertification due to climate change are causing chaos in many other countries in the Middle East as well as central and north Africa, fanning the flames of social revolutions and civil wars.[13] Such unrest poses major security threats to Israel and the West, with drought-induced hunger leaving populations angry, frustrated, and vulnerable to radicalization and recruitment. Drought, famine, and violence are also causing major migrations, furthering the potential for more chaos, instability, and violence.

Unless we take drastic action, the disruption, human rights tragedies, and economic costs of destabilization in countries like Syria and Iraq will

---

10   Andrew Johnson, "Retired Generals, Admirals Warn Climate Change Is a 'National Security Issue,'" *National Review*, May 14, 2014.

11   Julian Berger, "Darfur Conflict Heralds Era of Wars Triggered by Climate Change, UN Warns," *The Guardian*, June 23, 2007.

12   Mark Fischetti, "Climate Change Hardened Syria's Civil War," *Scientific American*, March 2, 2015.

13   Janpeter Schilling, et al., "Climate Change Vulnerability, Water Resources and Social Implications in North Africa," *Regional Environmental Change* 20, no. 15 (2020), https://doi.org/10.1007/s10113-020-01597-7.

no longer be outliers: they are essentially illustrative of what is already evident. Contrary to the myth popular among many climate change deniers, the world's temperature has risen significantly in recent years.[14] Every decade since the 1970s has been hotter than the previous one, and all twenty years of this century are among the twenty-one hottest years recorded since global temperature records started being kept in 1880 (the only other year in the top twenty-one is 1998). The year 2016 was the hottest globally, breaking the records held previously by 2015 and before that by 2014, the first time that there had been three consecutive years of record world temperatures. The six warmest years recorded are those from 2014 to 2019. July 2019 was the warmest month in recorded history, and scientists are forecasting that 2020 may be the hottest year on record.[15]

There is only one credible cause for this persistent warming trend, according to the climate scientists who measure its relationship to all of the natural and anthropogenic (human-caused) warming and cooling forces on Earth, from sunspots to tailpipes.[16]

Just as a person with a high fever suffers from many of its effects, our planet has experienced many negative consequences from the warmer global temperatures.

The number and severity of droughts, wildfires, storms, and floods have also increased. Such climate events have always occurred, but climate change has made them more frequent and destructive. They are also connected: as more moisture evaporates in warmer temperatures and warmer air holds more moisture, the potential for heavier storms is enhanced. Sea levels have risen, which exacerbates storm surges, and as the waters are warmer, more energy is added to the storms, meaning they are likely to be more destructive.[17]

A December 2019 report from the World Meteorological Organization was even more frightening, indicating that climate change

---

14   Many facts about recent temperature increases are in Stephanie Ebbs, "2018 Makes Last 5 Years the Warmest in History, Scientists Say, as Democrats Put Climate Change on the Agenda," *ABC News*, February 6, 2016.
15   Doyle Rice, "2020 Expected to be Earth's Warmest Year on Record, Scientsts Say," *USA Today*, April 16, 2020.
16   Dana Nuccitelli, "Study: Humans Have Caused All the Global Warming Since 1950," *The Guardian*, April 19, 2016.
17   Henry Fountain, "The Hurricanes, and Climate Change Questions, Keep Coming. Yes, They're Related," *The New York Times*, October 10, 2018.

was accelerating, with climatic conditions likely to get far worse in the near future.[18] Among the worrying trends cited in the report is that seas are warming and rising faster, putting many cities at risk of tidal flooding (there is already "sunny day flooding" in coastal cities like Miami, Florida, due to higher tides). Polar icecaps[19] and glaciers worldwide[20] have been melting rapidly, faster than scientific projections. Glaciers are "reservoirs in the sky," providing vital water for irrigating crops every spring, so their retreat will pose a major threat to future food supplies for the rising world population. These are melting at a pace many researchers did not expect for decades, and Arctic sea ice has declined so rapidly that the region may have ice-free summers by the 2030s.[21]

To give you a sense of just how rapidly this is occurring, in June 2019 temperatures in Greenland were 40°F above normal, causing the melting in a single day of two billion tons of ice, the equivalent of 800,000 Olympic swimming pools. The Arctic permafrost has begun to thaw seventy years before scientists had predicted only a few years ago, potentially liberating vast quantities of greenhouse gases that had been trapped underground for millennia. In the spring of 2019, Arctic sea ice coverage approached record lows.[22]

In addition to these ongoing system-transforming modifications of the planet, hundred-year or once-in-a-lifetime weather events are likely to become decade, half-decade, or even annual occurrences. Nor will they necessarily happen sequentially. For instance, on March 18, 2019, a deadly cyclone devastated several countries in southern Africa, causing almost a thousand deaths,[23] and catastrophic floods inundated several U.S. Midwestern states, possibly causing a "breaking point for farms,"

---

18 Henry Fountain, "Climate Change Is Accelerating: 'Things Are Getting Worse,'" *The New York Times*, December 4, 2019.
19 Damian Carrington, "Polar Ice Caps Melting Six Times Faster than in 1990s," *The Guardian*, March 11, 2020; and Theresa Braine, "Greenland Ice Sheets Melting Exponentially Faster Than in 1990s, Study Shows," *The Jerusalem Post*, December 15, 2019.
20 Stephanie Pappas, "How Fast Are Glaciers Melting? Just Listen to Them," *Scientific American*, May 29, 2018.
21 *Ibid.*
22 Thomas Gaulkin and Raymond Pierrehumbert, "Hooray, the Arctic Is Melting! Say WHAT?" *Bulletin of the Atomic Scientists*, June 25, 2019, https://thebulletin.org/2019/06/hooray-the-arctic-is-melting-say-what/.
23 Norimitsu Onishi and Jeffrey Mayo, "Cyclone Idai Destroys 'Ninety Percent' of a City of Half a Million in Southern Africa," *The New York Times*, March 18, 2019.

which were already experiencing falling incomes.[24] Different regions of the world will be able to handle crises such as these with relative ease or difficulty; however, no nation state will be able to absorb year upon year of ruinous climatic events and remain stable or prosperous.

Indeed, largely because of huge financial losses from such severe climate events, the same month of the floods in southern Africa and the American Midwest, Munich Re, one of the world's largest reinsurance companies, declared that some properties may soon be essentially uninsurable.[25] The company lost $24 *billion* in 2018 due to the severe, widespread wildfires in California. Their chief climatologist announced:

> If the risk from wildfires, flooding, storms or hail is increasing, then the only sustainable option we have is to adjust our risk prices accordingly. In the long run it might become a social issue. Affordability is so critical [because] some people on low and average incomes in some regions will no longer be able to buy insurance.[26]

CLIMATE CHANGE AND ISRAEL

Israel is especially threatened by climate change. Rising seas could cause the coastal plane, where much of Israel's population and infrastructure are located, to be inundated. Climatologists project that the Middle East as a whole will become significantly hotter and drier, and military experts believe that this makes instability, terrorism, and war more likely.[27]

In a report presented at the 2019 United Nations Framework Convention on Climate Change held in Madrid, Spain, between December 2 and December 13, the Israeli Ministry of Environmental Protection projected that the average temperature in Israel will rise by 0.9 to 1.2°C

---

24 Mitch Smith, Jack Healey, and Timothy Williams, "'It's Probably Over for Us': Flooding Pummels Midwest When Farmers Can Least Afford It," *The New York Times*, March 18, 2019.
25 Arthur Neslen, "Insurance Could Become Unaffordable, Due to Climate Change," *Bulletin of the Atomic Scientists*, March 22, 2019, https://thebulletin.org/2019/03/insurance-could-become-unaffordable-due-to-climate-change/.
26 *Ibid.*
27 Ruth Schuster, "Mideast Climate Change: Hotter, Drier, and More Dangerous," *Haaretz*, February 11, 2015.

by 2050, while rainfall will decrease by at least 15 to 25 percent by the end of the century.[28] To indicate how serious these projections are, the average world temperature rise since the start of the Industrial Revolution is 1.1°C; and Israel already faces a serious water problem during some years.

The gravity of the climate threats to Israel was captured in the December 4, 2019, headline in *The Jerusalem Post*: "Hot and Dry: Climate Report Spells Disaster." The ministry's report focused on four climate trends expected to negatively affect Israel: higher temperature, higher humidity, rising sea levels, and extreme weather fluctuations.[29] It warned that everyday Israeli life would be profoundly impacted, with more dangers of floods, famine, natural disasters, water contamination, and exacerbated tensions on the country's borders.[30] Israel is also vulnerable to the climate change–induced shortages that food and climate experts now believe the United States, China, and India could experience as severe weather and crop failures become annual events. Israel imports 90 percent of its grains and legumes.[31]

Israel received a potent reminder that these grim possibilities are no longer a distant threat. In May 2019, with temperatures throughout Israel near or above 40°C (104°F), "dozens of homes were burned to the ground and 3,500 people were evacuated from their homes . . . as more than 20 fires raged across the state."[32] Yet, despite these present and looming climate threats, Israel remains far behind most countries in responding to climate change.[33]

POTENTIAL TIPPING POINTS

It's clear that urgent preventive action is needed, not least because, as climate scientists warn, the present pace of climate change could speed

---

28 Lior Gutman, "Israel Will See Less Rain, Higher Temperatures by 2050," *CTech Newsletter*, December 3, 2019.
29 Idan Zonshine, "Hot and Dry: Climate Report Spells Disaster, *The Jerusalem Post*, December 4, 2019.
30 *Ibid.*
31 Ruth Schuster, "Revealed: Israel Is Dangerously Unprepared for Global Food Shortages," *Haaretz*, July 11, 2019.
32 Seth Frantzman, et al., "Thousands Evacuated as Homes Burned in Cross-country Heat-wave Inferno," *The Jerusalem Post*, May 24, 2019.
33 Schuster, "Revealed."

up dramatically if self-reinforcing positive feedback loops—vicious cycles in the climate system—trigger irreversible tipping points, causing climate change to spin out of control, beyond the reach of any mitigation.[34,35] Once the genie is out of the bottle—as massive polar ice sheets begin sliding into the sea, to give one example—there is no stuffing him back in. As Jerry Brown, the former governor of California, a state subjected to many severe climate events recently, commented: "Humanity is on a collision course with nature."[36]

The feedback loops can take several forms: stronger and more prevalent wildfires will burn more trees, which absorb CO_2. Carbon is released from the burning trees into the atmosphere, which warms the atmosphere more, exacerbating the potential for additional wildfires and other climatic events. Another feedback loop occurs when ice, a reflector of the sun's rays, melts. The darker soil or water revealed absorbs more of the sun's energy, causing more ice to melt, and faster. Yet another is that as temperatures go up, people use more air conditioning, which means more fossil fuels are burned, resulting in more greenhouse gas emissions, and thus more warming. This in turn leads to more people employing air conditioning . . . and the cycle continues and intensifies.

I'm afraid the news only gets worse. Prior to the December 2019 Madrid climate conference, scientists warned in the prestigious journal *Nature*[37] that irreversible climate tipping points are more likely and could occur at lower temperature increases than recently thought. Humans were, said the writers, in effect playing Russian roulette with Earth's climate by ignoring the growing risks.[38]

Will Steffen, a climate researcher with the Australian National University and co-author of the cautionary paper in *Nature*, told reporters: "What we're talking about is a point of no return, when we might actually

---

34 Fiona Harvey, "'Tipping Points' Could Exacerbate Climate Crisis, Scientists Fear," *The Guardian*, October 9, 2018.
35 Yasemin Saplakoglu, "The Planet Is Dangerously Close to the Tipping Point for a 'Hothouse Earth,'" *Live Science*, August 6, 2016.
36 David Siders, "'Humanity Is on a Collision Course with Nature, California Governor Says," *The National Memo*, May 19, 2014.
37 Timothy M. Lenten, et al., "Climate Tipping Points—Too Risky to Bet Against?" *Nature*, November 27, 2019.
38 Bob Berwyn, "Climate Tipping Points Are Closer Than We Think, Scientists Warn," *InsideClimateNews*, November 27, 2019.

lose control of this system, and there is a significant risk that we're going to do this. It's not going to be the same conditions with just a bit more heat or a bit more rainfall. It's a cascading process that gets out of control."[39]

The scientists warned of nine potential tipping points that are now active: Arctic sea ice; the Greenland ice sheet; the boreal forests; permafrost; the Atlantic meridional overturning circulation; the Amazon rainforest; warm-water corals; the West Antarctic Ice Sheet; and parts of East Antarctica.[40]

To illustrate how serious these potential tipping points are, if the major ice sheets on Greenland, West Antarctica, and part of East Antarctica collapsed, it would result in around ten meters (about 33 feet) of sea-level rise *worldwide*.[41] If tipping points were reached in rainforests, permafrost, and boreal forests, additional massive amounts of greenhouse gases would be released, amplifying warming, making other tipping points not only more likely, but closer in time.[42]

The study also showed that far from reducing the amount of CO_2 and other greenhouse gases in the atmosphere, we are adding to them, faster than ever. Climatologists have argued that concentrations of 350 parts per million (ppm) of atmospheric CO_2 is a threshold level for climate stability. The world has not only exceeded 400 ppm,[43] but the CO_2 level is continuing to grow.[44] In May 2019, data from the Mauna Loa Observatory in Hawaii showed that the atmospheric carbon dioxide level, which had hovered below 285 ppm for thousands of years prior to the Industrial Revolution, had surpassed 415 ppm, the highest value in human history.[45,46] Of course, every year that CO_2 emissions do not

---

39 *Ibid.*
40 *Ibid.* Also, University of Exeter, "Nine Climate Tipping Points Now 'Active,' Warn Scientists," *Science Daily*, November 27, 2019, https://www.sciencedaily.com/releases/2019/11/191127161418.htm.
41 *Ibid.*
42 *Ibid.*
43 Jonathan Watts and Agencies, "Global Atmospheric CO_2 Levels Hit Record High," *The Guardian*, October 30, 2017.
44 Josh Gabbatiss, "CO_2 Levels Expected to Rise Rapidly in 2019, Met Office Scientists Warn," *Independent*, January 25, 2019.
45 Ryan W. Miller and Doyle Rice, "Carbon Dioxide Levels Hit Landmark at 415 ppm, Highest in Human History," *USA Today*, May 13, 2019.
46 Chelsea Harvey, "CO_2 Emissions Will Break Another Record in 2019," *Scientific American*, December 4, 2019.

decrease, and especially if they increase, it becomes harder to meet any CO_2 reduction targets.

It's sometimes hard to grasp these seismic changes in human terms: the processes seem too vast and impersonal. However, the scope and scale of the effects of climate change cannot disguise the very real consequences to human well-being.

One area will be in the spread of illnesses caused by extreme weather, heat stress, and mosquitos, including malaria.[47] According to World Health Organization (WHO) expert Diarmid Campbell-Lendrum:

> WHO considers that climate change is potentially the greatest health threat of the 21st Century. The reason for that is that unless we cut our carbon emissions, we will continue to undermine our food supplies, our water supplies and our air quality—everything that we need to maintain the good health of our populations.[48]

Maria Neira, director of WHO's Department of Environment, Climate Change, and Health, told a news briefing at the December 2018 Madrid climate conference: "Health is paying the price of the climate crisis. Why? Because our lungs, our brains, our cardiovascular system is very much suffering from the causes of climate change which are overlapping very much with the causes of air pollution."[49] Yet less than one percent of international financing for climate action goes to the health sector, she said, calling it "absolutely outrageous."[50]

THE POWER OF DENIAL

Given the overwhelming evidence that confirms anthropogenic climate change, and the larger number of catastrophic meteorological events accompanying it, why are there still a considerable number of people, including some in power, who remain either skeptical or in denial? When

---

47 Stephanie Nebehay, "Climate Change Hits Health, Yet Funds Lacking: WHO," *Reuters*, December 3, 2019.
48 *Ibid.*
49 *Ibid.*
50 *Ibid.*

Ipsos MORI, one of the United Kingdom's largest market research companies, carried out a survey of people in twenty countries on the issue,[51] it discovered that only 54 percent of Americans agreed with the statement, "The climate change we are currently seeing is largely the result of human activity." This put the United States bottom of the list, ten points below the next lowest countries, Australia and Britain.

The survey also found that whereas 93 percent of people from China agreed with the statement, "We are heading for environmental disaster unless we change our habits quickly," only 57 percent of Americans concurred, again placing the United States last among the nations surveyed.

According to James Hoggan, author of *Climate Cover-Up: The Crusade to Deny Global Warming*, the oil, coal, and other industries that profit from the status quo are willing to go to great lengths to mislead people so they can continue to prosper. Hoggan, who was initially a skeptic about climate change, writes in the preface to his book that the industry's cover-up of climate change threats is a "story of betrayal, a story of selfishness, greed, and irresponsibility on an epic scale, . . . a story of deceit, of poisoning public judgment."[52]

Although the denialism is thankfully receding as we enter the third decade of this century, there are still conservative politicians and commentators who are downplaying the significance of climate change—most notoriously, U.S. Republican Senator James Inhofe, who called it the "greatest hoax ever perpetrated on the American people."[53]

No wonder some are confused. On one side you have vociferously opinionated media pundits, bloggers, and politicians like Senator Inhofe (who received close to a million dollars in campaign contributions from the oil and coal industries between 2000 and 2008) and Donald Trump (who has called climate change a Chinese "hoax")[54]; on the other are the

---

51   Michael Roppolo, "Americans More Skeptical of Climate Change than Others in Global Survey," *CBS News*, July 23, 2014.
52   James Hoggan, *Climate Cover-Up: The Crusade to Deny Global Warming* (Vancouver, BC: Greystone Books, 2009).
53   Michael Mann, et al., "Senator Inhofe on Climate Change," RealClimate, January 10, 2005, http://www.realclimate.org/index.php/archives/2005/01/senator-inhofe/.
54   Justin Worland, "Donald Trump Called Climate Change a Hoax. Now He's Awkwardly Boasting about Fighting It," *Time*, July 8, 2019.

genuine experts, typically more cautious in their assertions. For sure, a few examples of scientific misbehavior have occurred, unfairly seized upon and exaggerated by climate change deniers. But follow-up investigations have demonstrated that there were no efforts by the scientific community to mislead the public deliberately.[55]

In the end, the situation is too dire and the warning signs too stark for climate change to be a partisan issue, associated with the knee-jerk identities of our political parties. It is, I would suggest, the greatest moral, environmental, economic, and social justice issue of our time. Every aspect of our lives must be reconsidered: a shift to renewable forms of energy; improved transportation systems; more efficient cars and other means of transportation; the massive reduction of the production and consumption of animal-based foods; and lower population growth. All these, and more, need to be in service to lowering our greenhouse gas emissions and keeping future temperature rises to no more than another half—or at the most, one—degree Celsius.

I'm pleased to say that the Jewish voice on mitigating climate change is being heard. On October 29, 2015, a Rabbinic Letter on the Climate Crisis, signed by 425 rabbis, called for "vigorous action to prevent worsening climate disruption."[56] It is my hope that this initiative will inspire many more rabbis and additional Jews to play major roles in addressing climate threats.

Like many of you, I have a personal stake in the future of Israel and the world—one that is brought home to me whenever I hear of a couple getting married or a baby being born. In the last few years, three of my grandchildren have married, and one has given birth to a boy, making me and my wife great-grandparents. This child will be almost as old as I am now when the clock turns to 2100. What kind of world will he

---

55   Union of Concerned Scientists, "Debunking Misinformation About Stolen Climate Emails in the 'Climategate' Manufactured Controversy," December 8, 2009, https://www.ucsusa.org/resources/debunking-misinformation-about-stolen-climate-emails.
56   To see the signatories and read the letter, visit The Shalom Center, https://theshalomcenter.org/RabbinicLetterClimate.

live in? Will he have a house to call his own, or a homeland at all? Will he look back at his ancestors and wonder how it was possible they—we—didn't do more, when the evidence was so stark and compelling, and when we had the means in our hands, and on our plates, to make a difference?

6

THE ENVIRONMENT

Now the Lord God took the man [Adam], and He placed him in the Garden of Eden to work it and to guard it.

—*Genesis* 2:15

The earth was not created as a gift to you. You have been given to the earth, to treat it with respectful consideration, as God's earth, and everything on it [must be seen] as God's creation, . . . and to be respected, loved, and helped to attain their purpose according to God's will.

—*Rabbi Samson Raphael Hirsch*[1]

W hen confronted with the prospect of catastrophic climate change, it can be difficult to remember that there are other—although related—shocks that harm species and habitats, cause pollution and soil erosion, and lead to loss of biodiversity. As with climate change, the effects of human behavior on the planet's ecosystems are widely known and have been settled science for at least three decades.

In July 1992, a month after the world gathered in Rio de Janeiro for the United Nations Conference on Environment and Development (commonly known as the "Earth Summit"), 1,670 scientists—including 104 Nobel laureates (a majority of the then living recipients of the prize in the sciences)—issued a sobering statement titled "1992 World Scientists'

---

1   Rabbi Samson Rafael Hirsch, *Nineteen Letters* (Jerusalem/New York: Feldheim, 1969) (Rabbi Joseph Elias edition), Letter 4.

Warning to Humanity."[2] "Human beings and the natural world are on a collision course," their document began:

> Human activities inflict harsh and often irreversible damage on the environment and on critical resources. If not checked, many of our current practices put at serious risk the future that we wish for human society and the plant and animal kingdoms, and may so alter the living world that it will be unable to sustain life in the manner that we know. Fundamental changes are urgent if we are to avoid the collision our present course will bring about.

They issued a stern prescription for humanity:

> We the undersigned, senior members of the world's scientific community, hereby warn all humanity of what lies ahead. A great change in our stewardship of the earth and the life on it is required, if vast human misery is to be avoided and our global home on this planet is not to be irretrievably mutilated.

In 2017, a new generation of scientists returned to issue a second warning. Reflecting on those who issued the 1992 message, 15,364 signatories from 184 countries responded as follows:[3]

> On the twenty-fifth anniversary of their call, we look back at their warning and evaluate the human response by exploring available time-series data. Since 1992, with the exception of stabilizing the stratospheric ozone layer, humanity has failed to make sufficient progress in generally solving these foreseen environmental challenges, and alarmingly, most of them are getting far worse.
>
> Especially troubling is the current trajectory of potentially catastrophic climate change due to rising greenhouse gases from

---

2   Union of Concerned Scientists, "1992 World Scientists' Warning to Humanity," July 16, 1992, https://www.ucsusa.org/about/1992-world-scientists.html.

3   William J. Ripple, et al., "World Scientists' Warning of a Climate Emergency," *BioScience* 70, no. 1 (January 2020): 8–12, academic.oup.com/bioscience/article/70/1/8/5610806.

burning fossil fuels, deforestation, and agricultural production—particularly from farming ruminants for meat consumption. Moreover, we have unleashed a mass extinction event, the sixth in roughly 540 million years, wherein many current life forms could be annihilated or at least committed to extinction by the end of this century.

Humanity is now being given a second notice, as illustrated by these alarming trends. We are jeopardizing our future by not reining in our intense but geographically and demographically uneven material consumption and by not perceiving continued rapid population growth as a primary driver behind many ecological and even societal threats. By failing to adequately limit population growth, reassess the role of an economy rooted in growth, reduce greenhouse gases, incentivize renewable energy, protect habitat, restore ecosystems, curb pollution, halt defaunation [extinction of animal species], and constrain invasive alien species, humanity is not taking the urgent steps needed to safeguard our imperilled biosphere.

As with climate change, one of the main drivers of these harms to our ecosystems is animal agriculture.

THE IMPACT OF ANIMAL-BASED DIETS ON CLIMATE CHANGE

Many people express surprise when they learn about the contribution that animal-based diets make to climate change.[4] However, in 2006, the United Nations Food and Agriculture Organization (FAO) released a study, *Livestock's Long Shadow*, which found that livestock agriculture (at 14.5 percent) emits more greenhouse gases, per CO_2 equivalent, than all the cars, planes, ships, and other means of transportation worldwide

---

4   For an overview of animal agriculture's effect on the environment and climate change, see Christopher Schlottmann and Jeff Sebo, *Food, Animals, and the Environment: An Ethical Approach* (New York: Earthscan/Routledge, 2019). Another overview can be found in Tony Weis, *The Ecological Hoofprint: The Global Burden of Industrial Livestock* (London: Zed Books, 2013).

combined.[5] (Some have argued that the percentage is much higher.)[6] The FAO report also projected a possible doubling of meat consumption by the middle of this century[7] as newly affluent nations move up the food chain. Animal-centered agriculture is an outsized contributor to climate change mainly due to the emission of methane via enteric fermentation in cows, sheep, and goats—alongside land-use change.[8] Methane is about eighty-four times as potent a greenhouse gas as CO_2, even though (at twenty years) it lasts less time in the atmosphere.[9]

However, the livestock industry is responsible for many other threats to the environment. Before I show how environmental destruction is inimical to Jewish values, it's worth considering in detail how animal agriculture lays waste to the natural world.[10]

Each year, about a billion tons of precious topsoil are lost to erosion, either through overgrazing or poor or inefficient land use. Over half of all United States rangelands are overgrazed, with billions of tons of soil lost every year. Erosion is leading to lower yields and a reduction in soil fertility worldwide.[11]

Animal agriculture contributes to water pollution in several ways: excessive nitrogen and phosphorus from chemical fertilizers—much of it used (in the United States) to grow crops such as wheat, corn, and soy

5   Henning Steinfeld, et al., *Livestock's Long Shadow: Environmental Issues and Options* (Rome: FAO, 2006), http://www.fao.org/3/a0701e/a0701e00.htm. The FAO's original estimation that global livestock production was responsible for 18 percent of global GHGs was lowered to 14.5 percent in 2013.
6   Jeff Anhang and Robert Goodland in their November/December 2009 article, "Livestock and Climate Change," for *World Watch* magazine suggested the number was at least 51 percent.
7   Steinfeld, et al., *Livestock's Long Shadow*.
8   Brent Kim, et al., "The Importance of Reducing Animal Product Consumption and Wasted Food in Mitigating Catastrophic Climate Change," CLF Report, 2015, https://clf.jhsph.edu/publications/importance-reducing-animal-product-consumption-and-wasted-food-mitigating-catastrophic.
9   Environmental Defense Fund, "Methane: The Other Important Greenhouse Gas," n.d., https://www.edf.org/climate/methane-other-important-greenhouse-gas.
10 Much information about the negative environmental effects of animal-based diets, including many of the facts below, can be found in *Diet for a New America* by John Robbins, *Diet for a Small Planet* by Frances Moore Lappé, and *Eating Animals* by Jonathan Safran Foer. Additional valuable information on this issue is in the UN Food and Agriculture's report *Livestock's Long Shadow*, and in Bibi van der Zee, "What Is the True Cost of Eating Meat?" *The Guardian*, May 7, 2018.
11 John Sauven, "Why Meat Eaters Should Think Much More about Soil," *The Guardian*, May 16, 2017.

for animal feed—runs off into waterways, leading to eutrophication.[12] Animal waste from "lagoons" of excrement outside factory farms can leach or overflow into bodies of water, in addition to producing foul odors and flies.[13] Animals also produce pathogens (like *E. coli*) in their manure, as well as drug and hormone residue, feed additives, and toxic metals.[14]

Cattle are one of the leading causes of rainforest destruction: whether for grazing or to grow crops to feed to livestock around the world.[15] It has been estimated that over a hundred plant, animal, and insect species are lost every day due to the decimation of their habitats.[16] A May 2019 report by the Intergovernmental Science Policy Platform on Biology and Ecosystem Services (IPBES), written by 145 environmental experts from fifty countries, found that one million of the planet's eight million species are threatened with extinction, largely due to human actions, including animal-oriented agriculture and overfishing. Sir Robert Watson, IPBES chair, concluded: "The health of ecosystems on which we and all other species depend is deteriorating more rapidly than ever," and "transformative changes" are needed to save the planet.[17]

This loss of biodiversity is not only a tragedy for animals, but half of the world's plant species reside in tropical rainforests, and some may hold secrets for cures of some of today's deadly diseases.[18] A further worry is

12　World Resources Institute, "Sources of Eutrophication," n.d., https://www.wri.org/our-work/project/eutrophication-and-hypoxia/sources-eutrophication. See also, Tom Philpott, "The Gulf of Mexico Is About to Experience a 'Dead Zone' the Size of Connecticut," *Mother Jones*, June 17, 2016.
13　Christina Cooke, "North Carolina's Factory Farms Produce 15,000 Olympic Pools Worth of Waste Each Year," *Civil Eats*, June 28, 2016.
14　Purdue University, "CAFOs and Public Health: Pathogens and Manure," n.d. https://www.extension.purdue.edu/extmedia/id/cafo/id-356.html.
15　Yale School of Forestry & Environmental Studies, "Cattle Ranching in the Amazon Region," n.d., https://globalforestatlas.yale.edu/amazon/land-use/cattle-ranching; and FAO, "Cattle Ranching and Deforestation," Livestock Policy Brief 3, n.d., http://www.fao.org/3/a-a0262e.pdf.
16　Fred Pearce, "Global Extinction Rates: Why Do Estimates Vary So Widely?" Yale Environment 360, August 17, 2015, https://e360.yale.edu/features/global_extinction_rates_why_do_estimates_vary_so_wildly.
17　IPBES, "Media Release: Nature's Dangerous Decline 'Unprecedented'; Species Extinction Rates 'Accelerating,'" n.d., https://ipbes.net/news/Media-Release-Global-Assessment.
18　Walter Suza, "As Tropical Rainforests Disappear, So Do Potential Medicine Reservoirs," Undark, November 19, 2019, https://undark.org/2019/11/19/tropical-rainforest-disappear-potential-medicine-reservoirs/.

that the decrease of rainforests may reduce rainfall and weather patterns with potentially devastating effects on agriculture in many areas.[19]

ANIMAL AGRICULTURE, WATER, AND ENERGY

As part of a climate change mitigation strategy, international bodies such as the United Nations are urging us to reduce our fossil fuel dependency and conserve energy. Here, too, animal agriculture proves to be both fossil fuel–dependent and energy inefficient.[20]

The production of meat requires ten to twenty times more energy per edible ton than grain production. Indeed, growing feed crops for farmed animals requires considerable energy for plowing, pumping irrigation water, harvesting, producing pesticides and fertilizer, and transportation. Additional energy is needed to process those crops. Furthermore, the production of a pound of steak (500 calories of food energy) uses 20,000 calories of fossil fuels, most of which is expended to produce feed crops.[21]

Housing chickens and pigs in huge windowless sheds requires energy for lighting, artificial ventilation, and conveyor belts. Slaughterhouses also use energy and, because of the need to sluice away blood and viscera, are water intensive. In fact, animal foods require much more energy for processing, packaging, and refrigeration than do plant-based foods. Whereas it is true that the growing of any kind of food requires inputs of energy, it requires seventy-eight calories of fossil fuel to produce a calorie of protein obtained from feedlot-produced beef, but only two calories of fossil fuel to produce a calorie of protein from soybeans.[22]

---

19   Fred Pearce, "Rivers in the Sky: How Deforestation Is Affecting Global Water Cycles," Yale Environment 360, July 24, 2018, https://e360.yale.edu/features/how-deforestation-affecting-global-water-cycles-climate-change.
20   These examples are based on material from "Meat and the Environment: Facts and Resources," report produced by the Toronto Vegetarian Association, drawing from United Nations reports, February 2, 2007, https://veg.ca/2007/02/01/meat-and-the-environment/; and J. Frorip, et al., "Energy Consumption in Animal Production—Case Farm Study," Agronomy Research (Biosystem Engineering Special Issue) (2001) 1:39–48.
21   Frances Moore Lappé, Diet for a Small Planet, 20th Anniversary Edition (New York: Ballantine Books, 1992), 10.
22   Ibid., 74, 75.

Only 2.5 percent of the world's available water is potable, and only one percent is accessible.[23] Around 790 million people, or 11 percent of the world's population, lack access to safe drinking water.[24] Yet, in spite of the fact that fresh water is being depleted at an alarming rate as glaciers melt and aquifers shrink, our commitment to the very thirsty animal agriculture continues.

Almost a third of the world's water is consumed to produce meat and other animal products,[25] with 56 percent of the water in the United States (or 14 trillion gallons) used to grow crops to feed animals,[26] and between 20 and 33 percent of the world's fresh water consumption employed for animal agriculture.[27]

Because of the enormous amounts of water needed to produce feed crops for animals or to keep the animals themselves hydrated, an egg requires 53 gallons of water to produce; a pound of chicken, 468 gallons; a gallon of cow's milk, 880 gallons; and a pound of beef, 1,800 gallons. Just one hamburger requires up to 660 gallons of water to produce, the equivalent of about two months of showers for an individual. The production of one pound of steak uses 2,500 gallons of water, while only 25 gallons are required to produce a pound of wheat.[28] *Newsweek* calculated that "the water that goes into a 1,000 pound steer would float a Naval destroyer."[29]

As we saw earlier in this chapter, manure runoff from industrial farms pollutes ground water and rivers. In fact, one-third of rivers in

---

23   *National Geographic*, "Freshwater Crisis," n.d., https://www.nationalgeographic.com/environment/freshwater/freshwater-crisis/.

24   Centers for Disease Control and Prevention, "Global WASH Fast Facts," n.d., https://www.cdc.gov/healthywater/global/wash_statistics.html.

25   P. W. Gerbens-Leenes, et al., "The Water Footprint of Poultry, Pork and Beef: A Comparative Study in Different Countries and Production Systems," *Water Resources and Industry* Vols 1–2 (March–June 2013): 25–36.

26   Michael F. Jacobson, "Six Arguments for a Greener Diet: How a More Plant-based Diet Could Save Your Health and the Environment, Chapter 4: More and Cleaner Water" (Washington, DC: Center for Science in the Public Interest, 2006), https://cspinet.org/new/200608011.html.

27   Gerbens-Leenes, et al., "The Water Footprint of Poultry, Pork and Beef."

28   Nicholas Kristof, "Our Water-Guzzling Food Factory," *The New York Times*, May 30, 2015.

29   "The Browning of America," *Newsweek*, February 2, 1981. See also, John Vidal, "Meat-Eaters Soak up the World's Water," *The Guardian*, August 23, 2004.

the United States have been polluted by animal excrement, fertilizer, pesticides, and other toxic substances.[30]

JEWISH TEACHINGS ON THE ENVIRONMENT

Just as the Hebrew scriptures place an emphasis on compassion toward animals, so too they emphasize a commitment to the planet on which we all live. Perhaps the most fundamental Jewish environmental teaching is: "The land and the fullness thereof are the Lord's; the world and those who dwell therein" (Psalm 24:1). The land and its fruits are a sacred trust from God; they must be used to fulfill God's purposes.

In a sense, no person has absolute or exclusive control over their possessions. The idea that we are custodians of Earth, not its owners, is illustrated by the following story from Rabbi Shlomo Riskin:

Two men were fighting over a piece of land. Each claimed ownership and bolstered his claim with apparent proof. To resolve their differences, they agreed to put the case before the rabbi. The rabbi listened to their arguments but could come to no decision because both seemed to be right. Finally he said, "Since I cannot decide to whom this land belongs, let us ask the land." He put his ear to the ground and, after a moment, straightened up. "Gentlemen, the land says it belongs to neither of you but that you belong to it."[31]

There is an apparent contradiction between "The land and the fullness thereof are the Lord's; the world and those who dwell therein" (Psalm 24:1) and "The heavens are the heavens of the Lord, but the earth He gave to the children of men" (Psalm 115:16). The discrepancy can be resolved as follows: Before a person recites a *b'racha*—a blessing acknowledging God as the Lord and Creator of the land and all the bounty that flows from

30   Scott K. Johnson, "About a Third of US Rivers Contaminated with Agricultural Runoff," ArtsTechnica, April 8, 2013, https://arstechnica.com/science/2013/04/about-a-third-of-us-rivers-contaminated-with-agricultural-runoff/.
31   Story told by Rabbi Shlomo Riskin in *Biblical Ecology: A Jewish View*, a television documentary. As cited in my *Judaism and Global Survival* (New York: Lantern Books, 2002), 212.

it—it is indeed true that "the earth is the Lord's." But once a person has thoughtfully recited the *b'racha*, reflecting humbly on his or her place in the scheme of things, both as the beneficiary of God's earthly domain and its *steward* in His name, then indeed can it conscientiously be stated that "the earth He has given to humans" (*B'rachot* 30:5).

According to Judaism, the produce of the field does not belong solely to the person who farms the land. The poor are entitled to a portion:

> When you reap the harvest of your land, you shall not fully reap the corner of your field, nor shall you gather the gleanings of your harvest. And you shall not glean your vineyard, nor shall you collect the [fallen] individual grapes of your vineyard; you shall leave them for the poor and for the stranger. I am the Lord, your God. (Leviticus 19:9–10)

These portions set aside for the poor were not voluntary contributions based on kindness. They were, in essence, a regularly assessed payment. Because God was the true owner of the land, He claimed a share of His resources to benefit the poor and "the stranger"—including the immigrant or refugee.

To remind us that that "the Earth is the Lord's," and we must conserve it, the land must be allowed to rest and lie fallow every seven years. This is called the Sabbatical Year:

> Six years you may sow your land and gather in its produce. But in the seventh [year] you shall release it and abandon it; the poor of your people shall eat [it], and what they leave over, the beasts of the field shall eat. So shall you do to your vineyard [and] to your olive tree[s]. (Exodus 23:10–11)

Thus, the sabbatical year is a year of environmental conservation, of stewardship that benefits soil fertility, the poor, the hungry, and wildlife alike.

Judaism asserts there is one God who created our entire earthly ecosystem as a harmonious whole, in ecological balance, and that everything is interdependently connected. This vision is perhaps best expressed in Psalm 104:

> He [God] sends the springs into the streams; they go between the mountains.
> They water every beast of the field; the wild donkeys quench their thirst.
> Beside them the fowl of the heavens dwell; from between the branches they let out their voices.
> He waters the mountains from His upper chambers; from the fruit of Your works the earth is sated.
> He causes grass to sprout for the animals and vegetation for the work of man, to bring forth bread from the earth. . . .
> How great are Your works, O Lord! You have made them all with wisdom; the earth is full of Your possessions! (10–14, 24)

The talmudic sages were deeply concerned about preserving the environment and preventing pollution. "It is forbidden to live in a town which has no garden or greenery," they declared (*Kiddushin* 4:12; 66d). Threshing floors had to be placed far enough from a town that it would not be dirtied by chaff carried by the winds (*Baba Batra* 2:8). Tanneries had to be kept at least fifty cubits from a town and could be placed only on the east side of a town, so that odors would not be carried by the prevailing winds from the west (*Baba Batra* 2:8, 9). The rabbis express a sense of sanctity toward the environment: "The atmosphere (air) of the land of Israel makes one wise" (*Baba Batra* 158b).

The Psalms also give voice to this idea that God the Creator has appointed us to be partners in the work of creation:

> When I see Your heavens, the work of Your fingers, the moon and stars that You have established,
> What is man that You should remember him, and the son of man that You should be mindful of him?
> Yet You have made him slightly less than than the angels, and You have crowned him with glory and majesty.

You give him dominion over the work of Your hands; You have
placed everything beneath his feet. (Psalm 8:4–7)

The prohibition *bal tashchit* ("you shall not destroy"), which we came
across in chapter one, is based on Deuteronomy 20:19–20):

When you besiege a city for many days to wage war against it
to capture it, you shall not destroy its trees by wielding an ax
against them, for you may eat from them, but you shall not cut
them down. Is the tree of the field a man, to go into the siege
before you? However, a tree you know is not a food tree, you may
destroy and cut down, and you shall build bulwarks against the
city that makes war with you, until its submission.

This prohibition against destroying fruit-bearing trees in time of warfare
was extended widely by the Jewish sages into a general prohibition
against wastefulness. It is forbidden to cut down even a barren tree or
to waste anything if no useful purpose is accomplished (*Sefer Ha-Chinuch*
530): "Whoever breaks vessels or tears garments, or destroys a building,
or clogs up a fountain, or destroys food violates the prohibition of *bal
tashchit*" (*Kiddushin* 32a). In summary, *bal tashchit* prohibits the destruction,
complete or incomplete, direct or indirect, of all objects of potential value.

Rabbis considered the violation of *bal tashchit* very seriously. The
sage Rabbi Hanina attributed the early death of his son to the fact that
the boy had chopped down a fig tree (*Baba Kamma* 91b). Jews should be
taught when very young that it is a sin to waste even small amounts of
food (*B'rachot* 52b). Rav Zutra advised: "One who covers an oil lamp or
uncovers a naphtha lamp [actions that would cause a faster (hence wasteful) consumption of the fuel], transgresses the prohibition of *bal tashchit*"
(*Shabbat* 67b). Indeed, Rabbi Samson Raphael Hirsch observed that *bal
tashchit* is the first and most general call of God: We are to "regard things
as God's property and use them with a sense of responsibility for wise
human purposes. Destroy nothing! Waste nothing!"[32] He indicated that

---

32 Rabbi Samson Raphael Hirsch, *Horeb*, Dayan I Grunfeld, trans. (London: Soncino
    Press, 1982), Volume 2, 282.

destruction includes using more things (or things of greater value) than is necessary to obtain one's aim.[33]

In the spirit of *bal tashchit,* the following *midrash* (biblical commentary) contrasts the benefits of simplicity with the harms of excess:

> Two men entered a shop. One ate coarse bread and vegetables, while the other ate fine bread, fat meat, and drank old wine. The one who ate fine food suffered harm, while the one who had coarse food escaped harm. Observe how simply animals live and how healthy they are as a result. (*Ecclesiastes Rabbah* 1:18)

THE TEN NEW PLAGUES AND A NEW EXODUS

When I think of the threats to our land, water, and air; the existential threat to our climate; and other environmental perils that we face, I am reminded of the ten plagues that fell upon the Egyptians in Exodus.

Modern threats include: The rapid melting of polar ice caps, permafrost, and glaciers: all of which could precipitate a sudden and disastrous recalibration of Earth's climate, for which we are utterly unprepared, as well as destroy coastal communities and food-producing wetlands, and swallow entire nations. The destruction of the world's forests: a repository of biodiversity, carbon sequestration, rainfall production, climate regulation, natural capital, and numerous ecosystemic services. A series of deadly heat waves, with each five-year span hotter than the previous one. Increasingly widespread and severe wildfires because of warmer temperatures and the resultant drier conditions in many areas. Severe droughts that force huge population movements and the starvation of cities and regions, and lead to conflict.

Huge die-offs of species—a sixth great extinction. Widespread soil erosion and nutrient depletion—reducing fertility, causing further desertification, and severely compromising humanity's ability to feed itself. The pollution of waterways; the loss of potable water; the contamination by pesticides, inorganic fertilizers, and animal wastes from factory farms; as well as fallout from smokestack and tailpipe air pollution. Epidemics

---

33   *Ibid.,* 280.

of heart disease, many types of cancer, and other chronic degenerative diseases—largely due to gluttonous consumption of animal products and junk foods, sedentary lifestyles, and toxic environmental chemicals.

More hunger and famine because of a human population that is projected to approach 11 billion by 2100; greater affluence and urbanization leading to an exploding demand for animal products—all accompanied by reduced food production because of heat stress to plants and animals, and other damaging effects of climate change.

These modern "plagues" are different from those that confronted the Egyptians and the Jews. The Jews in Goshen were spared the biblical plagues, whereas every person on Earth is imperiled by the modern ones. The Egyptians were subjected to one plague at a time; these modern ones threaten us all at once. Instead of an ancient Pharaoh's heart being hardened, our hearts apparently have been hardened by the greed, materialism, and waste that are at the root of current environmental threats.

God inflicted the plagues to free the Israelites from oppression. But today we must apply God's teachings to save ourselves. Had Pharaoh heeded the warning of the first plague and simply let the Israelites go, there would have been no need for the nine others. Unfortunately, he did not. We must learn from Pharaoh's mistake and heed the warnings that are coming almost daily. We must apply our traditional Judaic teachings in the light of modern science to save our earthly homes, before we are destroyed because of our own hard-heartedness.

It is we ourselves who are the causes of these modern plagues, though it is future generations who will be most severely afflicted. Instead of recognizing that we are partners and co-workers with God in protecting the environment, modern commerce is driven by the unsustainable premise that nature is to be exploited for maximum profit, regardless of the long-term consequences. Whereas Judaism stresses that we are not to waste or unnecessarily destroy anything of value, wastefulness in the United States is so great that, with less than 5 percent of the world's people, the United States consumes 23 percent of the world's coal, 27 percent of its aluminum, and a quarter of the world's oil.[34]

Judaism asserts that a wise person considers the long-range consequences of their actions, including upon future generations. But today we are perilously focused on instant gratification and short-term gains. Although economies grow, environmental damage and destruction continue.

THE CALL OF THE HOUR

Since Jews are a small minority of the world's population (about 0.2 percent), even if every Jew became vegan (a very unlikely scenario), the effect on the climate and other environmental crises would be negligible. However, as Isaiah 49:6 declares, Jews are mandated to be a "light unto the nations," and being vegan is one way to carry this out. The power of a positive example should not be underestimated. It's my view that if many Jews became vegans or at least sharply reduced their consumption of meat and other animal foods, and if veganism and related issues became a major focus of Jewish life, members of other religions would notice and might also shift toward veganism. This could spur secular people to reduce their consumption of meat. A positive feedback loop could result, with veganism being accepted as the most rational diet, with many positive benefits to individuals and the world.

Given the extent of the crisis, it's essential that we in the Jewish community apply our rich tradition of environmental responsibility and stewardship to the world's fragile ecology. This means, for example, embracing an energy policy based not on destructive energy sources, but on CARE (conservation and renewable energy), consistent with Jewish teachings on environmental stewardship, creating jobs, protecting human life, and looking out for future generations.

Too often the Jewish establishment, like the rest of the world, has been silent while our climate is rapidly changing, our air is bombarded by poisons, our rivers and streams are polluted by industrial wastes, our fertile

---

34   *Scientific American*, "Use It and Lose It: The Outsize Effect of U.S. Consumption on the Environment," September 14, 2020, https://www.scientificamerican.com/article/american-consumption-habits/.

soil is eroded and depleted, and the ecological balance is endangered by the destruction of rainforests and other vital habitats.

The Jewish community must become more actively involved. We must proclaim that it is a *chillul Hashem* (a desecration of God's name) to pollute the air and water that God created pure; to slash and burn forests that existed before there were human beings; and to wantonly destroy the abundant resources that God has so generously provided for all of humanity to enjoy and be sustained by. We have a choice, as proclaimed in the Torah:

> This day, I call upon the heaven and the earth as witnesses [that I have warned] you; I have set before you life and death, the blessing and the curse. You shall choose life, so that you and your offspring will live. (Deuteronomy 30:19)

7

HUNGER

So far, we have charted the challenges of the climate crisis, environmental destruction, the cruel treatment of animals, and the issue of health: all of which are made worse by consuming animal products, and all of which would be mitigated, alleviated, repaired, or restored by leaving them off our plates. A further benefit of a vegan diet is that it has the potential to reduce the scandal of widespread world hunger. Given what we know about climate change's effects on food security—both its production and delivery—we've no time to lose to address this perennial problem.

We have already seen that Israel is potentially food insecure because of how dependent it is on imports.[1] Food experts believe that national emergency food reserves should last for at least a year, but Israel's are only enough to suffice for weeks or, at most, three months.[2]

However, Israel is relatively well off compared to other nations. Over 800 million people worldwide (over 10 percent of the world's population) are chronically hungry, and about nine million people die annually from hunger and its effects on health and resistance to disease.[3] The majority of these hungry people live in rural areas in developing regions and depend on agriculture to survive.

Hunger is a debilitating condition that involves far more than just missing an occasional meal. People who are chronically hungry and malnourished consistently lack the nutrients their bodies and minds

---

1   Ruth Schuster, "Revealed: Israel Is Dangerously Unprepared for Global Food Shortage," *Haaretz*, July 11, 2019.
2   *Ibid.*
3   Much of the material in this section is taken from Mercy Corps, "Quick Facts: What You Need to Know About Global Hunger," October 1, 2018, https://www.mercycorps.org/blog/quick-facts-global-hunger; and Hunger Notes, "2018 World Hunger and Poverty Facts and Statistics," WorldHunger.org, https://www.worldhunger.org/world-hunger-and-poverty-facts-and-statistics/.

need. This deprivation prevents them from being able to succeed in school, do well at work, and improve their lives. They often experience developmental disabilities and recurring illnesses, resulting in low productivity. They often must use most, if not all, of their financial and physical resources simply to provide some food for themselves and their families. This subsistence-level nutrition allows hunger to continue from generation to generation.

In many countries, male-dominated social structures limit education, financial services, and job opportunities for women, making them more vulnerable to poverty and hunger. Girls and women constitute about 60 percent of the world's hungry people. This impacts their children, since hungry, malnourished, or undernourished women often have complications during childbirth and deliver underweight babies, sometimes with irreversible mental and physical disabilities—another factor that augments the chances for continued poverty and hunger.

All of these debilitating facets of not having either enough food or adequate nutrition will be exacerbated by climate change.[4] A 2011 report from the National Academy of Sciences estimates that for every one degree Celsius rise in global temperature, there will be a 5 to 15 percent decrease in overall crop production. Without climate change mitigation, this means that there could be as much as a 35 percent decrease in legume and vegetable production by the end of this century.

Given that 80 percent of the world's crops depend on rainfall, unreliable rainfall patterns around the world could directly damage crop production, resulting in lower yields. Meanwhile, sea-level rise and more severe storms will flood croplands—potentially overwhelming drainage and sewage systems and allow toxins and pathogens from farms, roads, and lawns to enter the food supply.

As droughts grow longer and harsher, and as temperatures rise, evaporation and water shortages for irrigation will increase; pests, diseases, and invasive plant and insect species will expand their numbers

---

4   Material in this section is from Renee Cho, "How Climate Change Will Affect Our Food," State of the Planet: Earth Institute, Columbia University, July 25, 2018, https://blogs.ei.columbia.edu/2018/07/25/climate-change-food-agriculture/. See also, Concern Worldwide US, "How Climate Change Threatens Food Security—And Why We're All at Risk," October 23, 2019, https://www.concernusa.org/story/climate-change-food-security/.

and ranges, and will survive longer due to earlier springs and milder winters. More frequent heat waves will render livestock less fertile and more vulnerable to diseases, and leave them more vulnerable to droughts and severe storms. Warmer and more acidic seas (due to dissolved CO_2) threaten the already overfished oceans.

Veganism and Hunger

Perhaps the greatest scandal associated with hunger is that, although we have an abundance of cereal crops that we could feed to human beings, a large percentage of soy, corn, oats, and wheat is grown to feed farmed animals instead of people.[5] Indeed, the average person in the United States consumes almost five times as much grain (most of it indirectly, in the form of animal foods) as a person in a developing country. About 70 percent of the grain grown in the United States is fed to animals destined for slaughter.[6] Half of its arable land is devoted to feed crops or grazing,[7] with 95 percent of corn being directed to livestock feed.[8] What makes this especially shameful is that foods healthy for humans are converted into unhealthful animal products with the opposite characteristics.

It also wastes a colossal amount of land. An animal-based diet requires about 3.5 acres per person, whereas a vegan diet requires only about a fifth of an acre. For instance, it takes about a hundred calories of grain to deliver twelve calories of chicken or three calories of beef.[9]

---

5   The facts in this section and many additional facts relating diet and the utilization of resources can be found in *Diet for a New America* by John Robbins; *Beyond Beef* by Jeremy Rifkin; *Eating Animals* by Jonathan Safran Foer; and *Vegetarian Sourcebook* by Keith Akers. Also used are "Cowspiracy Facts," from the 2014 documentary film *Cowspiracy*, https://www.cowspiracy.com/facts.

6   Jeremy Rifkin, "There's a Bone to Pick with Meat Eaters," *Los Angeles Times*, May 27, 2002; John Robbins, *Diet for a New America: How Your Food Choices Affect Your Health, Happiness and the Future of Life on Earth*, 25th Anniversary Edition (Kindle, 2012).

7   US Department of Agriculture, "Farms and Farmland: Numbers, Acreage, Ownership, and Use," September 2014, https://www.nass.usda.gov/Publications/Highlights/2014/Highlights_Farms_and_Farmland.pdf.

8   US Department of Agriculture, "Feedgrains Sector at a Glance," n.d., https://www.ers.usda.gov/topics/crops/corn-and-other-feedgrains/feedgrains-sector-at-a-glance/.

9   Brad Plumer, "How Much of the World's Cropland Is Actually Used to Grow Food?" *Vox*, December 16, 2014.

Meanwhile, protein conversion rates are 9 percent for pork, 21 percent for poultry, and 3 percent for beef.[10]

This shocking waste and loss of food—and the finite resources, such as topsoil, water, phosphorus, and land that go into its production—is exacerbated by a global system that encourages raising animals or feed crops for export dollars. In spite of dedicating so much of its land and other resources to raising livestock, the United States is, as of 2020, the world's largest importer of beef.[11] For example, although Honduras suffers widespread poverty and malnutrition, it exports large amounts of beef to the United States.[12] In Central America, over half of the agriculturally productive land is used for livestock production, for the wealthy and for export.

The food being directed to farmed animals in the affluent nations could, if properly distributed, sharply reduce and possibly end both hunger and malnutrition throughout the world. A switch from animal-centered diets would free land and other resources that could be used to grow nutritious crops for people.

For all the waste and loss of water and land in food production, an enormous amount of food is wasted and lost *after* it has been grown. According to Feeding America, 72 billion pounds of food is wasted annually in the United States, even though 37 million Americans go hungry. That food is worth $218 billion; wastes 21 percent of fresh water; and occupies a fifth of landfill area.[13] So great is the amount of food lost (left in the fields to rot, unable to make it to market because of poor roads, lack of refrigeration, or because no one is there to pick it) or wasted (thrown away as leftovers, or because it's not considered suitable for sale) that it alone is responsible for *at least* 6 percent of global greenhouse gas (GHG) emissions. To put it another way, food waste is three times more GHG-intensive than aviation, and if it were its own country, food waste

---

10   Alon Shepon, et al., "The Opportunity Cost of Animal Based Diets Exceeds All Food Losses," *Proceedings of the National Academy of Sciences* 115, no. 15 (April 2018): 3804–09, https://doi.org/10.1073/pnas.1713820115.

11   Rob Cook, "World Beef Imports: Ranking of Countries," Beef2Live, https://beef2live.com/story-world-beef-imports-ranking-countries-0-106900.

12   Central America Link, "Honduras Exports Beef to United States," March 7, 2017, https://www.centralamericalink.com/news/honduras-exports-beef-to-united-states.

13   Feeding America, "How We Fight Food Waste in the US," n.d., https://www.feedingamerica.org/our-work/our-approach/reduce-food-waste.

would be the world's third greatest emitter, behind the United States and China.[14]

Animal products are part of that wasteful food chain—especially when, for instance, in the case of cow's milk, a glut in production means it becomes financially inefficient to bring milk to market;[15] or the market itself collapses and there is too much supply.[16] However, animal products represent their own particular waste and loss because of the choices to grow food to feed animals rather than people. In fact, a 2018 study found that the opportunity costs of animal-based diets exceeded all food losses because that lost food could have fed 350 million people.[17]

At a time when there is more than enough food produced annually to feed all of of the world's people if it were fed directly to them rather than to animals, the current widespread hunger is a true scandal.

JEWISH TEACHINGS ON HUNGER

Jewish teachings on hunger are very clear and send a powerful message: veganism is the way of life most consistent with Jewish values.

Feeding the hungry is a fundamental Jewish value. The Talmud states: "Providing charity for poor and hungry people weighs as heavily as all the other commandments of the Torah combined" (*Baba Batra* 9a). A *midrash* teaches:

> God says to Israel, "My children, whenever you give sustenance to the poor, I impute it to you as though you gave sustenance to Me." Does then God eat and drink? No, but whenever you give food to the poor, God accounts it to you as if you gave food to Him. (*Midrash Tannaim*)

---

14 Hannah Ritchie, "Food Waste Is Responsible for 6% of Global Greenhouse Gas Emissions," Our World in Data, March 18, 2020, https://ourworldindata.org/food-waste-emissions.
15 Jonathan Knutson, "'There's Too Much Milk'—Tough Times for Dairy Farmers," *AgWeek*, April 1, 2019.
16 P. J. Huffstutter, "U.S. Dairy Farmers Dump Milk as Pandemic Upends Food Markets," *Reuters*, April 3, 2020.
17 Shepon, et al., The Opportunity Cost."

On Yom Kippur, the holiest day of the Jewish year, while fasting and praying for a good, healthy year, Jews are told through the words of the Prophet Isaiah that the type of fast acceptable to God involves helping the hungry, among other positive acts:

> Is this not the fast I will choose? To undo the fetters of wickedness, to untie the bands of perverseness, and to let out the oppressed free. . . . Is it not to share your bread with the hungry? (Isaiah 58:6–7)

On Passover, Jews are reminded not to forget the poor. Besides providing *ma'ot chittim* (charity for purchasing matzah and other Passover necessities) for the needy, Jews reach out to them with the following words at Passover seders from the Haggadah:

> This is the bread of affliction which our ancestors ate in the land of Egypt. Let all who are hungry come and eat. Let all who are in need come and celebrate the Passover.

Jews are even admonished to help our enemies, if they are in need: "If your enemy is hungry, feed him bread to eat, and if he is thirsty, give him water to drink" (Proverbs 25:21). This is consistent with the Jewish teaching that the greatest hero is one who converts an enemy into a friend (*Avot de Rabbi Nathan*, chapter 23).

It is a basic Jewish belief that God provides enough for all. In our daily prayers, it is said, "You [God] open Your hand and satisfy every living thing [with] its desire" (Psalm 145:16). Jews are obligated to give thanks to God for providing enough food for us and for all of humanity. In the *bircat hamazon* (grace after meals), Jews thank God, "[w]ho feeds the whole world with goodness, grace, loving kindness, and mercy."

The blessing is correct. God has provided enough for all. Nature's bounty, if properly distributed and properly consumed, would sustain all people. Hundreds of millions of people are hungry today, not because of insufficient agricultural capacity, but because of unjust social systems and wasteful food production methods, including the squandering of crops to grow meat for the affluent.

The Jewish conscience on the subject of world hunger is eloquently summarized by Rabbi Marc H. Tanenbaum, former national interreligious affairs director of the American Jewish Committee, in words that remain as true today as when they were originally said:

> If one takes seriously the moral, spiritual, and humanitarian values of Biblical, Prophetic, and Rabbinic Judaism, the inescapable issue of conscience that must be faced is: How can anyone justify *not* becoming involved in trying to help save the lives of starving millions of human beings throughout the world—whose plight constitutes the most agonizing moral and humanitarian problem in the latter half of the 20th century?[18]

18 Rabbi Marc H. Tanenbaum, "Remarks following 'Report on Rome—The Challenge of Food and Population,'" 1974. In the Jacob Rader Marcus Center of the American Jewish Archives: MS-603: Rabbi Marc H. Tanenbaum Collection, 1945–1992. Series D. International Relations Activities. 1961–1992, http://collections.americanjewisharchives.org/ms/ms0603/ms0603.058.006.pdf, 11.

8

PEACE

O ne major argument that is often overlooked in making the case for a vegan diet is that it can reduce the potential for violence and war. We have already seen that climate change will dramatically affect our ability to feed the world, especially if we double down on our commitment to setting aside so much of the world's arable land and potable water for grazing or to grow food for animals to eat. We have likewise noted that hunger, environmental degradation, and catastrophic weather events will enlarge the number of migrants (whether in-country or beyond borders),[1] augmenting the strain on cities and border areas, and threatening security. It is hard to overemphasize the potential for chaos raised by such a situation, as Professor Michael T. Klare, an expert on the connections between scarcity and global security, wrote in *The Nation*:

> Two nightmare scenarios—a global scarcity of vital resources and the onset of extreme climate change—are already beginning to converge and in the coming decades are likely to produce a tidal wave of unrest, rebellion, competition and conflict. Just what this tsunami of disaster will look like may, as yet, be hard to discern, but experts warn of "water wars" over contested river systems, global food riots sparked by soaring prices for life's basics, mass migrations of climate refugees (with resulting anti-migrant violence) and the breakdown of social order or the collapse of states. At first, such mayhem is likely to arise largely in Africa,

---

1 The World Bank, "Climate Change Could Force Over 140 Million to Migrate Within Countries by 2050," World Bank Report, Press Release, March 19, 2018, https://www. worldbank.org/en/news/press-release/2018/03/19/climate-change-could-force-over-140-million-to-migrate-within-countries-by-2050-world-bank-report; and Francesco Bassetti, "Environmental Migrants: Up to 1 billion by 2050," Foresight, 2019, https://www. climateforesight.eu/migrations/environmental-migrants-up-to-1-billion-by-2050/.

Central Asia and other areas of the underdeveloped South, but in time, *all* regions of the planet will be affected.[2]

This is not a new concern. Long before climate change was acknowledged, Senator Mark Hatfield of Oregon observed in 1975:

> Hunger and famine will do more to destabilize this world; [they are] more explosive than all atomic weaponry possessed by the big powers. Desperate people do desperate things. . . . Nuclear fission is now in the hands of even the developing countries in many of which hunger and famine are most serious.[3]

We have also known for decades about the potential for our food choices to lead to conflict. Author and activist Jeremy Rifkin wrote in 1992:

> Feeding grain to cattle and other livestock while people starve has triggered bitter political struggles in developing countries and political strife between northern industrial nations and the poor nations of the southern hemisphere.[4]

Indeed, the awareness of the social costs of eating animals may go back to antiquity. The relationship between animal-based resource usage and conflict is dramatized by the following dialogue between Socrates and Glaucon from Plato's *Republic* on what happens when the healthy State is "no longer sufficient":

> [Socrates:] Will not tutors be also in request, and nurses wet and dry, tirewomen and barbers, as well as confectioners and books; and swineherds, too, who were not needed and therefore had no place in the former edition of our State, but

---

2   Michael T. Klare, "How Resource Scarcity and Climate Change Could Cause a Global Explosion," *The Nation*, April 22, 2013.

3   Mark Hatfield, "World Hunger: More Explosive than Atomic Weaponry," *World Vision* 19, February 1975, 5, https://wvusstatic.com/2019/magazine-archive/1970/WVUS%20Magazine%20FEB%201975.pdf.

4   Jeremy Rifkin, *Beyond Beef: The Rise and Fall of the Cattle Culture* (New York: Dutton, 1992), 2.

are needed now? They must not be forgotten: and there will be animals of many other kinds, if people eat them.

[Glaucon:] Certainly.

[Socrates:] And living in this way we shall have much greater need of physicians than before?

[Glaucon:] Much greater.

[Socrates:] And the country which was enough to support the original inhabitants will be too small now, and not enough?

[Glaucon:] Quite true.

[Socrates:] Then a slice of our neighbors' land will be wanted by us for pasture and tillage, and they will want a slice of ours, if, like ourselves, they exceed the limit of necessity, and give themselves up to the unlimited accumulation of wealth?

[Glaucon:] That, Socrates, will be inevitable.

[Socrates:] And so, we shall go to war, Glaucon. Shall we not?

[Glaucon:] Most certainly.[5]

War and violence have many causes, and it would be simplistic to suggest that a shift toward veganism would by itself eliminate all conflicts. However, in the centuries-long national struggles for natural resources, the fact that those resources are only going to be stretched thinner in the upcoming decades means that those struggles will be longer, more trenchant, and less easy to resolve. By adopting a diet that dramatically utilizes fewer resources, we provide a greater chance of reducing conflict.

JEWISH TEACHINGS ON PEACE

We don't have to call on Plato or the ancient Greeks to make a case for living more simply to avoid war. Judaism mandates a special obligation to

5   Benjamin Jowett, trans., *The Dialogues of Plato* (London: Macmillan & Co, 1892), 53–54. Quoted in Dudley Giehl, *Vegetarianism: A Way of Life* (New York: Harper and Row, 1979), 98.

work for peace. The Jewish scriptures do not command that Jews merely love peace or merely seek peace, but that we actively pursue it.

The rabbis of the Talmud note that there are many commandments that require a certain time and place for their performance, but with regard to peace, "Seek peace and pursue it" (Psalm 34:15) is a command to be followed at every opportune moment (*Leviticus Rabbah* 9:9). The famous Talmudic sage Hillel argued that we should "be of the disciples of Aaron, loving peace and pursuing peace" (*Pirkei Avot* 1:12).

On the special duty of Jews to work for peace, the sages commented: "Said the Holy one blessed be He: The whole Torah is peace and to whom do I give it? To the nation which loves peace!" (*Yalkut Shimoni Yithro* 27).

The rabbis of the Talmud used lavish words of praise to indicate the significance of peace:

> Great is peace, for God's name is peace . . . . Great is peace, for it encompasses all blessings. . . . Great is peace, for even in times of war, peace must be sought. . . . Great is peace since when the Messiah is to come, He will commence with peace, as it is said [Isaiah 52:7], "How beautiful upon the mountains are the feet [footsteps] of the messenger of good tidings, who announces peace." (*Leviticus Rabbah* 9:9)

> The whole Torah was given for the sake of peace, and it is said, "All its paths are peace." (Proverbs 3:17, *Gitin* 59b)

Many important Jewish prayers—such as the *Amidah* (also known as *Sh'moneh Esrei*), the *kaddish*, the priestly blessing, and the grace after meals—conclude with a prayer for peace.

Despite Judaism's historical aversion to idolatry, peace is so important that the rabbis taught: "If Israel should worship idols, but she be at peace, God had no power, in effect, over them" (*Genesis Rabbah* 38:6).

The Jewish tradition does not mandate absolute pacifism, or peace at any price. The Israelites often went forth to battle, and not only in defensive wars. But they always held to the ideal of universal peace and yearned for the day when there would be no more bloodshed or violence:

> And they shall beat their swords into plowshares, and their spears into pruning hooks; nations shall not lift sword against nation; neither shall they learn war anymore. And they shall dwell every man under his vine and under his fig tree, and no one shall make them move; for the mouth of the Lord of hosts has spoken. (Micah 4:3–4; see also Isaiah 2:4)

Judaism recognizes that violence and war often result from injustice, and that access to food is often at the root of conflict:

> The sword comes into the world because of justice delayed, because of justice perverted, and because of those who render wrong decisions. (*Pirkei Avot* 5:11)

The Hebrew word for war, *milchama*, is derived from the word *locham*, which means both "to feed" and "to wage war." The Hebrew word for bread, *lechem*, comes from the same root. This led the sages to suggest that lack of bread and the search for sufficient food tempt people to make war. The seeds of war are often found in the inability of a nation to provide adequate food for its people. Hence, very inefficiently using feed crops to fatten animals for slaughter, at the expense of feeding human beings, as discussed earlier, is a prime cause for war. In view of this, we could say that the slogans of the vegan and peace movements should, if you will excuse a pun, be the same: "All we are saying is give peas a chance."

When it came to the consideration of the welfare of animals as well as humans, the Jewish sages felt that the biblical laws related to kindness to animals were meant to condition people to be considerate of fellow human beings. Several medieval Jewish philosophers, including Rabbi Isaac Abarbanel (1437–1509) and Rabbi Joseph Albo (1380–1444), considered vegetarianism to be a moral ideal because it avoids the meanness and cruelty associated with meat consumption and the harsh treatment of animals.[6]

Regarding the biblical prohibition against taking a mother bird with her young, Nachmanides commented:

> The motivating purpose is to teach us the quality of compassion and not to become cruel; for cruelty expands in a man's soul, as is well known with respect to cattle slaughterers.[7]

Maimonides indicated that the general obligation with regard to *tza'ar ba'alei chayim* (avoiding causing pain to animals) is set down with a view to protecting us from acquiring moral habits of cruelty and learning to inflict pain gratuitously, and to be kind and merciful.[8] The *Sefer Hachinuch* compares the muzzling of an ox treading corn to the mistreatment of human beings:

> When a man becomes accustomed to have pity even upon animals who were created to serve us, and he gives them a portion of their labors, his soul will likewise grow accustomed to be kind to human beings.[9]

Rabbi Samson Raphael Hirsch stressed that vegetables are the preferable food to help make the human body an instrument of the soul and to implement its aims of holiness and proper actions.[10] He indicated that every food that makes the body too active in an aggressive direction makes people more indifferent and less sensitive to the loftier impulses of the moral life.[11] He also stated, "The boy who, in crude joy, finds delight

---

6   See Rabbi J. David Bleich, "Vegetarianism and Judaism," *Tradition* 23, no. 1 (Summer 1987).

7   Nachmanides, *Commentary on Deuteronomy* 22:6. Quoted in Martin D. Gaffe, ed., *Judaism and Environmental Ethics: A Reader* (Lanham, MD: Lexington Books, 2001), 354.

8   Moses Maimonides, *The Guide for the Perplexed*, 3:17. M. Friedlander, trans. Forgotten Books, 2008), 493–94.

9   *Sefer Hachinuch*, Mitzvah 596.

10 Rabbi Samson Raphael Hirsch, *Horeb*, Dayan Dr. I. Grunfeld, trans. (London: Soncino Press, 1962), Vol. 2, 328.

11 *Ibid.*

in the convulsions of an injured beetle or the anxiety of a suffering animal will soon also be dumb toward human pain."[12]

The prophet Isaiah (66:3) proclaimed: "Whoever slaughters an ox has slain a man." In its original context, this refers to insincere animal sacrifice. However, there are several ways of interpreting this verse from a vegan point of view. We might say that by eating animals, we are consuming the grain that fattened the animal; this grain could have been used to save human lives. Furthermore, in developing countries, the ox helps farmers to plow the earth and grow food. Hence the killing of an ox leads to less production of food and hence more starvation. Moreover, when a person is ready to kill an animal for his pleasure or profit, he may be more ready to kill another human being.

Judaism emphasizes the pursuit of justice and harmonious relations between nations to reduce violence and the prospects for war. The prophet Isaiah declared:

> And the deed of righteousness shall be peace, and act of righteousness [shall be] tranquility and safety until eternity. (Isaiah 32:17)

---

12 Quoted by Francine Klagsbrun, *Voices of Wisdom* (New York: Pantheon Books, 1980), 458.

9

THE FISHES OF THE SEA

Ihope I have demonstrated in the previous chapters the strong case to be made against eating animals—or at the minimum reducing meat consumption, not least because the realities of animal-based diets and agriculture are sharply inconsistent with basic Jewish mandates to take care of our health, treat animals with compassion, preserve the environment, conserve natural resources, share with hungry people, and seek and pursue peace.

However, many Jews and others who abstain from eating mammals and birds continue to eat fishes, sometimes arguing that the many problems associated with the production and consumption of other animal products do not apply to fishes. After all, these people reason, in many cases erroneously, fishes are not raised under extremely cruel, confined conditions on factory farms; unlike the raising of livestock, fishing does not contribute to climate change, cause the erosion and depletion of soil, require the destruction of forests to create pastureland and land to grow feed crops, or require huge amounts of pesticides and irrigation water. Also, they argue, the flesh of fishes is generally lower in fat than other animal products, and is often considered a healthy food.

Because these are widely held beliefs, and because fishes have regrettably generally not been considered as individual beings who suffer, it's worth dedicating a chapter to responding to these ideas and rethinking our attitude about sea animals and the oceans.[1]

---

1   I have used the unusual plural of "fishes" in order to emphasize how these animals are rarely considered as individuals. For more information on such issues, see Inhabitat, "35 Facts That Will Make You Never Want to Eat Fish Again," n.d., https://inhabit. com/35-facts-that-will-make-you-never-want-to-eat-fish-again/. For resources on facts about conditions for all kind of marine life, see Fish Feel, "Fact Sheets," n.d., http:// fishfeel.org/resources/facts/.

FISH SENTIENCE

Fishes are vertebrates with highly developed nervous systems. In the past fifteen years, Victoria Braithwaite and other ichthyologists have found significant evidence that fishes experience conscious pain, just like mammals and birds. Braithwaite has said: "More and more people are willing to accept the facts. Fish do feel pain. It's likely different from what humans feel, but it is still a kind of pain."[2]

When fishes are hauled up from the deep, the sudden change in pressure on their bodies causes painful decompression that often leads their gills to collapse and their eyes to pop out. As soon as fishes are removed from the water, they begin to suffocate. Hooked fishes struggle because of physical pain and fear. As Dr. Tom Hopkins, professor of marine science at the University of Alabama, describes it, getting hooked on a line is "like dentistry without novocaine, drilling into exposed areas."[3]

Fishes that are "farmed," as opposed to caught, live an existence no better than those land and air animals reared in intensive confinement.[4] Most trout, catfish, and many other species eaten in the United States are raised in modern "fish factories," which involves large-scale, highly mechanized production, much like the chicken industry.[5]

Like crowded broiler chickens, farmed fishes are crammed in enormous pools called raceways,[6] where they are pushed to gain weight far faster than is natural. The aim is to raise the greatest number of fishes per cubic foot of water in order to maximize profits. Under these very crowded, unnatural conditions, fishes suffer from stress, infections,

---

2   Quoted in Ferris Jabr, "It's Official: Fish Feel Pain," *Smithsonian,* January 8, 2018. See also, Victoria Braithwaite, *Do Fish Feel Pain?* (Oxford, UK: Oxford University Press, 2010). For ongoing research on fish cognition, see Jonathan Balcombe, *What a Fish Knows: The Inner Lives of Our Underwater Cousins* (New York: Farrar, Straus and Giroux, 2016).
3   Quoted in Animals Australia, "Unleashed," n.d., http://www.unleashed.org.au/animals/fish.php.
4   Katie Wells, "The Problems with Fish Farming," Wellness Mama, March 29, 2016, https://wellnessmama.com/105599/fish-farming/.
5   Animal Welfare Institute, "Fish Farming," n.d., https://awionline.org/content/fish-farming.
6   Worldwide Aquaculture, "Quick & Easy Fish Farming—the Raceway Aquaculture System," January 22, 2015, http://worldwideaquaculture.com/quick-easy-fish-farming-the-raceway-aquaculture-system/.

parasites, oxygen depletion, and gas bubble disease, akin to "the bends" in human beings. To prevent the spread of diseases among the fishes, large amounts of antibiotics are used—further reducing our ability to ward off infectious diseases in the future.[7]

Fishes are not the only animals to suffer because of people's appetite for their flesh. Egrets, hawks, and other birds who eat fishes might be shot or poisoned to prevent them from eating fishes at large uncovered pools where fishes are raised.[8] Also many non-target animals, including sea turtles, dolphins, sea birds, and other fishes, die horribly in commercial fishing nets. Indeed, the World Wildlife Fund observes that 300,000 cetaceans (aquatic mammals), 250,000 turtles, and 300,000 seabirds are caught annually as "bycatch," leading to their deaths. In fact, 40 percent (or 38 million metric tons) of fishes removed from the ocean are caught unintentionally. Most are thrown back into the sea, either dead, dying, or seriously injured, or disposed of on land.[9]

Further loss of life in the fishing industry occurs because farmed fishes are fed wild-caught fishes: one-third of all the seafood that is caught around the world is fed to farmed fishes. Wild-caught fishes (in the form of fish oil or feed) is in turn fed to pigs and poultry: one-quarter of all fish meal produced is fed to livestock.[10] Thus wild animals are being fed to farmed animals, and those farmed animals are in turn being fed to other farmed animals, before a human being eats the end result.

HEALTH

Fish is often considered a healthy food.[11] However, although fish is generally lower in fat than other animal foods, it has no fiber and virtually no complex carbohydrates. Fish also contains excessive amounts

7   Maisie Ganzler, "It's Time for Aquaculture to Start Kicking Its Drug Habit," *Forbes*, May 6, 2019.
8   Glen E. Gebhart., "Bird Predation on Fish Farms," Langston University, n.d., https://www.langston.edu/bird-predation-fish-farms.
9   World Wildlife Fund, "Bycatch—A Sad Topic," n.d., https://www.fishforward.eu/en/project/by-catch/.
10   Meg Wilcox, "Can Aquaculture Survive Without Forage Fish?" *Civil Eats*, August 16, 2018.
11   For more information, see Sofia Pinada Ochra, "Is Fish a Healthy Food, or Have We Just Let It Off the Hook?" Forks Over Knives, October 29, 2015, https://www.forksoverknives.com/wellness/is-fish-a-health-food-or-have-we-just-let-it-off-the-hook/#gs.5ee91i..

of protein and none of the protective phytochemicals and antioxidants found only in foods of plant origin. The average American consumes far more protein than required,[12] and much less fiber than is necessary.[13] The overconsumption of protein has been linked to several health problems, including kidney stones,[14] while the lack of fiber may contribute to several diseases related to the digestive process, such as colon cancer.[15]

Fish does possess the heart-protective omega-3 fatty acid EPA (eicosopentaenoic acid). But EPA is made by both fishes and humans from the essential omega-3 fatty acid, alpha-linolenic acid (ALA), and that in turn is made in the chloroplasts of green plants (for example, algae and spinach). ALA can be obtained from many plant foods, including green leafy vegetables, flaxseed, canola, soybean, walnut oils, tofu, pumpkin, and wheat germ, and these plant foods generally come without the nutritional hazards of fish flesh.[16]

In any case, the possible benefits of omega-3 fatty acids are largely limited to people at risk of heart disease, and for pregnant and breastfeeding women. The largest study of cholesterol levels, carried out in Framingham, Massachusetts, showed that people with cholesterol levels below 150 have virtually no such risk. Because people on well-balanced vegan diets generally have cholesterol levels below or around 150, the best way to maintain cardiac health is to follow such a diet, thereby ensuring that artery blockages don't occur in the first place.[17]

A major health hazard from eating fishes comes from the depredations we humans have caused in their natural environment. Fishes and shellfishes are repositories for the industrial and municipal wastes and

12 Sophie Egan, "How Much Protein Do We Need?" *The New York Times*, July 28, 2017.
13 Julia Belluz, "Nearly All Americans Fail to Eat Enough of This Actual Superfood," *Vox*, July 15, 2019.
14 Daniel Pendick, "5 Steps for Preventing Kidney Stones," Harvard Health Publishing, October 4, 2013, https://www.health.harvard.edu/blog/5-steps-for-preventing-kidney-stones-201310046721.
15 Cleveland Clinic, "New Study Points to Benefits of Fiber for Colon Cancer Survivors," November 2, 2017, https://newsroom.clevelandclinic.org/2017/11/02/new-study-points-to-benefits-of-fiber-for-colon-cancer-survivors/.
16 Cleveland Clinic, "Plant Sources of Omega-3s," n.d., https://my.clevelandclinic.org/health/articles/17651-plant-sources-of-omega-3s.
17 Physicians Committee for Responsible Medicine, "Lowering Cholesterol with a Plant-Based Diet," n.d., https://www.pcrm.org/good-nutrition/nutrition-information/lowering-cholesterol-with-a-plant-based-diet.

agricultural chemicals flushed into the world's waters.[18] Other pollutants that concentrate in sea creatures include pesticides; toxic metals including lead, mercury, cadmium, chromium, and arsenic;[19] dioxins; and radioactive substances such as strontium 90.[20] Because of biological magnification during movement up the food chain, these pollutants can reach levels much higher than that of the water in which the fishes live, and they have been linked to many health problems, including impaired behavioral development in young children. Nursing infants consume half of their mother's load of PCBs, dioxins, DDT, and other deadly toxins.

Many people feel a false sense of security when they change from red meat to a primarily chicken- and fish-based diet. However, as discussed in chapter three, the study by Dr. Dean Ornish showed dramatic improvements in the condition of patients with severe heart problems who switched to vegetarian, almost vegan, very low-fat diets. In sharp contrast, those who followed diets recommended by medical groups—such as the American Heart Association, which involve 30 percent of calories from fat, and include chicken without the skin, fish, and some dairy products—showed little improvement, and in most cases became worse.[21]

ENVIRONMENTAL IMPACTS

If you aren't convinced by the previous discussions about the pain fishes experience and by the harm eating fishes has on our health, perhaps you might be by the impact the fish industry has on Earth's environment.[22]

Researchers have found the biodiversity of the oceans rivals that of the tropical rainforests, but today the world is effectively "clear cutting" these precious underwater environments with our appetite for fishes. Modern

---

18 Environmental Defense Fund, "PCBs in Fish and Shellfish," n.d., http://seafood.edf. org/pcbs-fish-and-shellfish.

19 José G. Doréa, "Persistent, Bioaccumulative and Toxic Substances in Fish: Human Health Considerations," *Science of the Total Environment* 400, nos. 1–3 (2008): 93–114.

20 Jeff McMahon, "How Did Those Vermont Fish Get Radioactive?" *Forbes*, August 5, 2011.

21 Dean Ornish, et al., "Can Lifestyle Changes Reverse Coronary Heart Disease?" *The Lancet* 336, no. 8708 (July 21, 1990): 129–33.

22 Much of the material in this section is from Amber Pariona, "What Is the Environmental Impact of the Fishing Industry?" World Atlas, n.d., https://www.worldatlas.com/articles/what-is-the-environmental-impact-of-the-fishing-industry.html.

commercial fishing uses giant energy-intensive "factory" trawlers with huge nets that swallow up everything in their path. The result is that many of the world's major fisheries are depleted or are in serious decline, and others are considered overexploited. Some marine biologists believe that the oceans may be completely devoid of fishes by 2048.[23] Some waters that were once teeming with life are now so barren they have been compared to a "dust bowl."

Depleted fisheries generate negative outcomes throughout the entire marine ecosystem. Major predator–prey situations have been changed.[24] For example, a decline in pollock in western Alaska has caused a major decline in Stellar sea lions, which led to their being designated by the National Marine Fisheries Service as "threatened" in 1990 and "endangered" in 1997. Loss of sea lions deprived killer whales of their primary source of nutrition, and they have shifted to eating sea otters. As a result, sea otters have also seen a major decline since 1990, resulting in a surge by their prey, sea urchins. This trophic cascade demonstrates the ecological principle that "everything is connected to everything else."[25]

The environmental impact of aquatic farming is also cause for concern, which even the industry itself is forced to acknowledge.[26] First, wild stocks can be displaced by farmed fishes, who compete for food. Interbreeding pollutes the genetic pool.[27] Modern commercial fishing is extremely energy intensive. It requires as much as twenty calories of fossil fuel energy to produce one calorie of food energy from fish. Production of fish food is many times as intensive as the production of plant food, even when the plant foods are produced with modern technology.[28]

23 John Roach, "Seafood May Be Gone By 2048," *National Geographic*, November 2, 2006.
24 Mark V. Abrahams, et al., "Predator–Prey Interactions and Changing Environments: Who Benefits?" *Philosophical Transactions of the Royal Society B* 362, no. 1487 (May 1, 2007), doi.org/10.1098/rstb.2007.2102.
25 SeaWeb, "Collapse of Seals, Sea Lions & Sea Otters in North Pacific Triggered by Overfishing of Great Whales," September 24, 2003, https://www.sciencedaily.com/releases/2003/09/030924055244.htm.
26 Global Aquaculture Alliance, "What Is the Environmental Impact of Aquaculture?" April 22, 2019, https://www.aquaculturealliance.org/blog/what-is-the-environmental-impact-of-aquaculture/.
27 C. Roberge, et al., "Genetic Consequences of Interbreeding between Farmed and Wild Atlantic Salmon: Insights from the Transcriptome," *Molecular Ecology* 17, no. 1 (January 2008): 314–24.
28 James F. Muir, *Fuel and Energy Use in the Fisheries Sector: Approaches, Inventories and Strategic Implications* (Rome: UNFAO, 2015).

Where fishes are grown in artificial ponds, vast amounts of water are required as the medium of growth, to replenish oxygen, and to remove wastes from the aquatic system.[29] This great need for water has caused further environmental destruction too, as aquaculture is routinely sited on the coast, some of it cleared of mangrove forests, the prime breeding and spawning ground for many fishes.[30] Many of the world's mangrove forests have been cleared, drained, or filled, partly to make room for fish or shrimp farms, especially in Southeast Asia.[31]

SEEKING AND PURSUING PEACE

As we saw in the last chapter, Jewish sages, commenting on the fact that the Hebrew words for bread (*lechem*) and war (*milchamah*) come from the same root, deduced that shortages of grain and other resources made war more likely. The truth of their words is illustrated by battles over increasingly scarce fishes in many areas.[32] With many vessels scouring fished-out waters, confrontations between nations are inevitable, sometimes leading to fatalities.[33]

Humans have always depended on fishes from the sea, and since there have been fishermen, there have been conflicts over fishes. The open seas are often lawless; piracy remains common, and the fishing industry is a hotbed of modern-day slavery.[34] However, as population grows and incomes rise worldwide, the demand for food, especially protein, will rise as well. To maintain local political support, leaders must ensure access to the high-quality food, including fish, that their citizens demand. The supply of both wild and farmed fishes is not keeping up with demand.

---

29 James F. Muir, *Water Management for Aquaculture and Fisheries: Irrigation, Irritation or Integration?* Scotland: University of Sterling, Institute of Aquaculture, n.d.

30 Dyna Rochmyaningsih, "Aquaculture Is Main Driver of Mangrove Losses," Ecobusiness, June 28, 2017, https://www.eco-business.com/news/aquaculture-is-main-driver-of-mangrove-losses/.

31 Zoe Osborne, "The Environmental Hazards of Intensive Shrimp Farming on the Mekong Delta," *Pacific Standard*, July 2018; and Patrick Lee, "Mangrove Forests Disappearing," *The Star*, March 14, 2015.

32 Much of the material in this section is from Kate Higgins-Bloom, "Food Fight: Why the Next Big Battle May Not Be Over Treasure or Territory—But for Fish," *Foreign Policy*, September 12, 2018.

33 Matthew Green, "Plundering Africa: Voracious Fishmeal Factories Intensify the Pressure of Climate Change," *Reuters*, October 30, 2018.

34 Ian Urbina, "'Sea Slaves': The Human Misery that Feeds Pets and Livestock," *The New York Times*, July 27, 2015.

Wild populations of both migratory fishes, including tuna, and less mobile species, such as flounder, are being overfished. Pressure to meet rising demand for fishes furthers the potential for conflicts, as nations fish in contested waters or engage in illegal fishing, contrary to international maritime laws.

Scarcity has already caused China to have its fishing fleets go further and further afield, sometimes into disputed waters, in efforts to catch fishes. This has led to disputes with Indonesia and other nations over fishing rights in the South and East China Seas, as well as conflicts off the coast of Mauritania and Senegal.[35] Another factor that expands the likelihood of fish wars is warming temperatures that cause commercial fish species to move northward into territories controlled by other nations, producing conflicts with neighbors that are suddenly forced to share.[36]

In summary, the "production" and consumption of fish is harmful to human health, causes great suffering to fishes, threatens the ocean's biodiversity, wastes resources, and makes national conflicts more likely. Hence, an end to, or at least a sharp decline in, the consumption of fish and other sea creatures is both a societal imperative and a Jewish imperative.

---

35   Alfonso Daniels, "'Fish Are Vanishing'—Senegal's Devastated Coastline," *BBC*, November 1, 2018.
36   Craig Welch, "Climate Change May Spark Global 'Fish Wars,'" *National Geographic*, June 14, 2018; and Kendra Pierre-Louis, "Warming Waters, Moving Fish: How Climate Change Is Reshaping Iceland," *The New York Times*, November 29, 2019.

10

VEGANISM AND ANIMAL RIGHTS

M ost people think of veganism in the context of diet and lifestyle. And it's certainly true that many of those who espouse a plant-based diet are centered on health and wellness. Furthermore, because in terms of absolute numbers farmed animals constitute well over 90 percent of all the vertebrates deliberately killed by human beings—and because factory farming has massively increased the number that are raised and slaughtered for food, most animal advocates have over the last two decades concentrated their attention on changing people's diets.

However, as should be abundantly clear by now, many of us who call ourselves vegans consider ourselves practitioners of a philosophy of nonviolence and non-harm that impacts a wide range of choices. This philosophy has its origin or is paralleled in many faith traditions, including Judaism. In this chapter, I touch on a few of these other areas where animals are mistreated. The first is the use of animals for their skins (fur, wool, leather, and silk); the second is the use of animals in entertainment and sport (circuses, hunting, and racing); and the third is the use of animals in scientific experimentation. In each of these areas, I explain how these are not commensurate with either vegan or Jewish values.

FUR, WOOL, LEATHER, AND SILK

Jewish worshipers chant every Sabbath morning *Nishmat kol chai t'varech et shim'chah*, "The soul of every living being shall praise God's name." Yet some come to synagogues during winter months wearing fur coats that required the cruel treatment and slaughter of some of those living beings whose souls, we declare, are praising God.[1]

---

1   For more information about fur farming, visit Humane Society International, "Fur," n.d., https://www.hsi.org/issues/fur/.

For all its supposed connection to glamor and status, the killing of animals for their fur is a gruesome and sordid endeavor. Many of the smaller animals are either trapped or raised in tiny cages on "fur farms." Here, millions of foxes, beavers, minks, ocelots, rabbits, chinchillas, and other animals await death with little room to move and all their natural instincts thwarted. There is no regard for their physical, mental, or emotional well-being. These normally active animals go crazy and exhibit neurotic behaviors, such as compulsive movements and self-mutilation.[2] In the end, they suffer hideous deaths by electrocution rods thrust up their anuses, or through suffocation, poisoning (which causes painful convulsions), or having their necks broken. According to Fur for Animals,[3] one fur garment requires up to 400 squirrels, 200 chinchillas, 120 muskrats, 70 mink, 50 martens, 40 raccoons, 40 rabbits, 22 bobcats, 20 foxes, 12 lynx, or 15 wolves.

Larger animals—such as wolves and coyotes—are caught in steel-jaw leg traps and suffer slow, agonizing deaths. Some are attacked by predators, or freeze to death, or are in such tremendous pain that they chew off their own limbs to escape. It has been said that one can get a feel for the pain involved by slamming one's fingers in a car door. Tens of millions of wild animals are killed for their skins every year; several species have become endangered or have disappeared completely in some localities. Trappers discard millions of "trash" animals who do not have valuable skins, such as birds, each year. Dogs and cats are other frequent victims of these cruel devices. Many trapped animals leave behind dependent offspring who are doomed to starve.[4]

Whether they are raised on a farm or trapped, these animals undergo violent and abusive deaths, which are far from Jewish teachings on the dignity and sensibility of animals. Jewish scriptures and tradition recognize that the exploitation of animals and sometimes even killing of them

---

2   *BBC News*, "Inside a Russian Fur Farm" (video), April 27, 2016, https://www.youtube.com/watch?v=7LtiqFt6dC8.

3   Fur for Animals: Fighting the International Fur Trade, "How Many Animals Have to Die for a Fur Coat?" n.d., http://www.respectforanimals.org/how-many-animals-have-to-die-for-a-fur-coat/. The figure on wolves (and other animals) comes from FADA, "Clothing—Skins," n.d., http://faada.org/comercio-vestimenta-pieles.

4   See the Association for the Protection of Fur-Bearing Animals, "Trapping: Non-Targets," n.d., https://thefurbearers.com/the-issues/trapping/non-targets.

may have been necessary in the past for human survival. However, this does not apply to furs.

There are now many non-animal–based coats and hats, including "faux fur," that provide warmth and have the added advantage of being lighter and easier to care for than fur. As for style, imitation fur is produced at such a high level of quality that even among Hasidim there is a small but growing trend to wear synthetic *shtreimlach*.[5]

Thankfully, in recent decades religious authorities have been recognizing the cruelty of fur. Based on the prohibition of *tza'ar ba'alei chayim*, Rabbi Chaim David Halevy, former Sephardic Chief Rabbi of Tel Aviv, issued a *p'sak* (rabbinic ruling) in March 1992 mandating that Jews should not wear fur. Rabbi Halevy asked: "Why should people be allowed to kill animals if it is not necessary, simply because they desire the pleasure of having the beauty and warmth of fur coats? Is it not possible to achieve the same degree of warmth without fur?"[6]

Motivated by Rabbi Halevy's prohibition and by Israel's strict laws against mistreating animals, there have been several attempts to pass a law in the Knesset banning the manufacturing of fur in Israel, with an exception for Hasidic *streimels* for religious reasons. Had this law passed, it would have made Israel the only country in the world with such a ban. However, the bill has been blocked so far, despite widespread support.

Rabbi Yona Metzger, former Ashkenazic Chief Rabbi of Israel, ruled against fur imports from China, where animals are often skinned alive.[7]

Do we really need the Knesset to pass a law or rabbinical rulings to tell us what is right? In his book *The Jewish Encyclopedia of Moral and Ethical Issues*, Israeli author and educator Rabbi Nachum Amsel states: "If the only reason a person wears the fur coat is to 'show off' one's wealth or to be a mere fashion statement, that would be considered to be a frivolous and not a legitimate need."[8] Indeed, one has to wonder what kind of lesson young people are learning when they see worshippers arriving at

---

5   Gavriel Fiske, "Ultra-Orthodox Bigwig Calls for Synthetic Fur Hats," *The Times of Israel*, August 23, 2013.
6   Yonassan Gershom, *Kapporos Then and Now: Toward a More Compassionate Tradition* (Raleigh, NC: Lulu Press, 2015), 84–85.
7   World Jewish Congress, "Israeli Chief Rabbi Issues Edict on Furs," February 21, 2007, https://www.worldjewishcongress.org/en/news/israeli-chief-rabbi-issues-edict-on-furs.
8   Nachum Amsel, *The Jewish Encyclopedia of Moral and Ethical Issues* (Northvale, NJ: Aronson, 1994), 298.

the synagogue in fur coats on the Sabbath day. Instead of reinforcing the many beautiful Jewish teachings about compassion to animals, we are teaching them that expensive status symbols and conspicuous consumption are more important than respect for God's creatures.

If there were a reduction in the wearing of fur, not only would tens of thousands of animals benefit from our compassion and concern, but we, too, would benefit by becoming more sensitive and more humane Jews and civilized human beings. We would be setting an example for the rest of the world that says there is no beauty in cruelty.

When legislation was introduced into the New York City Council to ban fur sales in New York City in 2019,[9] Jewish Veg submitted a statement. It began: "As a national nonprofit organization supported by leading rabbis from across the denominational spectrum, Jewish Veg supports legislation to ban the sale of fur for one simple reason: Judaism mandates that we treat animals with exquisite and sensitive compassion, and the practices of the fur industry grotesquely violate this mandate." The statement concluded: "Actually, when it comes to Judaism, this legislation is itself an expression of our religious values, and thus we look forward to its passage. No civilized society, whether governed by religious or secular values, should blind itself to such suffering. Together, we will create a more compassionate world and a fur-free city."[10]

The ban on selling fur in New York City failed . . . for now. However, Los Angeles, San Francisco, and other cities around the world have banned its sale, and many countries have now moved to end fur farming, prohibit fur-farmed products from entering their countries, or restrict the importation of some furs.[11] Even the iconic stores are now following suit: Macy's and Bloomingdale's will no longer sell furs starting in 2021; and Calvin Klein, Ralph Lauren, Tommy Hilfiger, and now Michael Kors are no longer designing with it.[12]

---

9   Corey Kilgannon, "Fur Helped Build the City. Now Its Sale May Be Banned," *The New York Times*, May 16, 2019.
10 The full statement can be read at JewishVeg.org/Fur-Free-NYC.
11 PETA, "A Guide to the Fur-Free Revolution: These Places Have Banned Fur," n.d., https://www.worldjewishcongress.org/en/news/israeli-chief-rabbi-issues-edict-on-furs.
12 Ana Colón, "All the Fashion Brands That Have Banned Fur," *Glamour*, October 22, 2019.

Although many people think the production of wool is harmless since animals need not be killed in producing it, there are good reasons why vegans avoid wool.[13] In order to meet demand, sheep-sheering can be brutal and cruel. Not only can the sheep receive multiple cuts, but in a barbaric process called mulesing, farmers take large chunks of flesh and skin from lambs' backsides to prevent a maggot infestation—itself a result of the many folds of skin that merino sheep have been genetically engineered to have so as to boost the surface area for wool. Mulesing causes pain so severe that it can continue for weeks, and for some lambs it never ends.

Thick wool may be a benefit in the winter, but it can lead to heat stress in summer, especially in Australia, where many sheep are raised.[14] As with cows, sheep stomachs produce a substantial amount of methane: in fact, pound for pound, sheep and goats are the greatest GHG emitters of all farmed species.[15] Ending this cruel industry, therefore, would help reduce greenhouse gas emissions. It would also provide a welcome boost to the many cruelty-free, sustainable, and warm alternatives to wool, including hemp, ramie, bamboo, and microfibers. Obviously, wool is a byproduct of sheep, who are also bred for their flesh. Sheep for slaughter are shipped in their tens of thousands around the world—some from as far as Australia. In December 2018, Canadian photojournalist Jo-Anne McArthur wrote about her experience of seeing the *Bahijah*, en route from Australia to Egypt, unload a cargo of 22,000 sheep in Haifa. Israel, she writes, was expected to import 700,000 live animals in 2018, up from 200,000 in 2012. Sheep constituted by far the largest number of animals.[16]

Just as wool production helps support sheep farming, so too does leather for the meat industry—one that includes cows, buffalos, pigs, goats,

---

13   Material about some of the ethical and practical problems of wearing wool is taken from Vegan Life, "8 Reasons Not to Wear Wool This Winter," November 8, 2016, https://www.veganlifemag.com/8-reasons-not-wear-wool-winter/.
14   Meat & Livestock Australia, "Fast Facts: Australia's Sheep Industry," 2017, https://www.mla.com.au/globalassets/mla-corporate/prices--markets/documents/trends--analysis/fast-facts--maps/mla_sheep-fast-facts-2017_final.pdf.
15   Environmental Working Group, "Meat Eater's Guide to Climate Change & Health: Climate and Environmental Impacts," 2011, https://www.ewg.org/meateatersguide/a-meat-eaters-guide-to-climate-change-health-what-you-eat-matters/climate-and-environmental-impacts/.
16   Jo-Anne McArthur, "'We Could Smell the Boat Approaching': The Grim Truth about Animal Exports," *The Guardian*, December 11, 2018.

sheep, alligators, kangaroos, ostriches, horses, deer, elk, snakes, buffalo, oxen, yaks, kangaroos, elephants, sharks, stingrays, cats, and dogs.[17]

Tanning—as the Talmud recognized (*Baba Batra* 2:9)—is a filthy and polluting business.[18] Turning skin into leather involves application of a variety of polluting substances, including formaldehyde, mineral salts, coal-tar derivatives, and various oils, dyes, and finishes—some of them cyanide-based. It is also dangerous: Because of these chemicals, leather workers suffer from leukemia and some types of cancer at far higher rates than average workers.

Since their skin is considered a luxury product, unborn calves are sometimes mutilated for leather. Some are purposely aborted, while others are cut out of the bodies of slaughtered pregnant cows. Much of the leather sold in the United States is imported from India, where cows are either forced to march miles to slaughter in the heat and dust, without water or food, or they are trucked in horrendous conditions. They arrive exhausted, emaciated, and sometimes so malnourished that they can't stand up. Many suffer from broken bones, eye infections, and open wounds.[19]

There are many natural and synthetic substitutes for leather, including cotton, hemp, denim, and acrylic fiber. Synthetic pleather has the look and feel of real leather. Two Mexicans have created leather out of cactus leaves.[20] The product feels like animal-based leather, and is partially biodegradable, flexible, breathable, and lasts for at least ten years.[21]

---

17 Material below about problems wearing leather was obtained from Cistine Wells, "What's Wrong with Leather?" All-Creatures.Org, January 2013, https://www.all-creatures.org/articles/ar-whatswrong-leather.html; and Rachel Krantz, "7 Reasons Wearing Leather Is Actually the Opposite of Cute," *Bustle*, March 29, 2016, https://www.bustle.com/articles/149892-7-reasons-wearing-leather-is-actually-the-opposite-of-cute.

18 Andrew Tarantola, "How Leather Is Slowly Killing the People and Places That Make It," *Gizmodo*, June 3, 2014, https://gizmodo.com/how-leather-is-slowly-killing-the-people-and-places-tha-1572678618.

19 *New Internationalist*, "India's Holy Cash Cow," July 1, 2010, https://newint.org/columns/currents/2010/07/01/india-leather-cows. For an overview of the fashion industry's use of animal materials, see The Discerning Brute, "Massive Fashion Industry Studies Condemn Animal Materials," August 7, 2017, https://thediscerningbrute.com/home/2018/4/6/massive-fashion-industry-studies-condemn-animal-materials.

20 Jemima Webber, "Two Mexico Entrepreneurs Just Created Leather Out of Cactus Leaves," Live Kindly, November 26, 2019, https://www.livekindly.co/mexican-entrepreneurs-leather-cactus/.

21 *Ibid.*

Although not as clearcut as the reasons not to eat meat or to wear fur, the production of silk may involve harm as the silkworm cocoon is harvested. To begin the unraveling of the cocoons to produce silk threads, the cocoons are placed in boiling water, which kills the silkworms. It requires about fifteen silkworms to make a gram of silk thread. About ten thousand are killed to make just one silk sari.[22]

The irony is that a whole new industry is emerging that has the potential to completely reimagine how we might think about leather, silk, and other animal products. There are companies growing proteins to develop leather without the need for an animal, or from mycelium, or generating synthetic spider silk.[23] Some are manufacturing pet food (even for obligate carnivores) that supply all the nutrients without killing an animal, or by cultivating meat from a cell.[24] Others are fermenting milk using dairy proteins and enzymes.[25] However, it's in the area of meat production of all kinds that the most interest (and controversy) lies, and this is the subject of the next chapter.

CIRCUSES, HUNTING, AND RACING

Most of us probably grew up with images of the circus as a benign form of popular entertainment, with lion-tamers, tigers leaping through hoops, and dancing bears. Unfortunately, the realities of how the animals are trained to perform these actions and their lives on the road are far from glamorous or fun.[26] Animals, who are bred in captivity, are whipped to

---

22 Margherita Stancati, "Taking the Violence Out of Silk," *The Wall Street Journal*, January 4, 2011.

23 Eillie Anzilotti, "This Very Realistic Fake Leather Is Made from Mushrooms, Not Cows," *Fast Company*, April 2018, https://www.fastcompany.com/40562633/this-leather-is-made-from-mushrooms-not-cows; and John Cumbers, "Would You Buy a Bag Made of Mushroom Leather? A Jacket Made with Spider Silk: The Future of the Fashion Industry Is Here and It's Made with Biology," *Forbes*, September 17, 2019.

24 See Ernie Ward, et al., *The Clean Pet Food Revolution: How Better Pet Food Will Change the World* (New York: Lantern, 2019).

25 Knvul Sheikh, "Got Impossible Milk? The Quest for Lab-made Dairy," *The New York Times*, August 2, 2019.

26 For more on this subject, see Emma Brazell, "Circus Animals: 10 Reasons Why the US Needs to Ban Them Immediately," VT, August 16, 2017, https://vt.co/animals/stories/circus-animals-why-the-us-needs-to-ban-them/; and PETA, "Circuses: Three Rings of Abuse," n.d., https://www.peta.org/issues/animals-in-entertainment/circuses/.

be trained to obey commands on stage. Elephants are often beaten with bull-hooks (heavy batons with a sharp metal hook on one end), sometimes until they bleed.

When they are not performing they spend many hours of the day chained or in cages with barely enough space to turn around. Or they are crammed into filthy, cramped, sweltering, poorly ventilated tractor trailers. Because of the horrible conditions under which they live, circus animals often become depressed and despondent, resulting in abnormal behavior patterns, such as incessant pacing, head bobbing, and swaying, sometimes even harming themselves. It's not surprising then, that sometimes animals have lashed out—going on rampages, attacking their trainers, and causing human injuries and even deaths.

Thankfully, twenty-seven countries, including Israel, have banned circuses that use wild animals,[27] and cities and municipalities around the United States have done the same.[28] In 2017, Ringling Bros. & Barnum & Bailey's circus declared bankruptcy.[29] It's my belief that circuses that use animals will go the way of other "entertainments" that abuse animals, such as bear-baiting, cock-fighting, and dog-fighting, and be banned across the entire United States. We may also hope that rodeos and bull-fighting follow suit.

Throughout the ages, rabbis have strongly disapproved of hunting as a sport. A Jew is permitted to capture or kill animals only for purposes of food, or for what is considered an essential human need. But to destroy an animal for "sport" constitutes wanton destruction and is to be condemned. People who have access to plant-based foods do not need to hunt and, for them, the activity is fundamentally recreational, even if they eat the flesh of killed animals. Based on the statement not to stand "in the way of sinners" (Psalm 1:1), the Talmud prohibits association with recreational hunters (*Avodah Zarah* 18b).

27 Priya, "These 27 Countries Have Banned Wild-Animal Circuses," PETA UK, September 11, 2019, https://www.peta.org.uk/blog/these-26-countries-that-have-banned-wild-animal-circuses-are-making-england-look-really-bad/.
28 Four Paws in US, "Bans on Circuses," n.d., https://www.four-paws.us/campaigns-topics/topics/wild-animals/worldwide-circus-bans.
29 Natasha Daly, "Why All of America's Circus Animals Could Soon Be Free," *National Geographic*, May 20, 2017.

Rabbi Yechezkel Landau (1713–1793) once responded to a man wishing to know if he could hunt in his large estate, which included forests and fields, and still be consistent with Jewish teachings. Rabbi Landau's response is contained in his classic collection of *responsa, Nodah b'Yehudah*:

In the Torah the sport of hunting is imputed only to fierce characters like Nimrod and Esau, never to any of the patriarchs and their descendants. . . . I cannot comprehend how a Jew could even dream of killing animals merely for the pleasure of hunting. . . . When sport prompts killing, it is downright cruelty.[30]

It should be noted that meat from animals killed by hunting with a gun or bow is not kosher according to Jewish law, and not to be eaten, and therefore violates *bal tashchit*, the prohibition against unnecessary destruction or waste.

Like many other industries involving animals, the racing industry is built on the exploitation of animals, with cruelty and abuse common. Nina Natelson, founder and director of Concern for Helping Animals in Israel (CHAI), summarized the cruelty involved in horse racing in a personal email:

Thousands of horses are bred annually, but only the few fastest are chosen to race, with most of the rest sent to the slaughterhouse. Trained and raced by age two, before their bones have hardened, they often incur serious injuries. Pushed beyond their limits, they suffer bleeding in the lungs, which can be fatal, and chronic ulcers. They are drugged to improve performance and so they can race even while injured, which worsens the injury.

Corruption is inherent in this industry based on greed, so, for example, the legs of horses not fast enough to win have been broken to collect on insurance policies.

---

30 Quoted in Mark H. Bernstein, *Without a Tear: Our Tragic Relationship with Animals* (Champaign: University of Illinois Press, 2004), 80.

When the horses are too old to possibly win, at around six (though their natural lifespan is around 25), even former champions are often sent to a slaughterhouse. The US Congress held hearings on the industry due to the high level of breakdowns and deaths in training and on the track. At the hearings, industry leaders admitted that the industry could not police itself and asked the government to start policing for illegal drug use and other corrupt practices.

On July 30, 2006, Rabbi Shlomo Amar, the then Sephardic Chief Rabbi of Israel, issued a *p'sak halachah* (rabbinical ruling) against horse racing. The ruling concludes: "It seems self-evident that one ought . . . not to participate in horse-races—neither in establishing them, nor by watching them: because of the pain to animals caused thereby, because it is 'a dwelling place of scoffers,' and because it is 'playing with dice' [the Talmudic term for gambling]."[31] Among the reasons the chief rabbi cited for his conclusion was that racing involves the premature death of many horses, and this violates the Jewish law against wanton destruction.

Racing, he claimed, would lead to animals being euthanized and would create a risk that horse meat, which is not kosher, would be sold in Israel, violating Jewish law. He argued that using horses for racing was unnecessary, involved cruelty, and was conducted only for the purpose of making some rich people richer. Furthermore, Judaism discourages gambling because it enriches one person at the expense of another. Horse racing has come under considerable scrutiny in the United States, especially following the deaths of 495 thoroughbreds in 2018 alone.[32] The call for banning the "sport" in the United States is starting to become much louder.[33]

This chapter features only a few of the ways that animals are casually exploited for their bodies, outside of the consumption of their flesh or the drinking or fermenting of their "lacteal secretions," to use an industry

31 Concern for Helping Animals in Israel (CHAI), "Report of Chief Rabbi of Israel Against Racing," n.d., http://www.chai.org.il/en/campaigns/racing/campaigns_racing_psak.htm.
32 Rachel Fobar, "Why Horse Racing Is So Dangerous," *National Geographic*, May 2019.
33 Patrick Battuello, "The Time for Horse Racing Has Passed. It's Time to Outlaw It," *Washington Post*, October 8, 2019.

term.[34] Some of these industries, such as animals in entertainment, are dying out for lack of interest, an emerging recognition of their cruelty, or (for instance) through the astonishing verisimilitude of CGI in film. Some industries, such as the fur and seal skin trade, are only propped up by subsidies, which support a relatively small number of people who barely eke out a living from them.[35] However, there are others that are still given the validation of the state and the medical establishment, such as is the case with animal experimentation.

ANIMAL RIGHTS AND EXPERIMENTATION

Throughout this book, I have tried to make it clear that a commitment to the welfare of animals and the use of their bodies in animal agriculture has been a fundamental part of veganism, and what I consider to be the vegan identity. I have also argued that it should be part of our expression of Jewish values. That said, many animal advocates regard organized religion as an ideological opponent. The reasons for doing so are, I believe, in the case of Judaism a misconception held by both those who are religious and those who are secular animal advocates. I will address this in a moment, but first it is worth exploring what for many will be the most contentious aspect of veganism: the use of animals in scientific experimentation.[36]

Many still believe that experimentation on animals is necessary to find cures for diseases. Because Judaism places a priority on human life over that of animals, it is not, in principle, opposed to all uses of animals if there are significant benefits for humans that could not be obtained in any other way. Unfortunately, the manner by which experiments are conducted raises serious doubts about their efficacy, let alone their morality.

---

34 Jaya Saxena, "Got Lacteal Secretions? Virginia Tries to Limit the Legal Definition of Milk," *Eater,* January 31, 2020.
35 Ewa Demianowicz, "Canada's Government Needs to Stop Providing Subsidies for Fur," *Huffington Post* Canada, March 11, 2015.
36 Data about animal experimentation can be found at Do Something, "11 Facts about Animal Testing," n.d., https://www.dosomething.org/facts/11-facts-about-animal-testing. One of the most comprehensive overviews of the ethics and science surrounding the use of animals in science is in Hugh LaFollette and Niall Shanks, *Brute Science: Dilemmas of Animal Experimentation* (London and New York: Routledge, 1996). Ongoing information about animal experimentation can be found at Citizens for Alternatives to Animal Research and Experimentation (https://www.caareusa.org/).

In terms of the efficacy of experimentation, it is difficult to gain insight into a human disease by studying an artificially induced pathology in animals, no matter how similar the two diseases may seem. Indeed, because of differences between species, studies conducted on animals cannot reliably be extrapolated to humans. Many times, animals react to medicines differently than people do, and there is an ever-growing list of drugs that were deemed safe after very extensive animal testing, which later proved to be carcinogenic, mutagenic (causing birth defects), or toxic to humans.[37]

Guinea pigs generally suffer and sometimes die when given penicillin; aspirin causes birth defects in rats and mice, but not in people; aspirin is poisonous to cats; thalidomide was helpful when tested on laboratory animals, but caused birth defects in people; and insulin causes deformities in some laboratory animals, but not people. Animal test results can sometimes be devastating for human health. In a number of cases, effective therapies were delayed because of misleading animal models. For example, the animal model for polio resulted in a misunderstanding of the mechanism of infection, delaying the discovery of a vaccine.

Contrary to the assumption of many supporters of animal experimentation, key discoveries in areas such as heart disease and cancer were achieved through clinical research, observations of patients, and human autopsies, not through animal experiments. The greatest medical advancements in human health were likely the result of improved hygiene. Animal tests gave results that, at best, paralleled previous findings in humans. Furthermore, many alternative approaches to advancing medical knowledge have been developed that are often more accurate and cost effective. These include epidemiological studies, computer and mathematical models, genetic research, cell and tissue cultures, stem cell research, clinical pharmacology, diagnostic imaging (MRI, CAT, and PET scans), and autopsies.

A further challenge to animal experimentation is that it is expensive. Relying on animal experiments and transplants from animals keeps

---

37   For a comprehensive overview of the case against animal experimentation, see We Animals Media/NEAVS, *Gold Doesn't Rust: The Failing Standard of Animal Testing and Its Alternatives* (dir. Kelly Guerin, 2019), https://weanimalsmedia.org/project/gold-standard-turned-to-rust/.

society from considering its basic responsibility to boost preventive health measures that would reduce the number of expensive and extremely complex medical procedures required to remediate chronic conditions. If the billions of dollars spent on animal experimentation were instead directed to educating people to eat and live more healthfully, there would be far greater benefits for humankind.

Of course there are other factors that affect our health—including genetics—that are beyond our control, but lifestyle changes can make major differences in many cases. Perhaps because of the above factors, animal experimentation has produced relatively little progress in many areas of medicine. Despite (or perhaps because of) relying heavily on extensive animal experimentation for medical advancement, health costs in the United States and other countries have become very high, which has contributed to major budgetary problems in many cities and states and nationally, with the result that spending for many other human needs has been reduced.

Even if animal experiments were useful for health reasons, how can we account for the wasteful, unnecessary experiments? Must we force dogs to smoke to reconfirm the health hazards of cigarettes? Do we have to starve dogs and monkeys to understand human starvation? Do we need to cut, blind, burn, and kill animals to produce another type of lipstick, mascara, or shampoo?[38]

An animal rights position would argue that an individual animal's right to be free from torture or harm at our hands trumps any utility that the animal's use or death would provide to human beings. You don't have to hold such a view to recognize that animal experimentation is morally problematic. In the last two decades, the United States, the European Union, and countries around the world have either ended experimentation on great apes, granted them legal rights, or banned harmful research.[39] Bans on using animals for cosmetics testing are growing in number.[40]

38   Humane Society International, "About Cosmetics Animal Testing," March 6, 2013, https://www.hsi.org/news-media/about_cosmetics_animal_testing/.
39   Project R&R, "International Bans," n.d., https://www.releasechimps.org/laws/international-bans.
40   Tjasa Grum, "Global Ban on Animal Testing: Where Are We in 2019?" Cosmetics Design-Europe, March 5, 2019, https://www.cosmeticsdesign-europe.com/Article/2019/03/05/Global-ban-on-animal-testing-where-are-we-in-2019.

But so is use of animals in the United States—from sheep, pigs, cats, and dogs, to the proverbial guinea pigs—rising to 780,070 in 2018.[41]

It's possible that given the growth of personalized medicine[42] that one day experimentation on animals will become too blunt an instrument for diagnosis across species or for individual patients. It will either be obsolete, too expensive to be viable, or simply morally objectionable.[43] Until then, however, the most parsimonious approach should be replacement and reduction, and a commitment to prioritizing medicine that responds to human needs first. It is instructive that, in moments of crisis, such as the COVID-19 pandemic of 2020, animal experimentation has been sidelined in favor of direct human trials.[44]

JUDAISM AND ANIMAL RIGHTS

I will be the first to admit that institutional religion can be resistant to change; in fact, some of what attracts us to religions in the first place is that they hold values that we hope are not subject to the whims of fashion, political movements, or one individual's choice. Their rigor and structure can be appealing: a framework that supports our freedom and life goals rather than a prison or straitjacket that confines us. That said, all institutions, religious or otherwise, can fall victim to sclerosis, clericalism, literalism, and complacency—and that is also true of any issue that bedevils humanity, including our relationship with animals. Judaism, thankfully, has scriptural sources and a long history of interpreting them, and many fearless and compassionate sages who have called upon us both

---

41 Speaking of Research, "U.S. Statistics," n.d., https://speakingofresearch.com/facts/statistics/. To put that number in perspective, around nine billion chickens are killed each year for food in the United States alone, which is approximately 34,246 a minute. It thus takes only twenty-three minutes for the number of chickens killed to outstrip the entire population of animals used in research.

42 For more information, see "Personalized Medicine Coalition," http://www.personalizedmedicinecoalition.org/.

43 Patrick J. Kiger, "Will Alternative Technologies Make Animal Testing Obsolete? How Stuff Works," February 8, 2018, https://science.howstuffworks.com/innovation/scientific-experiments/will-alternative-technologies-make-animal-testing-obsolete.htm.

44 Nicoletta Lanese, "Researchers Fast-track Coronavirus Vaccine by Skipping Key Animal Testing First," *LiveScience*, March 13, 2020, https://www.livescience.com/coronavirus-vaccine-trial-no-animal-testing.html.

to reimagine the meanings of the scriptures for today *and* to look for the deeper truths within them.

Concerning Judaism, the negative presumption held by animal activists toward the religious and by the religious toward animal advocates is largely due to the misunderstanding of two important biblical verses that, when properly understood, actually endorse the struggle to improve conditions for animals.[45] The first misunderstanding is that the biblical teaching that humans are granted dominion over animals (Genesis 1:26, 28) gives us a warrant to treat them in whatever way we wish. As we discussed earlier, however, this biblical teaching does not mean we have the right to wantonly exploit them, and it certainly doesn't permit us to breed animals and then treat them as inanimate objects, designed solely to meet human needs, as is common today. For instance, if you hire a gardener to take care of your garden, you are in effect giving him or her "dominion." Of course, this does not give the gardener license to be destructive. Likewise, a mother has dominion over her infant, but this does not give her a right to mistreat the child.

In "A Vision of Vegetarianism and Peace," Rav Kook states:

> There can be no doubt in the mind of any intelligent person that [the Divine empowerment of humanity to derive benefit from nature] does not mean the domination of a harsh ruler, who afflicts his people and servants merely to satisfy his whim and desire, according to the crookedness of his heart. It is unthinkable that the Divine Law would impose such a decree of servitude, sealed for all eternity, upon the world of God, Who is "good to all, and His mercy is upon all His works" (Psalms 145:9), and Who declared, "The world shall be built with kindness" (Psalms 89:15).[46]

This view is reinforced by God, who gives humankind dominion over animals (Genesis 1:26, 28), but then prescribes vegan foods as the diet for humans (Genesis 1:29) and declares Creation "very good" (Genesis 1:31).

---

45 I want to express appreciation to Rabbi Dovid Sears for his contribution to this section.
46 Rav Kook, *A Vision of Vegetarianism and Peace*, Rabbi David Cohen, ed., Jonathan Rubenstein, trans. (2013), www.jewishveg.com/AVisionofVegetarianismandPeace.pdf.

Adam and Eve's original vegan diet was consistent with the stewardship that God entrusted to them and to all humankind. That "dominion" means responsible stewardship is reinforced by Genesis 2:15, which indicates that humans are to not only work the land, but also protect it. As indicated in the main text, Jews are to be coworkers with God in preserving the natural environment.

The second error is thinking that the biblical teaching that only human beings are created in God's image (Genesis 1:27, 5:1) means that God places little or no value on animals. The Torah declares that animals are also God's creatures, possessing sensitivity and the capacity for feeling pain. God is concerned that they be protected and treated with compassion and justice. In fact, the Jewish sages state that to be "created in the Divine Image" means that people have the capacity to emulate the Divine compassion for all creatures. "As God is compassionate," they teach, "so you should be compassionate."

In his classic work *Ahavat Chesed* ("The Love of Kindness"), the revered Chafetz Chayim (Rabbi Yisrael Meir Kagan of Radin) writes that whoever emulates the Divine love and compassion to all creatures "will bear the stamp of God on his person." Rabbi Samson Raphael Hirsch discusses the concept that human beings were created to "work it [the Garden of Eden] and to guard it" (Genesis 2:15). He observes that this actually limits our rights over other living things. He writes:

> The earth was not created as a gift to you. You have been given to the earth, to treat it with respectful consideration, as God's earth, and everything on it as God's creation, as your fellow creatures— to be respected, loved, and helped to attain their purpose according to God's will. . . . To this end, your heartstrings vibrate sympathetically with any cry of distress sounding anywhere in Creation, and with any glad sound uttered by a joyful creature.[47]

As the Lord is our shepherd, we are to be shepherds of voiceless creatures. As God is kind and compassionate to us, we must be considerate

---

47 Rabbi Samson Raphael Hirsch, *The Nineteen Letters* (Jerusalem/New York: Feldheim, 1969). Letter 4.

of the needs and feelings of animals. In addition, by showing compassion to animals through a vegan diet, we help fulfill the commandment to imitate God's ways.

Animal rights activists may argue, with some justification, that few religious communities are doing enough to end the many horrible abuses of animals today, especially in the meat industry. However, it would be a major mistake for animal activists to dismiss the various religious communities as unconcerned with the plight of animals. Rather, while respectfully challenging religious adherents to do more to live up to their religion's compassionate teachings about animals and to do more to reduce animal abuse, we should all seek ways to transcend our philosophical and theological differences, and seek common ground on which we may stand together for the benefit of animals and humanity.

11

THE FUTURE FOR CULTIVATED ANIMAL PRODUCTS

Previous chapters of this book have discussed the many negative effects of animal-based diets and agriculture, especially in exacerbating the consequences of climate change and other environmental threats. We have noted the epidemic of life-threatening conditions resulting from eating meat and other animal products, as well as the widespread mistreatment of farmed animals.

Many people believe that cultivated animal products can significantly reduce these problems. This chapter explores efforts to develop these substances, especially in Israel, and asks what their potential benefits might be. Are they kosher? Are they vegan? Should vegans support their development, and will consumers buy them?[1]

ORIGINS AND PROSPECTS

Cultivated meat—also known as "cultured," "lab-grown," "cellular," or "clean" meat—has been in development for around two decades, and, according to scientists working on the various components that make up the production of cultivated meat, is rapidly progressing toward production for consumers.

The "meat" is developed by taking a sample of muscle from an animal. Technicians then gather stem cells and, using nutrients and growth promotors, proliferate the cell to form fibers and muscle tissue.[2]

---

1   For an in-depth overview of this industry (as of July 2019), including the ethical, conceptual, economic, and technical issues that need to be overcome, see Brighter Green, *Beyond the Impossible: The Futures of Plant-based and Cellular Meat and Dairy*, https://brightergreen.org/wp-content/uploads/2019/11/Beyond-the-Impossible.pdf.
2   G. Owen Schaefer, "Lab-Grown Meat," *Scientific American*, September 14, 2018.

Dr. Yaron Bogin, executive director of the non-profit Modern Agriculture Foundation, which was established in 2014 with the aim of promoting and supporting research to implement the idea of cultivated meat, describes the process this way: "What we do, broadly speaking, is that we take a sample of cells from a cow or a hen, put them into bioreactors, add nutrients to them, cause the cells to divide and multiply and then we turn them into muscle cells, harvest them and make meatballs from them."[3]

Since 2013,[4] dozens of companies worldwide—including several in Israel—have been founded to create cultivated-meat equivalents of beef, pork, chicken, foie gras, kangaroo, tuna, and shrimp,[5] and they are attracting considerable financial investment.[6] Although cultivated meat start-ups hope to have marketable products relatively soon, they face several obstacles before they will be commercially viable.

When tissue engineer Mark Post first introduced a burger made from lab-grown meat in 2013,[7] it cost over $300,000 to produce and was considered too dry, because only muscle cells were cultivated—not a combination of muscle cells and fat cells.[8] Food experts believe that cultivated meat's taste will be improved through careful attention to texture, partly by adding fat cells to muscle cells, and by judicious supplementation with flavor enhancers. Much of the original cost was to source considerable amounts of a serum that was only used in laboratories. This substance was of an uneven quality and contained proteins from the fetuses of pregnant cows—which is obviously not vegan.[9]

Costs of production have decreased substantially since 2013, and Memphis Meats (another start-up) reported in 2018 that a quarter-pound

3   Ido Efrati, "Israeli Institutions Working to Bring Cultured Meat from Lab to Plate," *Haaretz*, April 30, 2017.
4   See, for example, Matt Simon, "Lab-Grown Meat Is Coming Whether You Like It Or Not," *Science*, February 16, 2016; and Synthego, "The Bench. Lab-Grown Meat Will Change the Food Industry Forever," May 15, 2019, https://www.synthego.com/blog/lab-grown-meats.
5   Cellbased Tech, "Lab Grown Meat Companies," n.d., https://cellbasedtech.com/lab-grown-meat-companies.
6   Sam Danley, "Cell-based Meats Approaching Scalability," *Food Business News*, January 27, 2020.
7   Henry Fountain, "A Lab-Grown Burger Gets a Taste Test," *The New York Times*, August 5, 2013.
8   Schaefer, "Lab-Grown Meat."
9   Matt Reynolds, "The Clean Meat Industry Is Racing to Ditch Its Reliance on Foetal Blood," *Wired* (UK), March 20, 2018.

of its lab-produced beef cost about $600 to produce.[10] Some industry leaders project that the cost of production could be only $10 by 2021,[11] a time frame that seems optimistic. (Whether one or more animal-free sera are or will be available by then remains a matter of conjecture.)[12] Moreover, moving from a lab to production facilities—such as the bioreactors in which the cells will be developed—will require the kind of scaling that has yet to be trialed.[13]

Other obstacles that will have to be surmounted are ensuring that the substance is produced hygienically, under appropriate regulatory structures, and is approved as safe to eat. Currently, in the United States, the Food and Drug Administration and the Department of Agriculture are working together to "address the many important technical and regulatory considerations that can arise with the development of animal cell–cultured food products for human consumption."[14] The cultivated meat industry has welcomed this expedited examination and believes their processes and products will meet the agencies' requirements.[15]

Concerned about what they perceive as impending competition, some traditional meat producers are arguing that cultivated products are not really meat and should not be labeled as such.[16] This is similar to

10 Schaefer, "Lab-Grown Meat."
11 Andres Gonzalez and Silke Cantrowitz, "The $280,000 Burger Could Be a More Palatable $10 in Two Years," *Reuters,* July 9, 2019.
12 Patrick Marx, "On Our Way to Animal-Free Cultured Meat," C2w International, May 2018, https://c2winternational.nl/2018-05/on-our-way-to-animal-free-cultured-meat/; and Jonathan Shieber, "Lab-Grown Meat Could Be on Store Shelves by 2022, Thanks to Future Meat Technologies," Techcrunch, October 10, 2019, https://techcrunch.com/2019/10/10/lab-grown-meat-could-be-on-store-shelves-by-2022-thanks-to-future-meat-technologies/.
13 Tristan Roth, "Scaling up Cultured Meat: The Technical Challenge," Medium, May 28, 2019, https://medium.com/the-ea-company/scaling-up-cultured-meat-the-technical-challenge-47fdac3d5aa5.
14 USDA, "USDA and FDA Announce a Formal Agreement to Regulate Cell-Cultured Food Products from Cell Lines of Livestock and Poultry," Press release, March 7, 2019, https://www.usda.gov/media/press-releases/2019/03/07/usda-and-fda-announce-formal-agreement-regulate-cell-cultured-food.
15 Matt Ball, "Closer to Your Table—USDA and FDA Reach Cell-Based Meat Milestone," Good Food Institute blog, March 8, 2019, https://www.gfi.org/closer-to-your-table-usda-and-fda-reach-cell.
16 Megan Poinski, "Cell-Based Meat Products Are Years Away, So Why Are States Making So Many Laws about Them?" Fooddive.com, February 12, 2020, https://www.fooddive.com/news/cell-based-meat-products-are-years-away-so-why-are-states-making-so-many-l/571071/.

campaigns by the meat and dairy industry to prevent plant-based burgers and drinks from being labeled *meat* and *milk*, respectively.[17] Other meat producers are planning to diversify their range of products by adding cultivated meat to their offerings.[18]

In spite of the significant obstacles that remain to be overcome by the cultivated meat companies, they are nonetheless committed to producing tasty, affordable products that will shift people's eating habits to being more ethical, healthy, humane, and environmentally sustainable. They are encouraged by surveys showing that two-thirds of the public is willing to try cultivated meat.[19]

THE BENEFITS OF CULTIVATED MEAT

One of the main benefits of cultivated meat is that it produces an almost identical substance to that derived from the slaughter of animals, with a significant reduction of their abusive treatment. The many horrors of factory farming—including the force-feeding of geese and the branding, dehorning, and castrating of cattle—would be eliminated, as would the genetic manipulation of these animals. Indeed, it is assumed that once the cell is extracted from the animal, these cells could be proliferated by themselves. Mosa Meat, a pioneering company in cell-based meat, believes that a single sample from a cow could produce enough muscle tissue to make 80,000 quarter-pound burgers.[20]

Another significant benefit from the resulting reduction in billions of animals raised for slaughter would be potentially dramatic decreases in many of the problems that have already been enumerated in this book: climate change, rapid species extinction; soil erosion and depletion; massive pollution of land, water, and air; destruction of tropical rainforests, coral reefs, and other valuable habitats; desertification; and so on. Without the need to feed so many animals, we could let large areas

17　Nathaniel Popper, "You Call That Meat? Not So Fast, Cattle Ranchers Say," *The New York Times*, February 9, 2019.
18　Cargill, "Protein Innovation: Cargill Invests in Cultured Protein," Press release, January 24, 2020, https://www.cargill.com/story/protein-innovation-cargill-invests-in-cultured-meats.
19　Kat Smith, "Almost 70 percent of Americans Want to Eat Clean Meat," Livekindly, August 16, 2018, https://www.livekindly.co/almost-70-of-americans-want-to-eat-clean-meat/.
20　*Ibid.*

of land lie fallow on a rotating basis, and thus restore its fertility, or even allow it to return to prairie, woodland, and forest, thus enabling carbon to be sequestered and animals to find natural habitats. With less need to grow crops for animal feed, fewer pesticides and chemical fertilizers would be necessary. Even though the lessening of animal agriculture would not in and of itself reverse climate change, it would be a major step in reducing its devastating consequences.

With the major shift from growing food for animals, we'd be able to direct our agricultural resources to feeding our world's malnourished and undernourished citizens, potentially saving the lives of many of the millions of people who die annually of hunger. We would save potable water, and potentially reduce pollution and greenhouse gas emissions—depending on how energy-intensive bioreactors might be, and where they source that energy. An added bonus would be that, since cultivated meat would have no added hormones and antibiotics and potentially be lower in saturated fat, it could have major health benefits. The current proliferation of antibiotic-resistant bacteria would be lowered, and there would be much reduced risk of animal-borne illnesses such as mad cow disease, salmonella, avian flu, swine flu, and coronaviruses. Furthermore, a world in which the stress on potable water, land, and (potentially) energy is lowered, and food may be more widely available, is one that will be more inclined toward peace.

Israel and Cultivated Meat

With at least five companies working on cultivated meat, Israel is a major player in efforts to produce cultivated meat, consistent with its status as a "start-up nation."[21] These Israeli start-ups, like many around the world, are driven by a mission to meet the needs of the world's ever-growing population and demand for food.

Food-giant Tyson, the largest meat producer in the United States and the second largest worldwide, has invested $2.2 million of

---

21   Recent articles on Israeli efforts to produce cultivated meat include: Eitan Halon, "Israeli Start-up to Build World's First Lab-grown Meat Production Facility," *The Jerusalem Post*, October 11, 2019; and Nir Goldstein, "The Race for Non-Meat Protein: How Israel Can Lead the World in Developing Food for the Future," *The Jerusalem Post*, November 10, 2019.

seed money in Jerusalem-based Future Meat Technologies.[22] Future Meat Technologies is developing a new generation of manufacturing technology that enables the cost-efficient production of muscle cells and fat, the core building blocks of cultivated meat.[23] Justin Whitmore, an executive vice president at Tyson, said: "This is our first investment in an Israel-based company and we're excited about this opportunity to broaden our exposure to innovative, new ways of producing protein. . . . We continue to invest significantly in our traditional meat business, but also believe in exploring additional opportunities for growth that give consumers more choices."[24]

On May 7, 2017, the Technion, the Israel Institute of Technology in Haifa, hosted the first Israeli international conference on the topic of cultivated meat, cleverly named "Future Meating."[25] Among the conference's local sponsors were Soglowek Food Industries and Strauss Israel, which, along with the Innovation Authority at the Economy and Industry Ministry, established an incubator for entrepreneurs about two years ago—the Kitchen FoodTech Hub.[26] Yaakov Nahmias, a bioengineering professor at Hebrew University and founder of Future Meat Technologies, has said: "Producing meat [by raising and slaughtering animals] is very inefficient," adding that "cultured meat by comparison, consumes a tenth of the water, land, and energy that current meat production requires."[27]

Israeli cultivated meat start-up Aleph Farms is working to go beyond burgers to produce lab-grown steak.[28] Seeking to tap into consumer concerns about animal welfare, health, and the environment, they hope to have their product on the market by 2021 at a reasonable price.[29]

22 JTA, "Tyson Foods to Invest in Israeli Company Developing Lab-Grown Meat," *Haaretz*, May 6, 2018.
23 *Ibid.*
24 *Ibid.*
25 Ido Efrati, "Israeli Institutions Working to Bring Cultured Meat from Lab to Plate," *Haaretz*, April 30, 2017.
26 *Ibid.*
27 MADAN, "Israeli Start-ups Make Lab-grown 'Clean Meat,'" March 4, 2019, http://madan.org.il/en/news/israeli-startups-make-lab-grown-clean-meat.
28 Lianne Back and Tova Cohen, "On the Menu Soon: Lab-Grown Steak," *The Jerusalem Post*, July 16, 2019.
29 *Ibid.*

Nir Goldstein, managing director of the Good Food Institute Israel, suggests how Israel can lead future lab-grown food development:

> So what has to be done so that we will see a successful meat substitute industry here? Simple. The government has to define alternative protein technology as a national priority assignment. Like cyber; like desalination technology. The Israel Innovation Authority must finance groundbreaking research studies through start-ups, in academia and in industry. The Agriculture, Economy, and Environmental Protection ministries must use the tools at their disposal to direct the Israeli food industry toward groundbreaking innovation—and the Health Ministry must quickly formulate a detailed program of activities for the regulation of cultured meat, so that Israel will also be the first country in the world in which the Israeli inventions can be consumed.[30]

WHY ARE SOME VEGANS AGAINST CULTIVATED MEAT?

Vegans and vegan organizations are generally in favor of any possibility of reducing or preferably ending the horrors of factory farming and the systemic cruelty toward animals that it involves.[31] However, some oppose the development of cultured meat. They observe that cultivated meat is not strictly vegan, since animals are used in its production (either as the subjects of a biopsy from which cells are drawn or in the medium, such as fetal bovine serum, within which *currently* cells are grown). They also note that cultivated meat is still the flesh of an animal. In responding to this, Paul Shapiro, author of *Clean Meat: How Growing Meat without Animals Will Revolutionize Dinner and the World*,[32] has said:

---

30   Goldstein, "The Race for Non-Meat Protein."
31   Arguments from some leading vegan activists against lab-grown meat can be found at Clean Meat Hoax, n.d., https://www.cleanmeat-hoax.com/animal-advocates-speak-out.html. A video of a panel discussion featuring four vegans who oppose lab-grown meat can be found at the United Poultry Concerns: 2019 Conscious Eating Conference, https://www.upc-online.org/videos/190315_announcing_the_videos_for_the_conscious_eating_conference_2019.html.
32   Paul Shapiro, *Clean Meat: How Growing Meat without Animals Will Revolutionize Dinner and the World* (New York: Simon & Schuster, 2018).

Clean [Cultivated] meat is not an alternative to meat: It is meat. The cells grow as they would in an animal's body, which creates actual meat, not a meat alternative. So, clean meat isn't really for vegans. Clean meat will be for people who are more likely to go to KFC. The goal is to provide a type of meat that meat eaters can consume while causing much less harm. All that said, for vegans who are vegan solely to avoid harming animals, clean meat does seem to alleviate that concern.[33]

Critics observe that the promotion of cultivated meat obscures the reality that the simplest and best way to create a healthy, sustainable, and ethical world food system is through a plant-based diet; that its promotion helps the meat industry in its wider strategy of preserving animal agriculture; and reinforces the myth that people need meat for their health and happiness. One final critique is that with humans running out of time to save the world, the commercialization of cultivated meat may not come soon enough because of many technical problems still to be solved.[34] Some have suggested that the supposed health and environmental benefits of lab-grown meat may be exaggerated, especially since eating animal flesh, whether from a farmed animal or from a laboratory, is likely to contain fat and cholesterol. They are concerned at how much energy may be required to power bioreactors.

Noting the presence of and investment in cultivated meat by multinational food companies such as Cargill, Perdue, Tyson, and Smithfield, which profit mightily from the current slaughter of billions of animals, these critics are skeptical at whether the promise of cultivated meat ending industrialized animal production will be met. Moreover, they state, promoting cultivated meat as the "solution" to food-related problems diverts attention away from the delicious and popular plant-based food alternatives, and from the massive mistreatment of animals raised on factory farms and other negatives of animal agriculture. Furthermore, the emphasis on cultivated meat implies that the vegan

33   Midge Raymond, "Is So-called Clean Meat Vegan? Paul Shapiro Has the Answer," *VegNews*, January 2018, https://vegnews.com/2018/1/is-so-called-clean-meat-vegan-paul-shapiro-has-the-answer.
34   See Sam Bloch, "The Hype and the Hope Surrounding Lab-Grown Meat," *The New Food Economy*, July 23, 2019.

movement has failed and that developing meats of different kinds is the way of the future.

One final question is worth asking: Is cultivated meat kosher? Yes, according to Israeli Orthodox Rabbi Yuval Cherlov, a member of the Tzohar Rabbinical Organization, who ruled that cloned (or cultured) meat is not subject to the rules that apply to the consumption of regular meat.[35] He added that "cloned meat produced [even] from a pig shall not be defined as prohibited for consumption—including with milk."[36] As cultivated meat approaches commercial availability, its kosher status will be discussed at greater length by rabbinic authorities, but the consensus so far is that it is kosher.[37]

In view of the many deleterious and destructive practices and outcomes of animal agriculture that I've enumerated in this book's previous chapters, I believe everything possible should be done to reduce the consumption of meat and other products from animals, given the urgency of rapid changes needed in order to avert a climate catastrophe and other environmental threats to humanity. I consider the ideal diet to consist of locally grown organic fruits, vegetables, nuts, seeds, whole grains, and legumes; and because there has already been outstanding progress in producing plant-based burgers and other animal substitutes that are increasingly receiving wide acceptance and acclaim (even from meat-loving consumers) because their taste and texture are virtually indistinguishable from present commercial meat-based burgers, vegans should prioritize promoting these plant-based foods even more than cultivated meat. In addition, I want and would expect cultivated meat to be thoroughly tested before it becomes commercially available to make sure there are no significant unanticipated problems or negative side effects.

---

35 JTA, "Rabbi Says Meat from Genetically Cloned Pig Could be Eaten by Jews, Including with Milk," *Haaretz*, March 25, 2018.
36 *Ibid.*
37 Gabriella Gershonson, "No Animals Were Harmed in the Production of This Steak," *The Tablet*, June 11, 2019; and Bruce Friedrich, "Why Clean Meat Is Kosher," Good Food Institute blog, June 22, 2017, https://www.gfi.org/why-clean-meat-is-kosher.

Finally, whether or not a vegan decides to consume cultivated meat, I think vegans in general should support efforts to produce such products that are tasty, affordable, and healthy, because they have the potential to markedly reduce animal suffering, climate change, environmental degradation, hunger, life-threatening ailments, and other negative effects of eating conventional meat.

12

LIVING AS A VEGAN AND A JEW

In this book I have attempted to present the evidence that the world is in the throes of a climate catastrophe. Self-reinforcing positive feedback loops (vicious cycles) are moving the climate system toward irreversible tipping points. If we fail to act rapidly and decisively, these will bring massive climate disruptions, with calamitous results for all life on Earth. Because animal agriculture is a major cause of global warming, a shift toward veganism is key to the effort to avert this climate catastrophe. Such a shift is becoming easier than ever, thanks to monumental progress in simulating popular animal foods with plant-based and animal cell–based ingredients.

As this book documents, many potentially fatal diseases can be prevented and in some cases reversed by positive lifestyle changes, including a vegan diet; in an age of resource scarcity, diets full of animal products require far more land, energy, water, and other resources per person than plant-based diets; and although the world already produces more than enough food to feed every person on the planet, we waste it through turning so much of it into animal feed. In addition, climate change will only exacerbate tensions around the planet as desperate refugees flee droughts, wildfires, storms, floods, and other severe climate events, making terrorism and war more likely.

These issues animate my life, and they impact what food I place in my mouth. Although I have been a vegan for many years, I still encounter the assumption that my diet is a deprivation—an ascetical practice that runs contrary to a deeper biological or emotional need that I may have to eat animal products. It is as if vegans are expected at any moment to throw up their hands and return to eating meat and dairy, relieved of their burden of conscience.

No doubt there are some people who may feel deprived, or may indeed relish the notion that they are practicing some kind of austerity. As with all regimens, there's a danger that someone might adopt a restrictive vegan diet as a cover for orthorexia, particularly as a way of getting attention or feeling empowered by controlling the body's urges.[1]

For me, however, veganism is a life-affirming and life-giving diet and set of values that is about plenitude and pleasure. It offers a daily reminder of our responsibilities as stewards of creation and environmental remediation, and it provides me with a way to protest the sheer insanity that non-vegan diets represent. It offers a prospect of peace and security for all.

In fact, veganism couldn't be further removed from deprivation or denial. Not only are there an astonishingly wide variety of plant-based foods, fruits, vegetables, nuts, seeds, pulses, and grains, but cuisines from all over the world offer thousands of dishes that are either already vegan or can easily be made so. Indeed, over the last couple of decades vegan options have moved from health food stores, co-ops, and stores selling ethnic foods, to supermarkets all over the United States and many other places around the world. Tofu, tempeh, and seitan—to name some of the classic formulations of bean curd and wheat gluten, respectively—have now been supplemented with an ever-expanding range of plant-based burgers, sausages, crumbles, and slices; an enormous array of cheeses made of various kinds of nuts, and many varieties of yogurts, milks, and butters; and a panoply of vegan juices, smoothies, and snacks sit alluringly on or near the check-out counter.

That said, if you're persuaded by anything you've read in these pages and want to go vegan, it might be wise to prepare yourself: either by reducing animal products over time, or by filling your kitchen cabinets before taking the leap. Many of us, when we began, were concerned (unreasonably) that we would not be getting enough protein. Don't worry. As long as you are eating sufficient calories via a variety of wholesome plant-based foods, you'll meet all your protein needs. However, if you are concerned, then a few good sources of plant-based protein are nuts,

---

1   For more on orthorexia and veganism, see Plenty Vegan, "You Are Not What You Eat: Instagram, Veganism & Orthorexia," n.d., https://plentyvegan.com/you-are-not-what-you-eat-instagram-veganism-orthorexia-2/.

seeds, lentils, tofu, and tempeh. Many common foods such as whole grain bread, broccoli, spinach, potatoes, corn, and peas add to protein intake.

The only caution doctors and dietitians have regarding your vegan diet is to make sure you take a B_{12} vitamin supplement. B_{12} (cobalamin) is an essential mineral found in microbes, which because of the destruction of the health of our soil and our sanitized food system, are becoming much less common. Nonetheless, they are necessary. Thankfully, many vegan foods are fortified with B_{12}. However, always consult your doctor about any aspects of your diet, and ask to be tested for your B_{12} levels.[2] You do not have to be an expert on all aspects of nutrition as long as you know the basics and are willing to learn more.

In every instance, be sure to eat a wide variety of foods, preferably in season, rather than depend on a limited selection of foods with which you were previously familiar. Experiment with new foods; dare to improvise! Invite people over to share your food; approach each meal positively and with joy.

If you fancy yourself a chef, hundreds of cookbooks are in print catering to all kinds of tastes and culinary interests, and there are innumerable videos online showing you how to make any dish from scratch. Several magazines, hundreds of blogs, and monthly food festivals and annual conferences provide you with many opportunities to learn more about veganism and encounter the diversity of lifestyles, attitudes, and interests shared by vegans.

Become familiar with vegan restaurants in your area, and if you have questions related to kosher vegan dining, then consult a trusted rabbinical authority. Associate with other vegans and vegetarians and become friendly with health-minded people for mutual support and reinforcement. A sense of community is important, even if socialization is mostly by telephone or on social media. This is especially the case for children: they should know that there are others with diets similar to theirs.

---

2   See Michael Greger, MD, "Vitamin B_{12}. Nutrition Facts," n.d., https://nutritionfacts.org/topics/vitamin-b12/; and Virginia Messina, "The Vegan RD," n.d., https://www.theveganrd.com/vegan-nutrition-101/vegan-nutrition-primers/vitamin-b12-a-vegan-nutrition-primer/. B_{12} deficiency affects not only vegans. See Rise of the Vegan, "B_{12}: Why It's Not Just a Vegan Issue," February 19, 2017, https://www.riseofthevegan.com/blog/b12-is-not-just-a-vegan-problem.

Community is also valuable because you will find that, although the larger society in which you move is much more accommodating to your diet than it used to be, misconceptions and hurdles exist. This is particularly true of social occasions. If you are invited to a wedding, bar/bat mitzvah, or dinner at a home, respectfully let your hosts know beforehand that you are a vegan. Generally, they will comply cordially and they may enjoy preparing a special meal for you and other guests. If they ask "why?" use this as an opportunity to respectfully educate them, using the information in this book and books in the bibliography.

If you feel it would be an imposition for your host to prepare something special for you, offer to bring a vegan dish. This will not only relieve the pressure on the host, but will also provide the opportunity to introduce the host and other guests, whose knowledge of and experience with vegan food may be limited, to something really wonderful! Situations such as these can often lead to stimulating discussions on why one chose to be vegan.

My advice is to not become overly obsessed with label-reading or purity tests. Our aim as conscious eaters should be to consume food that is as health-giving as possible; to source that food locally and seasonally; to pay attention to the rights of workers who picked or prepared that food; and to try to live as lightly on the land as possible. These are high barriers to leap, and it may be difficult because of our life circumstances to surmount them all at once. So, if you accidentally eat something that contains an animal product; or if you find it hard to reduce your intake of junk food or high-fat oils or artificial sweeteners in your diet; or if you tend to enjoy food out of a can more than you do freshly grown— then don't take yourself to task too much. Animal products are in many everyday items; it is impossible to be perfect.

The Active Vegan

"How can you tell if someone is vegan?" runs a set-up to a joke that's familiar to vegans. "Don't worry," comes the answer. "They'll tell you."[3]

---

3   Korinne Bricker, "How Can You Tell If Someone Is Vegan? Don't Worry, They'll Tell You," Medium, March 14, 2017, https://medium.com/@korinnebricker/how-can-you-tell-if-someone-is-vegan-dont-worry-they-ll-tell-you-4eec13254f03.

As you can probably tell from reading this book, I am passionately committed to veganism, and I am not alone. We can see how much is wrong with our current treatment of animals, and how consequential that maltreatment is for the environment, human health, and the future of the planet, so that it is hard not to want to tell everyone we meet about the problem and the remedy, as we see them. Many of us see it as a moral imperative to change people's minds as well as their practices, before it is too late.

It's likely that once you adopt a vegan lifestyle you will become an activist; or, you will be seen by others as an activist, simply by the choices you make at the dinner table. That's why it is valuable to be well informed and knowledgeable—and also, as it turns out, why it's important to remember that you likely were once *not* a vegan. Openness, attentiveness, and modesty are virtues. In the heat of new awareness it can be hard to remember how you might have reacted to someone if they'd berated you for eating animals; your ideas will be more welcome and probably better received if you treat people's questions with respect and respond in the appropriate tone. That applies with family members, friends, colleagues at work, local or national officials, businesses, and associations you approach. It even applies with your doctor. Because medical school has traditionally not incentivized the role of diet in general health, your doctor may know less than you do about your diet. Respectfully, help deepen their knowledge of the many health benefits of a vegetarian or vegan diet.

You can also present your veganism to the world less vocally: on bumper stickers or with buttons; donating books on veganism for your local library; writing to the editors of newspapers, penning op-eds, starting your own blog, or using a social media site. You can offer cooking demonstrations; join a group providing vegan food for the homeless or the elderly; or set up your own co-op, restaurant, or food cart.

In all such matters, it's important to not let the perfect become the enemy of the good. If your correspondents or interlocutors are not willing to become vegans, encourage them to at least make a start by giving up red meat and/or having one or two meatless meals a week (perhaps Mondays and Thursdays, which were traditional Jewish fast days).

Furthermore, remember that veganism is only part of our struggle for a more just, peaceful, compassionate, environmentally sustainable world. All of us should try to affect public policy with regard to vegan-related issues, including preserving health, showing compassion to animals, conserving natural resources, helping hungry people, and seeking and pursuing peace.

If you are Jewish, you can ask your rabbi to raise issues around veganism and the treatment of animals in your synagogue, or ask whether you can do this yourself. You can request that meat and other animal products not be served at synagogue and Jewish organizational functions and celebrations—or at least that healthy vegan options be provided. Groups such as the International Jewish Vegetarian Society and Jewish Veg (formerly Jewish Vegetarians of North America) provide many resources to help you with your facts and arguments.

Ask Jewish school principals and camp directors to provide students with nutritious vegan options, and even see whether trips can be arranged to visit a slaughterhouse or factory farm (if that is possible in your area). You can veganize your festivals. (See Appendix C.)

If you ever feel frustrated or overwhelmed by the many crises facing the world today and the difficulties in trying to help shift people toward vegan diets, please consider the following. Jewish tradition teaches, "You are not obligated to complete the task, but neither are you free to desist from it" (*Pirkei Avot* 2:21). We must make a start and do whatever we can to improve the world. Judaism teaches that a person is obligated to protest when there is evil and to proceed from protest to action. Judaism also teaches that the world is evenly balanced between good and evil and that each person's actions can determine the destiny of the entire world.

Even if little is accomplished, trying to make improvements will prevent the hardening of your heart and will affirm that you accept moral responsibility. The very act of consciousness raising is meaningful because it may lead to future changes. Also, as you plant seeds of information, you never know what positive things might eventually result.

Veganism is my practice and my journey. In this book, I've tried to show that veganism is the diet and lifestyle most consistent with fundamental Jewish teachings, which oblige us to preserve our health, treat animals with kindness, protect and preserve the environment, feed the hungry, and pursue peace. I hope I have demonstrated, using the wisdom of the sages and the scriptures, that the exploitation of animals is an egregious violation of the Jewish obligation to be kind to animals. I have suggested that Jews, including those who observe *kashrut*, have freedom of dietary choice, and that choice should not be based solely on habit, convenience, or tradition. Instead, it should be animated by an ethical consideration of the impact the food we eat has upon our fellow human beings, the animals with whom we share this planet, and the planet itself.

Furthermore, Jewish traditions call upon us to be active agents in the fight to avert catastrophic climate change, while promoting peace, justice, and compassion for all. We must strive for *tikkun olam*, to repair a broken world. And we can do it in the way that fits our interests, skills, and personality: from "being the change" we wish to see in the world, to engaging in respectful one-on-one conversations, to writing, tweeting, leafleting, voting, and demonstrating.

I believe the principles I've articulated are not only *my* vision of Judaism, but are fundamental truths of the faith. Judaism teaches us that God's compassion is over all His works (Psalms 145:9), that the righteous individual considers the well-being of animals (Proverbs 12:10), and that Jews must refrain from *tza'ar ba'alei chayim*, the needless infliction of pain on animals. Judaism calls upon us to engage boldly and unshirkingly in the struggle against injustice, oppression, and idolatry, and to proclaim that God is the Creator of all life, and that His holy attributes of kindness, compassion, and just benevolence are to be emulated by us, His children.

Judaism asserts that every person is created in God's image (Genesis 1:26, 5:1) and is precious and invaluable, and directs us to work with God to preserve and perfect the world as stewards of Earth's resources to ensure that God's bounties are used for the benefit of all (see Genesis 2:15). Judaism cautions us that nothing useful should be selfishly or frivolously wasted or destroyed (*bal tashchit*, based on Deuteronomy 20:19, 20), and bids us to love other people as ourselves and to be kind to strangers. For, note the scriptures, "we were strangers in the land of Egypt," and we should be compassionate toward others who are poor, homeless, orphaned, widowed, or simply members of other species.

It is a Judaic priority to relieve hunger. One who feeds a hungry person is considered, in effect, to have fed God Himself. Judaism mandates that we must seek and pursue peace. Great is peace, for it is one of God's names, all of God's blessings are contained in it, and it will be the Messiah's first blessing. Judaism likewise exhorts us to pursue justice, to work toward a social order in which every person is able to obtain through meaningful and dignified work a secure and fulfilling life. And that, finally, the Jewish people are mandated to be a "light unto the nations," compassionate followers of a compassionate God, setting a positive example for others to follow.

For these reasons, and much more, I am proud to be a Jew. I am proud of our wonderful and universal teachings. Applying them to the world today is vital if we are to steer our endangered civilization onto a sustainable path. I hope that if you are Jewish, and even if you are of another faith, or no faith at all, you will join in the mission to apply these values to the challenges of today. I hope my efforts will help to revitalize Judaism and return disaffected Jews to its embrace. It is also my hope that this book will provoke respectful discussions within the Jewish community, and beyond. Such discussions can lead us to a vegan world in which "they shall neither harm nor destroy on all My holy mount" (Isaiah 11:9).

The futures of Judaism and our imperiled planet depend on it. There is no Planet B!

Acknowledgments

First, I wish to express my thanks to God by reciting the traditional Jewish blessing (*Shehechiyanu*) pronounced when a person reaches a milestone in life: "Blessed are You, our God, King of the universe, Who has kept us alive and sustained us, and brought us to this season."

In writing this book, I was very fortunate to have received input from a wide variety of dedicated and extremely knowledgeable individuals about the important issues considered.

I want to express much appreciation to Jonathan Wolf for his many years of providing valuable suggestions for my Judaica books. I want to abundantly thank Rabbi Yonassan Gershom, a long-time vegetarian activist and author of several books, including *Kapporos Then and Now: Toward a More Compassionate Tradition*, for his very valuable suggestions over many years, many of which are also reflected in my previous book, *Who Stole My Religion: Revitalizing Judaism and Applying Jewish Values to Help Heal Our Impaired Planet.*

Rabbi Dovid Sears, a Breslov *chasid* and author of several Judaica books, provided many valuable suggestions on possible cooperation between activists for better conditions for animals and religious Jews.

The following. listed alphabetically, reviewed many chapters of the book and provided significant input: Sud Baumel, long-time editor of the *Aquarian* magazine; Steve Kaufman, chair of the Christian Vegetarian Association; Lewis Regenstein, long-time vegan activist and author; Jayn Meinhardt and David Sickles, long-time vegan activists, and Rabbi Barry Singer.

Paul Shapiro, author of *Clean Meat: How Growing Meat Without Animals Will Revolutionize Dinner and the World*, and Matt Ball, senior media relations specialist for the Good Food Institute (GFI), provided very significant suggestions for the chapter on cultivated (lab-grown) meat.

People who reviewed one or more chapters of the manuscript and made helpful suggestions include Professor Daniel Brook, PhD; author Judy Carman; Jonathan Danilowitz; Professor David Faiman, PhD; Bruce Friedrich, founder and director of the Good Food Institute; Batzion Shlomi; and Yossi Wolfson, coordinator of the Israeli Jewish Vegetarian Society.

The following people made important suggestions that helped me select the title for this book: Lisa Apfelberg, Rabbi Susan Conforti, Lionel Friedberg, Jayn Meinhardt, Tom Meinhardt, Rabbi David Rosen, Rabbi Barry Silver, Steve Schuster, and Batzion Shlomi.

I want to thank Rabbi David Rosen for his wonderful foreword and the valuable advice he provided for many aspects of this book.

I appreciate Igor Fershtenfeld for his valuable computer help.

I can't begin to find the words to thank Martin Rowe, president of Lantern Publishing & Media, for his very thorough editing, which enlivens and strengthens much of this book, and for everything else he did to get this book published as efficiently as possible.

The contributors named above do not necessarily agree with everything in this book, nor did I always use their suggestions. Although everyone mentioned was very helpful in the writing process, I take full responsibility for the final selection of material and interpretations, as well as any errors. I apologize in advance to any contributors whom I might have inadvertently omitted.

I wish to express deep appreciation to my dear wife, Loretta; our children, Susan (and David) Kleid, David, and Devorah (and Ariel) Gluch; and my grandchildren: Shalom Eliahu, Ayelet Breindel, Avital P'nina, and Michal Na'ama Kleid; and Eliyahu, Ilan Avraham, Yosef, Yael Shachar, Talya Nitzan, and Ayala Neta Gluch, and my first and only great-grandson, Netta Nissenboim, for their patience, understanding, and encouragement, as I took time away from family responsibilities to gather and write this material.

Finally, I wish to thank in advance everyone who will read this book and send me ideas and suggestions for improvements, so that I can more effectively help work to revitalize Judaism and increase awareness of how the application of Judaism's eternal values can help shift our imperiled planet onto a sustainable path.

Appendix A

Voices of Veg*nism

Reinforcing the message of a vegan revolution in Israel and worldwide, with momentum toward veganism accelerating, I present statements from Jewish vegan and vegetarian activists, in alphabetical order.

Jeffrey Spitz Cohan *is executive director of Jewish Veg, formerly Jewish Vegetarians of North America. He speaks frequently on Jewish vegetarianism and veganism and related topics throughout the United States and Canada.*

In September 2017, seventy-five rabbis signed a statement circulated by Jewish Veg, urging their fellow Jews to transition to plant-based diets. For many of the rabbis, a main motivation to sign stemmed from one simple reason: The Torah mandate of *tza'ar ba'alei chayim* is being grotesquely violated in modern animal agriculture, making the method of slaughter a moot point.

Tza'ar ba'alei chayim is the Torah mandate to prevent and alleviate animal suffering. Sadly, a kosher *hechsher* on a package of meat does not mean the animal was treated humanely. The issue here is not whether *shechita*, kosher slaughter, is better or worse than any other type of slaughter. The issue is that the kosher meat companies do not raise their own animals. They buy their animals from the same cruel industry that supplies Oscar Meyer and Tyson—in other words, the secular meat industry.

Rather than go into graphic detail, suffice it to say that the standard practices on factory farms, animal-auction houses, animal-transport vehicles, and feedlots are unspeakably cruel, a desecration of God's name, and a clear-cut violation of *tza'ar ba'alei chayim*.

In Judaism, a mitzvah cannot be enabled by an *aveirah*, a sin. So, no matter how careful a *shochet* is, it just doesn't matter. A grievous sin, actually many sins, were committed to get the animal to that point. Meat nowadays cannot be considered truly kosher.

It's really that simple.

Rabbi Gabriel Cousens is a U.S.-based vegan holistic physician, homeopath, psychiatrist, family therapist, ayurvedic practitioner, and Chinese herbalist. In addition, he's a leading diabetes researcher, ecological leader, spiritual master, and founder and director of the Tree of Life Foundation and Tree of Life Center U.S. He is the bestselling author of There Is a Cure for Diabetes, Conscious Eating, Spiritual Nutrition: Six Foundations for Spiritual Life, Creating Peace by Being Peace, Torah as a Guide to Enlightenment, *and* Depression Free for Life. *He is considered one of the leading live-food vegan medical doctors and holistic physicians, and a world expert on spiritual nutrition.*

Current meat-consumption practices contradict Torah values and therefore diminish *kedusha* (holiness) in at least seven areas—health; cruelty to animals; respect for God's creation; avoiding wastefulness; feeding the hungry; pursuing peace; and following the Ten Speakings, commonly known as the Ten Commandments.

In my work as an actual genetic Levite and thriving *frum* (Jewishly observant) Jewish vegan (since 1973), and as an author of thirteen books on spirituality and vegan nutrition, including *Torah as a Guide to Enlightenment*, I have added the following reasons for considering Jewish veganism to be the new *kashrut* because of its powerful effect in uplifting *Am Yisrael* and the whole world.

In the larger context, veganism as the new *kashrut* is not a new idea and goes back to *Gan Eden*. "And HaShem Elohim [God] commanded the man, saying: 'Of every tree of the garden, you may freely eat . . . '" (Genesis 2:16), " . . . and you shall eat the herbs of the field" (Genesis 3:18).

"God did not permit Adam and his wife to kill a creature and to eat its flesh. Only every green herb shall they all eat together."[1] "Adam was not permitted meat for purposes of eating."[2]

Holistic Torah vegetarianism is the consciousness of sanctifying ourselves and creating holiness for ourselves in the act of eating. It involves experiencing and choosing to invoke the holiness both in the raising of the food as well as in the eating of the food. What and how we eat is both the cause and effect of our consciousness. In essence, Holistic Torah vegetarianism turns the continuum of eating into an act of sanctification and holiness, which in turn helps us maintain our holiness in the act of eating. Vegan as the New Kosher is best suited for the protection of the germ cell and the continuation of the generations to be. The teaching "be fruitful and multiply" (Genesis 1:28) is followed by the vegan directive in Genesis 1:29, as the dietary approach to be fruitful and multiply. Immediately after God gave humankind dominion over animals (Genesis 1:26), He prescribed vegan foods as the diet for humans (Genesis 1:29).

A vegan diet in Judaism contains a moral symmetry that is concerned for human health, for animal life, for nature. It holds the deepest level of moral, ethical, and Torah insight that what is good for human health and spirit is also good for the health of the planet and all life on it. Beyond all question, our future and the survival of this planet depend upon the consciousness of holistic Torah veganism. Holistic Torah veganism supports the strengthening of spiritual sovereignty and expansion of consciousness. The spiritual evolution that emerges from that is the irresistible force pushing us to a thousand years of peace.

Lionel Friedberg *is a documentary film producer, director, cinematographer, and writer who has written and produced films for Animal Planet, CBS, PBS, the History Channel, the Discovery Channel, and the National Geographic Channel. He produced and directed, along*

---

1   Rashi's commentary on Genesis 1:29. Quoted in Barbara Allen, *Animals in Religion: Devotion, Symbol and Reality* (London: Reaktion Books, 2016), 168.
2   Talmud *Bavli, Sanhedrin* 59b.

with his wife, Diana (a professional film editor), the Jewish Vegetarians of North America-sponsored movie A Sacred Duty: Applying Jewish Values to Help Heal the World *as a labor of love and dedication, thus enabling the video to be produced and widely distributed.*

Old habits are hard to break. But when it comes to survival—for ourselves, for our children, for our fellow beings, for our society, for our planet—there are some things that need critical reassessing and adjusting. What we put on our plates and in our mouths, and how we live our lives, affects every single one of us. When I realized this some forty years ago as a filmmaker trying to make sense of our world and its ever-growing sets of challenges, I recognized that those morsels of dead flesh, those eggs and bodily fluids of non-human beings, that I was swallowing at every mealtime were having a profound effect on the environment, on the creatures from which we were obtaining them, and on my own personal health. The moral, physical, and health costs of maintaining an unsustainable Western diet derived from animal foods were becoming too great. I had to do something about it. Fortunately, there were those who showed me the way, and I have never looked back since becoming a vegan.

It is not only about ethics, moral conviction, and religious teachings. Modern science is as clear as a bell on the terrifying cost of clinging to a non-vegan diet. Whole tracts of virginal land, from the Amazon rainforest to the verdant plains of the Americas, are being plowed over to grow genetically modified soybeans to feed cattle who are injected with poisonous chemicals to cause excessive and rapid growth, merely to provide us with a cheap hamburger. The world's oceans are rapidly becoming devoid of life as overfishing trawls and sucks the last remaining organisms from the depths. . . .

It is up to every single one of us to help make a difference and right these awful wrongs. And it begins at a very simple place . . . on the dinner plate. That is not difficult to accomplish. And that is why I am a vegan.

Alex Hershaft, PhD, is a Holocaust survivor and an animal rights pioneer, as well as co-founder and president of the Farm Animal Rights Movement (FARM). Formed in 1976, FARM is the oldest organization promoting the idea that animals should not be raised for food. Working with Jewish Veg, he has frequently talked about how his experience as a Holocaust survivor inspired him to speak out for defenseless animals.

I chose the vegan lifestyle in 1981, and regret only not having done it much earlier. I did it for health—mine and my family's, the animals, and our endangered planet. Consumption of animal meat and dairy products has been linked conclusively with elevated risks of stroke, heart disease, cancer, and other chronic killer diseases. Today, at age 85, I still work out every day and dance on weekends, and my mind is still active.

A number of undercover investigations in the past decades have provided ample evidence that animal agriculture inflicts mind-boggling abuses on the animals it raises for food. Animal agriculture is responsible for more emissions of human-induced greenhouse gases than any other industrial sector, including transportation. It dumps more pollutants into our water supplies than all other human activities combined. It is chiefly responsible for the destruction of forests and other wildlife habitats.

All forms of oppression, including the Holocaust, must have social sanction in order to succeed. Given social sanction, some of the nicest and most enlightened people in the world, including our best friends, will engage in and/or subsidize atrocities and murder of sentient beings.

That social sanction is first manifested to a four-year-old, when we tell him or her that society has decreed that Rex on the sofa is to be fed, watered, walked, and cherished, but Babe on his plate, equivalent in nearly every respect, is to be abused, killed, cut into small pieces, and shoved into his face. Discrimination and oppression will never end until each of us assumes personal responsibility for our actions, to minimize any harm we may be causing, however unintentionally. This to me is what veganism is all about.

Jews, who have been associated with some of history's most egregious oppression, should be particularly sensitive to this issue and go vegan.

Rabbi Asa Keisar is an Israeli religious scholar who writes and speaks widely, arguing that veganism is a Torah imperative and the ideal diet for humanity. In 2015, he wrote the book Velifnei Iver, *"Before the Blind," because of his belief that those who promote meat and other animal products are violating the Torah commandment: "Do not put a stumbling block before the blind" (Leviticus 19:4). Keisar argues in his book that Jews are not permitted to eat meat, dairy products, or eggs, because the modern industrial production of these foods violates Jewish teachings on compassion to animals. Keisar has given away copies of his book to thousands of Israeli yeshiva students and has lectured at yeshivas, universities, and high schools throughout Israel. A video of his lecture on YouTube has been viewed over two million times.*

Reuven Rivlin, Israel's president, who is a vegetarian, wrote a letter to Keisar on November 13, 2017, praising his work promoting veganism as a Jewish and moral imperative. Rivlin wrote: "You are doing groundbreaking work, nothing less than a true revolution."

Today we are witnessing a phenomenon that is growing daily—the moral cry of people from all over the world in the face of the cruel abuse currently occurring in the animal food industry. With nearly 15 percent of the Israeli population choosing a plant-based diet, Israel may be on track to becoming the first vegan country in the world. Such an achievement would be a global *Kiddush Hashem* (sanctification of God's name) that would cause the image of the State of Israel to skyrocket.

We would become a role model for other nations in our values of morality, justice, and peace. Justice and peace begin with how we treat those who are below us, i.e., under our sovereignty—animals and plants—as the prophet Hosea says regarding the end of days: "I will make a covenant for them with the animals of the field and the birds of heaven and the creeping creatures of earth" (Hosea 2:18). This means there will first be peace between people and animals, and only then "I will abolish bow and arrow from the earth and all will dwell safely."

I will conclude with a quote from Reuven Rivlin, the vegetarian president of Israel, in a letter to me: "Returning to the caring sensitive Jewish heart and imparting the knowledge that veganism is not only a moral imperative but also a Jewish one, is no doubt an important step toward the desired change. It is my hope that in the coming years more and more people will join your just journey so that the Jewish people and the State of Israel will soon become a 'light unto the nations' (Isaiah 49:6) and pride itself, among other things, in having a moral and conscientious policy toward animals."

David Krantz *is a co-founder, president, and chairperson of Aytzim (Hebrew for "trees"), parent organization of the Green Zionist Alliance, Jewcology, EcoJews, Jews of the Earth, and Shomrei Breishit: Rabbis and Cantors for the Earth. He is editor of the* Jewish Energy Guide. *He has spoken about Israeli, Jewish, and interfaith environmentalism on four continents.*

Rav Kook posits at the time of the Torah we were not ready for the ideal—but that eating meat, with the limitations of kashrut, was only a step toward meat abstinence. After all, we cannot overcome the paradox of meat consumption. All animals are God's creation, and God has given them life the same as us, a life that flows in the blood of their veins. So the Torah prohibits the consumption of blood. But try as we might, we cannot eliminate the blood of flesh. We salt, we dry, we cook; the blood may become less viscous, it may escape the eye, but it remains nonetheless, a reminder that our bloodlust—if even simply a desire to taste flesh—has brought the life of one of God's creations to an end. Do we refuse to move beyond the bloodlust of our ancestors? Or do we choose to live the biblical ideal?

Today, we face the threat of another flood, as the higher temperatures from climate change—driven significantly by greenhouse gases released through the raising of over 60 billion animals annually for slaughter and consumption—melt the ice caps and raise sea levels, slowly inundating coastal communities. After the biblical flood God promised not to destroy the Earth again (Genesis 8:21)—however, this time we are doing it ourselves. Adherence to the biblical ideal of consuming plants instead of animals would have helped mitigate this climate crisis; meat abstinence is part of the solution. We also have an ethical obligation to do so (*For the Perplexed of the Generation* 10:6). And if that is found insufficient motivation, from an environmental perspective, widespread meat abstention—and its corresponding decline in carbon emissions, water and energy consumption, and land use—is necessary for our own survival. As we face a planetary emergency, it is past time for us to choose the biblical ideal, and to choose to refrain from eating our fellow animals. (Copyright © David Krantz)

Nina Natelson is founder and director of Concern for Helping Animals in Israel (CHAI) and its Israeli sister group Hakol CHAI.
The new kashrut and the vegan revolution are born of our longing for a deeper spiritual existence, a closer connection to the Divine in all that lives, and an acceptance of our power and responsibility to act as stewards of Creation. As we become conscious of the impact of our daily choices on our fellow humans, animals, and the entire planet, we can learn which cause the least harm and the most good. Aligning our choices with our beliefs and words builds integrity and transforms our lives into a visible expression of our beliefs. Our ability to inspire and lead others grows, and we become a force for good in the world, drawing us closer to God and speeding a return to Eden.

All religions are based on the Golden Rule, which conforms to the universal law of cause and effect—the energy we send out rebounds with equal or greater force, or, simply put, what goes around comes around. Asked to state their deepest desire, attendees of our education conferences unanimously respond "to live in a kinder world." By becoming vegan, we take a giant leap toward making that hoped-for vision a reality.

Rabbi Yonatan Neril is founder and executive director of the Interfaith Center for Sustainable Development and of Jewish Eco Seminars, which reveal the connection between religion and ecology and mobilize people to act. He developed faith-based vegan infographics and recorded videos of leading rabbis speaking on Jewish veganism. Neril became vegan after viewing the overcrowded and filthy conditions of chicken sheds in Israel. Seeing that made him recognize that eating eggs contributes to the

suffering of chickens. He completed a B.A. and an M.A. from Stanford University, focusing on global environmental issues, and received rabbinical ordination in Israel.

There are close to four chickens for every person on the planet. Chickens are the most populous animal or bird on planet Earth, and the vast majority of the world's 24 billion chickens live in industrial sheds in order to produce eggs or be slaughtered for meat. Global egg production has doubled in just the past twenty-five years.

So my heart goes out to the tens of billions of chickens in the world living in sheds. Most chickens produced in factories will never touch the ground or see the light of day. The incredible, edible egg is bound up in so much suffering for the chicken that produces it. They are produced in a factory similar to how we produce iPhones and refrigerators. But these are living beings. They are more than egg-laying machines.

How we treat the mother chicken is part and parcel of how we're treating mother Earth. The Jewish mystical tradition teaches that humans exile the feminine presence of God from Earth when humanity does not act righteously.

Eggs are sold in boxes with pictures of free chickens, but that's not the case for the vast majority of egg-producing chickens. Companies that sell eggs effectively lie to consumers by misleading them to believe that the chickens that produced the eggs were free and in nature. Consuming mainstream eggs means keeping chickens in industrial sheds.

We try to be ethically, morally, and spiritually aware. There are few foods bound up in suffering as much as eggs. There is a major gap between what is happening to tens of billions of chickens, and the practice of morality in modern life. The time has come to make a change. We can start by reducing or eliminating our personal consumption of eggs.

Lewis Regenstein *is president of the Interfaith Council for the Protection of Animals and Nature, and the author of the essay "Commandments of Compassion: Jewish Teachings on Protecting the Planet and Its Creatures,"* Replenish the Earth, *and other writings on Jewish teachings about*

animals. He also writes a column for the Jewish Georgian newspaper, sometimes discussing vegetarianism, veganism, and animal rights.

The massive, ongoing, and increasing devastation of the natural environment has become a critical and imminent threat to our survival. The ecological systems on which the lives of humans and, indeed, all of God's Creation, depend, are endangered. Nothing short of a revolution in our way of thinking and acting is now required. A major part of that revolutionary change is to put into practice our responsibility to treat animals compassionately that is mandated and stressed throughout the Bible and Jewish laws and literature.

It is not hard to believe that a merciful God would want His laws to be interpreted in a way that would minimize or eliminate the suffering of animals.

The sixteenth-century Code of Jewish Law (*Schulchan Aruch*) announces: "It is forbidden, according to the law of the Torah, to inflict pain upon any living creature. On the contrary, it is our duty to relieve the pain of any creature, even if it is ownerless or belongs to a non-Jew."

The Talmud even ordains that a person must provide for his animals before eating anything, and declares that one should not have an animal unless one can properly feed and care for it (*Yerushalmi Keturot* 4:8, 29a; *Yevanot* 15). Another Hebrew teaching is that "a Jew should not sell his animal to a cruel person" (*Sefer Hassidim* 13c, #142, 64).

The biblical prohibition against working animals on the Sabbath (Exodus 20) is a very important concept in Judaism, appearing in the holiest of the laws, the Ten Commandments. Psalm 36 proclaims: "Man and beast you save, O Lord. How precious is thy steadfast love." And Proverbs 12:10 suggests there are two types of people: "A righteous person has regard for the life of his animal, but the tender mercies of the wicked are cruel."

Indeed, the Jews invented the concept of kindness to animals some four thousand years ago. There is an entire code of laws (*tza'ar ba'alei chayim*, the requirement "to prevent the suffering of living creatures") mandating that animals be treated with compassion. Jews are not allowed to "pass by" an animal in distress or animals being mistreated, even on the Sabbath.

Given these and many other clear laws and teachings forbidding causing unnecessary suffering of animals, the Jewish People, commanded to be "a light unto the nations," should do all we can to eliminate such suffering by abandoning an unhealthy animal-centered diet that requires the massive and unavoidably cruel raising and slaughter of intelligent creatures.

Yael Shemesh is a professor in the Bible Department at Bar-Ilan University and chair of the Fanya Gottesfeld Heller Center for the Study of Women in Judaism. She believes veganism will soon spread widely because social media and other technology are enabling people to become more aware of it and, quoting Victor Hugo, "Nothing is as powerful as an idea whose time has come."

Judaism means taking personal responsibility alongside the aspiration to improve the world. So does veganism.

Genesis 1:29–30 shows that the diet instituted by God at the dawn of Creation was purely plant-based, for humans as well as for animals. Following the flood, when Noah and his family left the ark, God permitted them to eat meat, but it was clearly not God's initial intent; it was done with obvious discomfort, just as was God's permission for a Jew to marry an *eshet yefat to'ar*—a non-Jewish woman captured in war. Now, do we have to sanctify this reluctantly given compromise and cling to it, or should we try to transcend it and return to the original Divine intention?

There are two main factors leading to the conclusion that it is proper to aspire for veganism to receive the status of the ideal *kashrut* in our generation, and to act in order to realize this ideal. The first is the inconceivable cruelty practiced toward animals in the modern food industries, which of course did not exist in biblical times, nor in those of the sages and in fact ever, until the Industrial Revolution. Today animals in this industry are treated as though they were a product to which almost anything can be done for profit. This stands in complete contradiction to the prohibition against hurting animals, and the *halakhic* demand to take into account both their physical and mental needs.

The second reason that I want to see veganism as *kashrut* for our generation is the abundance in which we live today, which eliminates the need to consume products whose production involves such excruciating cruelty to animals. For us to avoid consumption of animal products is a relatively small concession, while such continued consumption is fatal— as it means the continuation of lives of indescribable suffering from birth to death.

Charles Stahler is co-director (with his wife, Debra Wasserman) of the Vegetarian Resource Group (VRG), an organization that works with businesses, schools, and consumers to provide information about and advocate for vegetarian and vegan lifestyles. The organization is highly respected for providing clear, objective, accurate information through its magazine, Vegetarian Journal. *Before being involved with VRG, Charles was a leader in the early days of Jewish Vegetarians of North America.*

Having grown up keeping kosher, when I became vegetarian forty-four years ago, and then vegan forty-two years ago, it was easy not to eat animal products. It didn't matter that there weren't all the exciting vegan foods and restaurants that are available today. Experience in being kosher in a non-kosher world made it simple. Judaism has trained us as a people to think and study, and to do what we believe is right, no matter the actions of people around us and without judging others.

While exhibiting at a health fair, a health educator mentioned to me that she had an Orthodox client who was addicted to cigarettes and couldn't give up the habit, but on Shabbat, totally abstained from smoking. Being Jewish allows us to make decisions, have beliefs, and take actions beyond what's in front of us. While we are not monks and are here to experience what we have been given, we appreciate and see life through a lens larger than ourselves. Though for our health, the environment, and following Torah, we don't have to be totally vegan, committing to being vegan is something we can do and makes sense because of the teachings and practices of our Judaism.

Yossi Wolfson is an attorney who's been involved with the animal rights movement in Israel since the 1980s. After serving as the spokesperson for the Israeli Society for the Abolition of Vivisection, he cofounded Anonymous for Animal Rights, now renamed Animals Now, the prominent and proactive Israeli animal rights group. He served as coordinator for Animals in Agriculture and was a member of the legal department at Let the Animals Live. Currently, Yossi is coordinator and on the board of the Jewish Vegetarian Society in Jerusalem. Among the campaigns that he has worked on are the successful efforts to ban animal circuses, animal dissections in schools, force-feeding of geese and ducks, and veal crates. His current activism includes important work such as leafleting, lecturing, legal action, and lobbying.[3]

The ethos of Judaism that I was raised on was the pursuit of justice, suspicion toward power, and intolerance toward oppression. Abraham, Jeremiah, Rosa Luxemburg—the shadows of such Jewish heroes could be seen through the lenses of this version of Judaism, marching behind Rabbi Abraham Joshua Heschel and the Reverend Dr. Martin Luther King from Selma to Montgomery, Alabama, in March 1965.

A chicken in the meat industry is deprived of all the bliss this world can provide. Her animality taken away, she becomes the raw material for an industrial complex she will never understand. This is tyranny, injustice, and torture. Veganism is the simple action one cannot avoid in the face of this.

Another prime aspect of Judaism, for me, is that it is down-to-earth. It is not primarily about philosophy, spirituality, and dogmas, but about the way one behaves. Correct view, intention, and speech may be important—but correct action is what one is ultimately judged for. In the face of current realities, veganism is correct action.

Blindly applying the institutional system of *Halacha* can reach absurdity. Greens, high in pesticides (to avoid insects), and a tortured chicken: Is this a kosher meal? While there is a *halachic* case for veganism, for me the case is in the words of Isaiah: "Is this not the kind of fasting I have chosen:

3   Much of this information is taken from an interview on the podcast "Our Hen House," Episode 193: https://www.ourhenhouse.org/YossiWolfsonEpisode193.pdf.

to loose the chains of injustice and untie the cords of the yoke, to set the oppressed free and break every yoke?" (Isaiah 58:6). Change "fasting" to "feasting" and you will have veganism as the new *kashrut*.

Rabbi David Wolpe is a leading U.S. conservative rabbi, named the Most Influential Rabbi in America by Newsweek *in 2012. He has authored eight books and is the spiritual leader of Sinai Temple in Los Angeles. He writes a weekly column in the New York–based* Jewish Week, *which sometimes discusses vegetarianism and animal rights.*

"It is impossible to imagine the Master of all things, Who has mercy on all creation, making it impossible for the human race to survive except by shedding blood, even the blood of animals." So wrote Rav Kook, the great scholar and mystic. He had famous precursors, including Abravanel, who wrote (on Exodus 16:4): "Eating meat is not essential to one's nutrition. Rather it is a matter of gluttony . . . and gives rise to a cruel and evil temperament."

There are good reasons—health, environmental impact and sustainability, and the sheer cruelty of factory farming—that make vegetarianism desirable. After all, by the industry's own claims, in the United States, about 3 million pounds of antibiotics are given yearly to humans and 17.8 million pounds to livestock, who frequently live in appalling conditions. The same people for whom eating a dog or cat is unthinkable eat animals as alive and aware. And sadly, no—*kashrut* does not ensure kindness.

Ultimately, it resolves to questions of conscience and appetite. We eat 150 times as many chickens as less than a century ago, and 50 billion birds suffer and are slaughtered each year to slake our appetites. Even so-called free range chickens can be debeaked, drugged, force-molted, and cruelly slaughtered.

This is the moral question. What's your moral answer?

Shmuly Yanklowitz *is founder and director of Shamayim v'Aretz, a vegan organization. He is an "Open Orthodox" rabbi who is the author or editor of sixteen books, including* Jewish Veganism, Jewish Veganism and Vegetarianism, *and* Kashrut and Jewish Food Ethics. Newsweek *and the* Daily Beast *named him as one of the most influential rabbis in America, and* The Forward *called him one of the most influential Jews of 2016. In addition, he founded or co-founded Uri L'Tzedek, an Orthodox social justice organization; YATOM, the Jewish Foster and Adoption Network; and Torat Chayim, a "progressive minded" Orthodox rabbinic association.*

Throughout history, Jews have tried to understand the logic behind commandments, of which the *kashrut* laws are among the most debated. In addition to the technical laws of *kashrut*, there is the prohibition of causing pain to animals, the mandate to pursue the holy path, and the warning against becoming a scoundrel within the boundaries of the technical laws.

A large portion of the Jewish community today does not ask ethical questions with regard to *kashrut*. Their primary concerns when it comes to food purchases relate to health and finances. A growing number of Jews are gaining inspiration from the notion that *kashrut* helps create communities committed to justice. Veganism leads the way in this regard.

I personally believe that Jewish tradition demands more from us. And without following these precepts, I fear that the essence of *kashrut* will wither away. Maimonides argued: "Animals feel very great pain, there being no difference regarding this pain between man and other animals."

Why should we be unconcerned about this pain if our tradition is so adamant about these values? We must not acquiesce to the power of broader consumer trends. Our moral tradition and billions of sentient creatures depend on it.

Appendix B

DIALOGUE BETWEEN A JEWISH VEGAN ACTIVIST AND A RABBI

It is vital to conduct respectful dialogues within the Jewish community on whether Jews should be vegetarians, or even vegans. In the spirit of this debate, I have imagined a dialogue as a means of encouraging readers to conduct such debates with local rabbis, educators, and other Jewish leaders. These are, of course, my own thoughts, and you are free to adapt your own.

Scene: A Jewish vegan activist meets his or her rabbi in the latter's office.

Jewish Vegan Activist (JVA): Shalom, Rabbi.

Rabbi: Shalom. Good to see you.

JVA: Rabbi, I have been meaning to speak to you for some time about an issue, but I have hesitated because I know how busy you are. But I think this issue is very important.

Rabbi: Well, that sounds interesting. I am never too busy to consider important issues. What do you have in mind?

JVA: I have been reading a lot recently about the impacts of animal-based diets on our health and the environment and about Jewish teachings related to our diets. I wonder if I can discuss the issues with you, and perhaps it can be put on the synagogue's agenda for further consideration.

153

Rabbi: I would be happy to discuss this with you. But I hope that you are aware that Judaism does permit the eating of meat. Some scholars feel that it is obligatory to eat meat on Shabbat and holidays.

JVA: Yes, I recognize that Judaism permits people to eat meat. Jewish vegetarians and vegans understand that people have a dietary choice, but we feel that this choice should consider basic Jewish teachings and how animal-based diets and modern intensive livestock agriculture impinge on these teachings. For example, we should recognize the tension between the permission to consume animals and the extremely cruel treatment they now receive on factory farms. With regard to eating meat on Shabbat and holidays, according to the Talmud (*Pesachim* 109a), since the destruction of the Temple, Jews are not required to eat meat in order to rejoice on sacred occasions. This view is reinforced in the works *Reshit Chochmah* and *Kerem Shlomo* and Rabbi Chizkiah Medini's *Sdei Chemed*, which cites many classical sources on the subject. Several Israeli chief rabbis, including Shlomo Goren, late Ashkenazic Chief Rabbi of Israel, and Shear Yashuv Cohen, late Ashkenazic Chief Rabbi of Haifa, were vegetarians or vegans. Also, Rabbi Lord Jonathan Sacks, former Chief Rabbi of the United Kingdom, is a vegetarian, and Rabbi David Rosen, former Chief Rabbi of Ireland, is a vegan.

Rabbi: We also should recognize that there is much in the Torah and the Talmud about which animals are kosher and about the proper way to slaughter animals. So eating meat is certainly not foreign to Judaism.

JVA: Yes, but there is also much in the Torah and our other sacred writings that point to veganism as the ideal Jewish diet. For example, God's initial intention was that people be vegans: "And God said: 'Behold, I have given you every seed bearing herb, which is upon the surface of the entire earth, and every tree that has seed bearing fruit; it will be yours for food'" (Genesis 1:29).

The foremost Jewish Torah commentator, Rashi, says the following about God's first dietary plan: "God did not permit Adam and his wife to kill a creature to eat its flesh. Only every green herb were they to all eat together." Most Torah commentators, including Rabbi Abraham Ibn Ezra, Maimonides, Nachmanides, and Rabbi Joseph Albo, agree that human beings were initially vegans.

In addition, Rabbi Abraham Isaac Hakohen Kook, first chief rabbi of pre-state Israel and a major Jewish twentieth-century writer and philosopher, believed that the Messianic period would also be vegan. He based this on Isaiah's powerful prophecy that "a wolf shall live with a lamb, . . . and a lion, like cattle, shall eat straw. . . . They shall neither harm nor destroy on all My holy mount" (Isaiah 11:6–9). Hence the two ideal times in Jewish thought—the Garden of Eden and the Messianic period—are vegan.

Rabbi: I have to tell you one thing that concerns me. Jews historically have had many problems with some animal rights groups, which have often opposed *shechita* (ritual slaughter) and advocated its abolishment. Some have even made outrageous comparisons between the Holocaust and the slaughter of animals for food.

JVA: Jews should consider switching to veganism not because of the views of animal rights groups, whether they are hostile to Judaism or not, but because it is the diet most consistent with Jewish teachings. It is the Torah, not animal rights groups, that is the basis for observing how far current animal treatment is from fundamental Jewish values. As Samson Raphael Hirsch put it: "Here you are faced with God's teaching, which obliges you not only to refrain from inflicting unnecessary pain on any animal, but to help and, when you can, to lessen the pain whenever you see an animal suffering, even through no fault of yours."[1]

Rabbi: Another concern is with two teachings in Genesis: The Torah teaches that humans are granted dominion over animals

---

1   See Samson Raphael Hirsch, "Do Not Destroy!" in *Judaism and Human Rights*, Milton R. Konvitz, ed. (New York: Routledge, 2017), 259–64.

(Genesis 1:26) and that only people are created in the Divine Image (Genesis 1:27, 5:1). I fear that vegetarians are promoting a philosophy inconsistent with these Torah teachings, hence potentially reducing the sacredness of human life and the dignity of human beings.

JVA: I think that if we consider how Judaism interprets these important verses, we can go a long way to reduce this potential problem. As you know, Jewish tradition interprets "dominion" as responsible guardianship or stewardship: we are called upon to be co-workers with God in improving the world. Dominion does not mean that people have the right to wantonly exploit animals, and it certainly does not permit us to breed animals and treat them as machines designed solely to meet human needs.

This view is reinforced by the fact that immediately after God gave humankind dominion over animals, God prescribed vegan foods as the diet for humans (Genesis 1:29). Although the Torah proclaims that only human beings are created "in the Divine Image," animals are also God's creatures, possessing sensitivity and the capacity for feeling pain. God is concerned that they are protected and treated with compassion and justice. In fact, the Jewish sages state that to be "created in the Divine Image" means that people have the capacity to emulate the Divine compassion for all creatures. "As God is compassionate," they teach, "so you should be compassionate."

Rabbi: Yes, these are good points, but some vegans elevate animals to a level equal to or greater than that of people. This is certainly inconsistent with Judaism.

JVA: Vegans' concern for animals and their refusal to treat them cruelly does not mean that vegans regard animals as being equal to people. There are many reasons for being vegan other than consideration for animals, including concerns about human health, environmental threats, and the plight of hungry people.

Because humans are capable of imagination, rationality, empathy, compassion, and moral choice, we should strive to end the unbelievably cruel conditions under which farm animals are currently raised. This is an issue of sensitivity, not an assertion of equality with the animal kingdom.

Rabbi: Another issue to be considered is that, with all the problems facing humanity today, can we devote much time to consider animals and which diets we should have?

JVA: Vegan diets are not beneficial only to animals. They improve human health, help conserve food and other resources, and put less strain on endangered ecosystems. In view of the many threats caused or worsened by today's intensive livestock agriculture (such as climate change, deforestation, and rapid species extinction), working to promote veganism may be the most important action that one can take for environmental sustainability. In addition, a switch toward veganism would reduce the epidemic of heart disease, various types of cancer, and other chronic degenerative diseases that have been strongly linked to the consumption of animal products.

Rabbi: Perhaps I am playing the devil's advocate here, but by putting vegan values ahead of Jewish teachings, aren't vegans, in effect, creating a new religion with values contrary to Jewish teachings?

JVA: Jewish vegans are not placing so-called vegan values above Torah principles, but are respectfully challenging the Jewish community to apply Judaism's splendid teachings in all aspects of our daily lives. Jewish teachings about treating animals with compassion, guarding our health, sharing with hungry people, protecting the environment, conserving natural resources, and seeking peace are all best applied through vegan diets.

Rabbi: What about the Torah teachings about animal sacrifices and that Jews had to eat *korban Pesach* (the Passover sacrifice) and parts of other animal sacrifices?

JVA: The great Jewish philosopher Maimonides believed that God permitted sacrifices as a concession to the common mode of worship in biblical times. It was felt that had Moses not instituted the sacrifices, his mission would have failed and Judaism might have disappeared. The Jewish philosopher Abarbanel reinforced Maimonides' position by citing a *midrash* that indicates that

God tolerated the sacrifices because the Israelites had become accustomed to sacrifices in Egypt, but that He commanded they be offered only in one central sanctuary in order to wean the Jews from idolatrous practices. Rav Kook and others believed that in the Messianic period, human conduct will have improved to such a degree that animal sacrifices will not be necessary to atone for sins. There will be only non-animal sacrifices to express thanks to God.

Rabbi: You have correctly pointed out that Jews must treat animals with compassion. However, the restrictions of *shechita* minimize the pain to animals in the slaughtering process, and thus fulfill Jewish laws on proper treatment of animals.

JVA: Yes, but can we ignore the cruel treatment of animals on factory farms in the many months, and sometimes years, prior to slaughter? Can we ignore the removal of calves from their mothers shortly after birth, often to raise them for veal; the killing of over 250 million male chicks annually immediately after birth at egg-laying hatcheries in the United States; the placing of hens in cages so small that they can't raise even one wing; and the many other horrors of modern factory farming?

Rabbi: As a rabbi, I feel that I must point out that if Jews do not eat meat, they will be deprived of the opportunity to fulfill many *mitzvot*.

JVA: By not eating meat, Jews are actually fulfilling many *mitzvot*: showing compassion to animals, preserving health, protecting the environment, conserving natural resources, and helping to feed the hungry. And by abstaining from meat, Jews reduce the chance of accidentally violating several prohibitions of the Torah, such as mixing meat and milk, eating non-kosher animals, and eating forbidden fats or blood. There are other cases where Torah laws regulate things that God would prefer people not do. For example, God wishes people to live in peace, but he provides commandments relating to war, knowing that human beings will quarrel and seek victories over others. Similarly, the Torah's permission to take a female captive in wartime is a concession to human weakness. Indeed, the sages go to great lengths to deter people from taking advantage of such dispensations.

Rabbi: Judaism teaches that it is wrong not to take advantage of the pleasurable things that God has provided. Since people find it pleasurable to eat meat, is it not wrong to refrain from eating meat?

JVA: Can eating meat be pleasurable to a sensitive person when he or she knows that, as a result, their health is endangered, grain is wasted, the environment is damaged, and animals are being cruelly treated? One can indulge in pleasure without doing harm to living creatures. There are several other cases in Judaism where actions that people may consider pleasurable are forbidden or discouraged—such as the use of tobacco, drinking liquor to excess, having sexual relations out of wedlock, and hunting.

Rabbi: As you know, the laws of *kashrut* are very important in Judaism. But a movement by Jews toward veganism would lead to less emphasis on *kashrut*, and eventually possibly a disregard of these laws.

JVA: I believe that there would be just the opposite effect. In many ways, becoming a vegan makes it easier and less expensive to observe the laws of *kashrut*. This might attract many new adherents to keeping kosher, and eventually to other important Jewish practices. As a vegan, one need not be concerned with mixing *milchigs* [dairy products] with *fleishigs* [meat products]; waiting three or six hours after eating meat before being allowed to eat dairy products; storing four complete sets of dishes, extra silverware, pots, pans, etc.; and many other considerations incumbent upon the non-vegan who wishes to observe *kashrut*.

Rabbi: I must express a concern for the livelihoods of some of my congregants and other Jews. If everyone became vegans, butchers, *shochtim* [slaughterers], and others dependent for a living on the consumption of meat would lack work.

JVA: There could be a shift from the production of animal products to that of nutritious vegan dishes. In England during World War II, when there was a shortage of meat, butchers relied mainly on the sale of other foods. Today, businesses that previously sold meat and other animal products could sell tofu, miso, falafel, soy burgers, and vegan *cholent* [Sabbath hot dish]. Besides, the shift toward veganism would be gradual, providing time for a transition to other jobs.

The same kind of question can be asked about other moral issues. What would happen to arms merchants if we had universal peace? What would happen to some doctors and nurses if people took better care of themselves, stopped smoking, improved their diets, and so on? Immoral or inefficient practices should not be supported because some people earn a living in the process.

Rabbi: If veganism solves some problems, doesn't it create others? For example, if everyone became vegan, wouldn't animals overrun Earth?

JVA: Respectfully, this concern is based on an insufficient understanding of animal behavior. For example, there are millions of turkeys around at Thanksgiving not because they want to help celebrate the holiday, but because farmers breed them for dinner tables. Dairy cows are artificially inseminated annually so that they will constantly produce milk. Before the establishment of modern intensive livestock agriculture, food supply and demand kept animal populations relatively steady. An end to the manipulation of animals' reproductive lives to suit our needs would lead to a decrease, rather than an increase, in the number of animals. We are not overrun by animals that we do not eat, such as lions, elephants, and crocodiles.

Rabbi: Instead of advocating veganism, shouldn't we alleviate the evils of factory farming so that animals are treated better, less grain is wasted, and fewer health-harming chemicals are used?

JVA: The breeding of animals is big business. Animals are raised the way they are today because it is very profitable. Improving conditions for animals would certainly be a positive step, but it has been strongly resisted by the meat industry since it would push up already high prices. Why not abstain from eating meat as a protest against present policies while trying to improve them? Even under the best of conditions, why take the life of a creature of God, "Whose mercies are upon all His works" (Psalm 145:9), when it is not necessary for proper nutrition?

Rabbi: If vegan diets were best for human health, wouldn't doctors recommend them?

JVA: Although still relatively a small number, more and more doctors do recommend vegan, or at least vegetarian, diets. Unfortunately, although doctors are devoted to the well-being of their patients, many lack information about the basic relationship between food and health, because nutrition is not sufficiently taught at most medical schools. Also, many patients are resistant to making dietary changes. The accepted approach today seems to be to prescribe medications first and perhaps recommend a diet change as an afterthought. However, there now seems to be burgeoning awareness on the part of doctors about the importance of proper nutrition; but the financial power of the beef, dairy, and egg lobbies and other groups that gain from the status quo prevents rapid changes. Experts on nutrition, including the American and Canadian dietetic associations, stress the many health benefits of plant-centered diets.

Rabbi: Some of my congregants would respond: *I enjoy eating meat. Why should I give it up?*

JVA: If one is solely motivated by what will bring pleasure, perhaps no answer to this question would be acceptable. But as you well know, Judaism wishes us to be motivated by far more: doing *mitzvot*, performing good deeds and acts of charity, sanctifying ourselves in the realm of the permissible, helping to feed the hungry, pursuing justice and peace, etc. Even if one is primarily motivated by considerations of pleasure and convenience, the negative health effects of animal-centered diets should be considered. One cannot enjoy life when one is not in good health.

Rabbi: Well, I am sure there are other questions that should be addressed. But I think you have made a very strong case for having a broad discussion of the Jewish and universal issues related to our diets. Please help form a committee with members of different viewpoints and set up a forum at which all of the issues related to our diets can be discussed.

Appendix C

THE JEWISH VEGAN YEAR

Meat-eating is valorized in our cultures because it is often associated with festivity, rituals, heritage, family, and tradition. Furthermore, to be able to eat meat is considered in many cultures to be a signifier of wealth, status, and even masculinity; to offer meat to your guests is likewise a facet of hospitality and largesse.

It's my conclusion that although putting meat on our dinner tables for family gatherings or to welcome visitors may once have been a significant symbol of our willingness to sacrifice something of value on behalf of others (an animal that we owned, for example), this is neither necessary nor true for the majority of the world's population. Unfortunately, eating meat for many is a thoughtless, insignificant act: fast food and a throwaway culture have made it a disposable item. The time is ripe, therefore, to reinvest the meaning of our rituals and festivals by removing the animal entirely from the plate and honoring the deeper impulses that lead us to commemorate our rituals with food that is plant-based.

Judaism is rich with holidays, and Jewish teachings are reflected in them. As Rabbi Irving Greenberg has written: "The Holy Days are the unbroken master code of Judaism. Decipher them and you will discover the inner sanctum of your religion. Grasp them and you hold the heart of the faith in your hand."[1] In this appendix I reconsider each of the Jewish holidays and the Jewish Sabbath (Shabbat) from a vegan perspective. In order to make each section complete in itself—so that readers can

---

1   Rabbi Irving Greenberg, *The Jewish Way: Living the Holidays* (New York: Summit Books, 1988), 17.

build talks, articles, discussions, and programs around Jewish teachings about veganism and related issues on any Jewish holiday—there is some repetition of facts, quotations, and ideas.

ROSH HASHANAH

Rosh Hashanah is the Jewish New Year, when Jews take stock of our lives and consider new beginnings. Perhaps the most significant and meaningful change that we can make during this major Jewish holiday is a shift away from diets that have devastating effects on our health and that of our imperiled planet. Although many Jews seem to feel that the celebration of Rosh Hashanah requires the consumption of chopped liver, gefilte fish, chicken soup, and roast chicken, there are many inconsistencies between the values of this holiday and the realities of animal-centered diets.

For instance, although Jews ask God for a healthy year, many Jews and others consume foods that have been linked to heart disease, strokes, several forms of cancer, and other life-threatening ailments. We implore "our Father, our King" on Rosh Hashanah to "keep the plague from your people"; however, high-fat, animal-based diets are causing a plague of degenerative diseases that have resulted in soaring medical bills, threatening health care systems.

Jews pray on the Jewish New Year that God "remove pestilence, sword, and famine," yet many Jews and others have diets that contribute to these conditions, because of grain that could feed people being fed to animals destined for slaughter, as millions of people die annually because of hunger and its effects; and the waste of valuable resources, which helps to perpetuate the widespread hunger and poverty that often lead to instability and war.

Jews commemorate the creation of the world on Rosh Hashanah, yet livestock agriculture is a major contributor to many global threats, including climate change, soil erosion and depletion, air and water pollution related to the production and use of pesticides and chemical fertilizer, and the destruction of tropical rainforests and other habitats that are essential to wildlife and ultimately ourselves.

Whereas Jews pray on Rosh Hashanah for God's compassion during the coming year, many Jews, as well as most other people, partake in diets that involve animals being raised for food under very cruel conditions: in crowded, confined cells, where they are denied fresh air, exercise, and any emotional stimulation, prior to being slaughtered.

Judaism teaches that our fate for the new year is written on Rosh Hashanah and sealed on Yom Kippur, but that repentance, prayer, and charity can cancel or reduce a negative Divine decree. However, the fate of farmed animals is determined before they are born, and there is no way they can change it.

Although the Torah and Prophetic readings on Rosh Hashanah describe the great joy of both Sarah and Hannah when they were blessed with sons after it seemed that both were destined to be childless, meat-and-dairy-centered diets require the taking of animal babies from their mothers shortly after their birth.

Rosh Hashanah is a time when we are to "awake from our slumber" and mend our ways. Nonetheless, the consumption of meat on Rosh Hashanah means that we continue the habits and actions that are so detrimental to our health, to animals, to hungry people, and to ecosystems.

Although we symbolically cast away our sins at *tashlich* during Rosh Hashanah, the eating of meat means a continuation of the "sins" associated with our diets, with regard to the treatment of animals, protecting our health, polluting the environment, and wasting food and other resources. Rosh Hashanah is meant to be a time of deep contemplation when we carefully examine our deeds, yet most meat eaters ignore the many moral problems related to their diets.

We speak of God's "delighting in life" on Rosh Hashanah. Even so, the standard American diet annually involves the brutal treatment and deaths of billions of animals, as well as many human deaths due to insufficient food in poor countries and too much health-damaging food in the wealthy countries.

Rosh Hashanah has a universal message and involves the prayer that "[a]ll the world's people shall come to serve [God]." In spite of this, many of the world's people suffer from chronic hunger, which denies them the necessary strength and will for devotion, while meat and fish from the choicest land and most bountiful waters of their countries are exported to meet gustatory demands in the United States and other developed countries.

Rosh Hashanah is a time of joy (along with sincere meditation). However, animals on factory farms never have a pleasant day, and millions of people throughout the world are too involved in worrying about their next meal to be able to experience many joyous moments.

In view of these and other contradictions, I hope that Jews will enhance their celebrations of the beautiful and spiritually meaningful holiday of Rosh Hashanah by making it a time to begin striving even harder to live up to Judaism's highest moral values and teachings by moving toward a vegan diet.

YOM KIPPUR

There are many connections that can be made between the solemn Jewish holiday of Yom Kippur, the Day of Atonement, and veganism.

On Yom Kippur, Jews pray to the "Living God," the "King Who delights in life," that they should be remembered for life and be inscribed in the "Book of Life" for the new year. Yet, typical meat-intensive diets have been linked to heart disease, stroke, several types of cancer, and other chronic degenerative diseases that annually shorten the lives of millions of people. In this holiday, Jews pray to a "compassionate God," Who remembers His creatures for life. Yet, there is little compassion involved in modern intensive livestock agriculture (a.k.a. factory farming), which involves the cruel treatment and slaughter of over nine billion farmed animals annually just in the United States.

On Yom Kippur, Jews pray to God, "Who makes peace," to be inscribed into the "Book of Life, Blessing, and Peace." Yet, animal-centered diets, by requiring vast amounts of land, water, energy, and other resources, help to perpetuate the widespread hunger and poverty that often lead to instability, violence, and war.

Jews are told through the words of Isaiah in the morning prophetic reading that the true purpose of fasting is to sensitize us to the needs of the hungry and the oppressed, so that we will work to end oppression and "share your bread with the hungry" (Isaiah 58:6,7). Yet, 70 percent of the grain produced in the United States is used to fatten up farmed animals, while millions of the world's people die annually from lack of adequate food.

One of the most important messages of Yom Kippur and the preceding days is the importance of *teshuvah*, of turning away from sinful ways, from apathy, and from a lack of compassion and sensitivity, and returning to Jewish values, ideals, and *mitzvot*. Veganism is also a way of making a significant turn away from a diet that has many harmful effects to one that is consistent with basic Jewish teachings.

The Yom Kippur liturgy includes a prayer with this statement: "We are God's flock, and God is our shepherd." Since Judaism teaches that people are to imitate God in His acts of compassion and caring, shouldn't we be treating God's defenseless creatures compassionately, in the ways that we want God to treat us?

On Yom Kippur, Jews ask for forgiveness for the sin of "casting off responsibility." Veganism is a way to assume responsibility for our health, for animals, for the environment, and for the world's hungry people. This period is a time for reflection and soul searching, a time to consider changes in one's way of life and make decisions for improvement. Hence, it is an excellent time to switch to a diet that has so many personal and societal benefits.

According to the Jewish tradition, our fate is sealed on Yom Kippur for the coming year. But repentance, charity, and prayer can avert a negative decree. However, people have determined the fate of animals before they are born, and there is virtually no possibility of a change in the cruel treatment and early slaughter that awaits them.

Yom Kippur is the Day of Atonement, a day of being, in effect, at one with God. One way to be more at one with God is by adopting a plant-based diet, and thereby not harming animals, since "God's mercies are upon all His works" (Psalm 145:9). Yom Kippur also teaches that, although it is often difficult, old habits can be broken. Thus, the days surrounding Yom Kippur provide a good period to break habits related to our consumption of animal products.

The afternoon service for Yom Kippur includes the reading from the Book of Jonah, which relates how he was sent to warn the people of Nineveh that they must do *teshuvah*, change their sinful ways, in order to avoid destruction. Today, the whole world is like Nineveh, in need of redemption, and in danger as never before from a variety of environmental threats. Today, in a sense, vegans are playing the role of Jonah, pointing out that a shift from intensive animal agriculture with significant negative effects on the environment, and a shift to vegan diets, have become global imperatives, necessary to move us from our current perilous path. The Book of Jonah also shows God's concern for animals. It ends with God's statement: "Should I not then spare the great city of Nineveh with more than 120,000 human beings . . . and much cattle?"

On Yom Kippur, one of the many sins we ask forgiveness for is "the sin we committed before You in eating and drinking." This can be interpreted in terms of the harm that animal-based diets do with regard to human health, animals, the environment, and hungry people. We're also forbidden to wear leather shoes for this holiday. One reason is that it is not considered proper to plead for compassion when one has not shown compassion to God's creatures.

Rabbi Israel Salanter, one of the most distinguished Orthodox rabbis of the nineteenth century, failed to appear one Yom Kippur eve in time for the sacred *Kol Nidre* prayer. His congregation became concerned, for it was inconceivable their saintly rabbi would be absent or late on this very holy day. The congregants sent out a search party. After much time, their rabbi was found in a Christian neighbor's barn. On his way to the synagogue, Rabbi Salanter had come upon one of the neighbor's calves, lost and tangled in the brush. Seeing the animal in distress, he freed him and led him home. His act of compassion represented the rabbi's prayers on that Yom Kippur evening.

In summary, a shift to veganism is an important way to do *teshuvah*, to turn away from a diet that is harmful in many ways to one that is in accord with the many compassionate and wise teachings and values that Yom Kippur represents.

SUKKOT, SHEMINI ATZERET, AND SIMCHAT TORAH

The Sukkot holiday, including Shemini Atzeret (the Eighth Day of Solemn Assembly) and Simchat Torah, is known as the "Season of Rejoicing," since people's worries about the success of the harvest are over. There is much vegan flavor associated with these festivals. Since one must be in good health in order to fully rejoice, the many health benefits of a vegan diet and the knowledge that such diets are not harmful to hungry people or animals are factors that can enhance rejoicing.

Sukkot commemorates the forty years when the ancient Israelites lived in the wilderness in frail huts and were sustained by manna. According to Isaac Arama (1420–1494), author of *Akedat Yitzchak* and other tomes, the manna was God's attempt to reestablish a vegan diet for the Israelites. Sukkot is the Jewish harvest festival, called the "Feast of Ingathering." Hence, it can remind us that many more people can be sustained on vegan diets than on animal-centered diets that presently require almost 70 percent of the grain produced in the United States being fed to animals raised for slaughter, while millions of people die annually due to malnutrition and its effects.

Sukkahs, the temporary structures that Jews dwell in during Sukkot, are decorated with pictures and replicas of apples, oranges, bananas, peppers, carrots, and other fruits and vegetables, never with meats or other animal products. Besides the *sukkah*, the main ritual symbols for Sukkot are related to the plant kingdom. The Torah states: "And you shall take for yourselves on the first day, the fruit of the hadar tree [an *etrog* or citron], date palm fronds, a branch of a braided tree, and willows of the brook, and you shall rejoice before the Lord your God for a seven day period" (Leviticus 23:40). These four species represent the beauty and bounty of Israel's harvest.

On Simchat Torah, Jews complete the annual cycle of Torah readings and begin again, starting with the first chapter of Genesis, which contains God's first dietary law: "And God said: 'Behold, I have given you every seed bearing herb, which is upon the surface of the entire earth, and every tree that has seed bearing fruit; it will be yours for food'" (Genesis 1:29). The Torah, along with prophetic and talmudical interpretations, is the source of the fundamental Jewish mandates that point to veganism as the ideal diet today: to take care of our health, treat animals with compassion, protect the environment, conserve natural resources, help hungry people, and seek and pursue peace.

On Shemini Atzeret, Jews pray for rain and plead to God that it should be for a blessing, not a curse. This is a reminder of the preciousness of rainwater to nourish the crops so that there will be a successful harvest. Also, according to the Talmud (*Rosh Hashanah* 1.2), the world is judged on Sukkot with regard to how much rainfall it will receive.

In the days when the Temple stood in Jerusalem, there was a joyous "water drawing ceremony" (*Simchat Bet Shueva*), designed to remind God to pour forth water when it was needed. Modern intensive livestock agriculture requires huge amounts of water, much of it to irrigate feed crops for animals. An animal-centric diet requires many times as much water as a strict vegan diet.

Sukkot is a universal festival, with at least three indications that Jews consider not only their own welfare, but also the fate of all of the world's people. First, in Temple days, there were seventy sacrifices for the then-known seventy nations of the world; second, the *lulav* (the palm frond) is waved in all directions, to indicate God's rule over and concern for the entire world; third, the roof of the *sukkah* is made only of natural materials such as wood and bamboo, and must be open sufficiently so that people inside can see the stars, to remind them that their concerns should extend beyond their immediate needs and should encompass the world. In a similar way, veganism not only considers a person's health, but also encompasses broader concerns, including the global environment, the world's hungry people, and the efficient use of the world's resources.

Moving out of comfortable homes to dwell in relatively frail *sukkahs* symbolizes the concept that it is not our power and wealth that we should rely on; rather, our fate is in God's hands. And it is God who originally provided vegan diets for people, and created us with hands, teeth, and digestive systems most conducive to eating plant foods.

Dwelling in *sukkahs* also teaches us that no matter how magnificent our homes, no matter how extensive our wealth and material possessions, we should be humble and not be overly concerned about our status. Veganism is also an attempt to diminish the importance of status symbols, often represented by expensive meat dishes, such as steak.

Finally, Sukkot's prophetic readings point to the universal Messianic transformation of the world. According to Rav Kook, first chief rabbi of pre-state Israel, based on the prophecy of Isaiah ("a wolf shall live with a lamb, . . . and a lion, like cattle, shall eat straw. . . . They shall neither harm nor destroy on all My holy mount" [Isaiah 11:6–9]), the Messianic period will be vegan.

In summary, a shift to veganism is a way to be consistent with the many values and teachings related to the joyous festivals of Sukkot, Shemini Atzeret, and Simchat Torah.

CHANUKAH

The festival of Chanukah celebrates the rededication of the Temple during the Maccabean Revolt. According to the Book of Maccabees, the Maccabees lived on plant foods to "avoid being polluted like the rest," since kosher meat could not be obtained when they hid in the mountains to avoid capture and to engage in guerrilla war against the Syrian Greeks.

The foods associated with Chanukah, *latkes* (potato pancakes) and *sufganiyot* (fried donuts), are vegetarian and potentially vegan; the oils used in their preparation are reminders of the oil employed to light the menorah in the rededication of the Temple.

Chanukah represents the triumph of non-conformity. The Maccabees fought for their inner beliefs, rather than conforming to external pressure. They were willing to say: "This I believe, this I stand for, this I am willing to struggle for." Today, vegans represent non-conformity. At a time when most people in the wealthier countries think of animal products as the main part of their meals, and when McDonald's and similar fast-food establishments are expanding, vegans are resisting and insisting that there is a better, healthier, more humane way to eat.

Chanukah represents the victory of the few, who practiced God's teachings rather than the values of the surrounding society, over the many. Today, vegans are a small minority in most countries, but they believe that—consistent with God's original prescribed diet (Genesis 1:29) and religious mandates to preserve our health, treat animals with compassion, protect the environment, preserve natural resources, share with hungry people, and pursue peace—veganism is the diet most consistent with Jewish values.

Chanukah commemorates the miracle of the oil that was enough to light the menorah for only one day, but miraculously lasted for eight days. A switch to veganism on the part of the world's people could result in an even greater miracle: the end of the scandal of world hunger, which results in the death of about nine million people annually, while over a third of the world's grain is fed to animals destined for slaughter.

Chanukah also commemorates the rededication of the Temple in Jerusalem after it was defiled by the Syrian Greeks. The Hebrew root of the word *Chanukah* means "dedication." Today, a shift to veganism could be a major factor in the rededication and renewal of Judaism, because it would show that eternal Jewish values are relevant to everyday Jewish life and to addressing current critical problems, such as climate change, hunger, pollution, resource scarcity, and soaring health-care expenditures.

The Hebrew root of the word *Chanukah* also means "education," and Jewish vegans believe that many Jews would switch toward vegan diets if they were educated about the horrible realities of factory farming and the powerful Jewish mandates about taking care of our health, showing compassion to animals, protecting the environment, conserving resources, and helping hungry people.

Candles are lit during each night of Chanukah, symbolizing a turning from darkness to light, from despair to hope. According to the prophet Isaiah, the role of Jews is to be a "light unto the nations" (Isaiah 49:6). Veganism can be a way of adding light to the darkness of a world filled with slaughterhouses, factory farms, and vivisection laboratories, as well as other examples of oppression.

On the Sabbath during Chanukah, the prophetic portion indicates that difficulties can best be overcome "not by might and not by power, but by my spirit, says the Lord of hosts" (Zechariah 4:6). Today, Jewish vegans are arguing that the way to a better world is not by exercising our power over animals, but by applying the spirit of God, whose "mercies are upon all His works" (Psalm 145:9).

At the morning services during each day of Chanukah, there is a recitation of *Hallel*, the psalms of praise from Psalms 113 to 118. During the Sabbath of Chanukah and every other Sabbath during the year, the morning service has a prayer that begins, "The soul of all living creatures shall praise God's name." Yet, it is hard for animals to rejoice and join in the praise of God when annually in the United States alone over nine billion animals are killed for their flesh after suffering from very cruel treatment on factory farms.

TU BISHVAT

Tu Bishvat is the most vegan of Jewish holidays because of its many connections to vegan themes and concepts. During the Tu Bishvat Seder, fruits and nuts are eaten; songs are sung and biblical verses recited related to trees and fruits. It's the only sacred meal where only vegan foods are eaten, consistent with the diet in the Garden of Eden, as indicated by God's first, completely vegan, dietary law: "And God said: 'Behold, I have given you every seed bearing herb, which is upon the surface of the entire earth, and every tree that has seed bearing fruit; it will be yours for food'" (Genesis 1:29).

The Talmud refers to Tu Bishvat as the New Year for Trees. It is considered to be the date on which the fate of trees is decided for the coming year. In recent years, one of the prime ways of celebrating Tu Bishvat, especially in Israel, is through tree-planting. Veganism also reflects a concern for trees. One of the prime reasons for the destruction of tropical rainforests today is to create pasture land and areas to grow feed crops for cattle. To save an estimated five cents on each imported fast-food hamburger patty, we are destroying forested areas in Central and South America, where at least half of the world's species of plants and animals live, and threatening the stability of the world's climate. It has been estimated that every vegan, by not eating meat, saves an acre of forest per year.

Both Tu Bishvat and veganism are connected to today's environmental concerns. Many contemporary Jews look on Tu Bishvat as a Jewish Earth Day, and use Tu Bishvat seders as a chance to discuss how Jewish values can be applied to reduce many of today's environmental threats. When God created the world, God was able to say, "It is very good" (Genesis

1:31). Everything was in harmony as God had planned—the waters were clean, the air was pure.

But what must God think about the world today? What must God think when the rain He sends to nourish our crops is often acidic due to the many chemicals poured into the air by our industries? When the abundant species of plants and animals that God created are becoming extinct in tropical rainforests and other threatened habitats, before we are even able to discover, study, and catalog them? When the fertile soil that God provided is rapidly being depleted and eroded? When the conditions that God designed to meet our needs are threatened by climate change?

An ancient *midrash* has become all too relevant today:

> In the hour when the Holy one, blessed be He, created the first person, He showed him the trees in the Garden of Eden, and said to him: "See My works, how fine they are; now all that I have created, I created for your benefit. Think upon this and do not corrupt and destroy My world, For if you destroy it, there is no one to restore it after you." (*Ecclesiastes Rabbah* 7:28)

Both Tu Bishvat and veganism embody the important teaching that "The land and the fullness thereof are the Lord's" (Psalm 24:1) and that people are to be its stewards, to see that its produce is available for all God's children. Property is a sacred trust given by God; it must be used to fulfill God's purposes. No person has absolute or exclusive control over his or her possessions. With their concern about the preservation and expansion of forests and their focus on plant-based foods, both Tu Bishvat and veganism reflect this important Jewish teaching.

Tu Bishvat and veganism both reflect the Torah mandate that we are not to waste or destroy unnecessarily anything of value. It is interesting that this prohibition, *bal tashchit* ("you shall not destroy"), is based on concern for fruit-bearing trees, as indicated in the following remarkable Torah prohibition:

> When you besiege a city for many days to wage war against it to capture it, you shall not destroy its trees by wielding an ax

against them, for you may eat from them, but you shall not cut them down. Is the tree of the field a man, to go into the siege before you? However, a tree you know is not a food tree, you may destroy and cut down, and you shall build bulwarks against the city that makes war with you, until its submission. (Deuteronomy 20:19–20)

This Torah mandate of *bal tashchit* is consistent with veganism, since, compared to plant-based diets, animal-centered diets require the use and depletion of far more land, water, energy, and other agricultural resources.

Tu Bishvat reflects a concern about future generations. In ancient times it was customary to plant a cedar sapling on the birth of a boy and a cypress sapling on the birth of a girl. The cedar symbolized the strength and stature of a man, whereas the cypress signified the fragrance and gentleness of a woman. When the children were old enough, it was their task to care for the trees that were planted in their honor. It was hoped that branches from both types of trees would form part of the *chupah* (bridal canopy) when the children married. Another example of the Jewish concern for the future expressed through tree-planting is in the following story: Choni (the rainmaker) was walking along a road when he saw an old man planting a carob tree. Choni asked him: "How many years will it take for this tree to yield fruit?" The man answered that it would take seventy years. Choni then asked: "Are you so healthy a man that you expect to live that length of time and eat of its fruit?" The man answered: "I found a fruitful world because my ancestors planned for me. So I will do the same for my children."

Veganism also reflects concern about the future since this diet puts a minimal strain on Earth and its ecosystems and, as indicated above, requires far less water, land, energy, and other scarce agricultural resources than animal-centered diets.

On Tu Bishvat, it is customary to recite Psalm 104, as well as other psalms. Psalm 104 indicates how God's concern and care extends to all creatures, and illustrates that God created the entire Earth as a balanced, unified organism:

He [God] sends the springs into the streams; they go between the
mountains.

They water every beast of the field; the wild donkeys quench
their thirst.

Beside them the fowl of the heavens dwell; from between the
branches they let out their voices.

He waters the mountains from His upper chambers; from the
fruit of Your works the earth is sated.

He causes grass to sprout for the animals and vegetation for the
work of man, to bring forth bread from the earth. . . .

How great are Your works, O Lord! You have made them all
with wisdom; the earth is full of Your possessions!

Veganism also reflects concern for animals and all of God's creation,
since for many people it is a refusal to take part in a system that involves
the cruel treatment and annual slaughter of nine billion farmed animals
in the United States alone, and, as indicated above, puts so much stress
on Earth and its resources.

Both Tu Bishvat and veganism are becoming popular today: Tu
Bishvat because of building interest in and concern about nature and
environmental issues; and veganism because of growing concern about
health, the treatment of animals, the environment, and the proper use of
natural resources.

PURIM

The joyous festival of Purim shares many connections with veganism.
According to the Talmud, Queen Esther, the heroine of the Purim story,
was a vegetarian while she lived in the palace of King Achashverosh. She
was thus able to avoid violating the kosher dietary laws while keeping her
Jewish identity secret.

During Purim it is a mitzvah to give *mat'not evyonim* (added charity
to poor and hungry people). In contrast to these acts of sharing and
compassion, animal-based diets involve the feeding of almost 70 percent

of the grain in the United States to animals, while an estimated nine million people die of hunger and its effects annually.

During the afternoon of Purim, Jews have a *seudah* (special festive meal), at which family and friends gather to rejoice in the Purim spirit. Serving only vegan food at this occasion would enable all who partake to be consistent with Jewish mandates to preserve health, protect the environment, share with hungry people, conserve resources, and treat animals with compassion.

On Purim, Jews emphasize unity and friendship by sending gifts of food (*shalach manot*) to friends. Vegans act in the spirit of unity and concern for humanity by having a diet that best shares Earth's abundant resources. Because of the deliverance of the Jewish people that it commemorates, Purim is the most joyous Jewish holiday. By contrast, animals on factory farms never have a pleasant day, and millions of people throughout the world are too involved in worrying about their next meal to be able to experience many joyous moments.

Mordechai, one of the heroes of the Purim story, was a nonconformist. The Book of Esther affirms: "And all of the king's servants . . . bowed down and prostrated themselves before Haman. . . . But Mordechai would not bow down nor prostrate himself before him" (Esther 3:2). Today, vegans represent non-conformity. At a time when most people in the wealthier countries think of animal products as the main part of their meals, when McDonald's and similar fast-food establishments are expanding, vegans are resisting and insisting that there is a better, healthier, more humane diet. Purim commemorates the deliverance of the Jews from the wicked Haman. Today, veganism can be a step toward deliverance from modern problems such as climate change, hunger, pollution, and resource scarcities.

Purim commemorates the time when conditions for the Jews changed from sorrow to gladness and from mourning to celebrating. Today, a switch to veganism could result in positive changes for many people, since plant-based diets would reduce health problems and hunger.

Jews hear the reading of the Megillah twice during Purim, in order to reeducate themselves about the terrible threats that faced the Jewish people and their deliverance.

Jewish vegans believe that if Jews were educated about the horrible realities of factory farming and the powerful Jewish mandates about taking care of our health, showing compassion to animals, protecting the environment, conserving natural resources, and helping hungry people, they would seriously consider switching to vegan diets.

PASSOVER

Passover and veganism? Can the two be related? After all, what is a Passover Seder without gefilte fish, chicken soup, chopped liver, chicken, and other meats? And what about the shank bone to commemorate the paschal sacrifice? And doesn't Jewish law mandate that Jews eat meat to rejoice on Passover and other Jewish festivals?

More Jews are becoming vegans while being consistent with the spirit and substance of Jewish teachings. Contrary to a common perception, Jews are not required to eat meat at the Passover Seder or any other time. According to the Talmud (*Pesachim* 109a), since the destruction of the Temple in Jerusalem, Jews need not eat meat to celebrate Jewish festivals. This concept is reinforced by scholarly articles by Rabbi Alfred Cohen in the *Journal of Halacha and Contemporary Society* and Rabbi J. David Bleich in *Tradition* magazine. Also, Israeli chief rabbis—including Rabbi Shlomo Goren, late Ashkenazic Chief Rabbi of Israel, and Rabbi Sha'ar Yashuv Cohen, late Ashkenazi Chief Rabbi of Haifa—were strict vegetarians.

The use of the shank bone originated in the time of the Talmud as a means of commemorating the paschal lamb. However, since the talmudic scholar Rabbi Huna argues that a beet can be used for this purpose, many Jewish vegetarians and vegans substitute a beet for the bone. The important point is that the shank bone is a post-biblical symbol and no meat need be eaten at the seder.

Jewish vegans see their values reinforced by several Passover themes. For instance, at the seder, Jews say, "Let all who are hungry come and eat." As on other occasions, at the conclusion of the meal, *bircat hamazon* (blessings of thanks for the food) is recited to thank God for providing food for the world's people. These practices seem inconsistent with animal-centered diets, which involve the feeding of 70 percent of the grain grown in the United States to animals destined for slaughter, while an estimated nine million of the world's people die of hunger and its effects annually.

Although he is not a vegetarian, Rabbi Jay Marcus, former Spiritual Leader of the Young Israel of Staten Island, saw a connection between simpler diets and helping hungry people. He commented on the fact that *karpas* (eating of greens) comes immediately before *yahatz* (the breaking of the middle matzah) for later use as the *afikomen* (dessert) in the seder service. He concluded that those who live on simpler foods (greens, for example) will more readily divide their possessions and share with others.

Many Jewish vegans see comparisons between the oppression that their ancestors suffered and the current plight of the billions of people who presently lack sufficient food and other essential resources. Vegan diets require far less land, water, energy, pesticides, fertilizer, and other resources, and thus enable the better sharing of God's abundant resources, which can help reduce global hunger and poverty.

Moreover, the main Passover theme is freedom. As we relate the story of our ancestors' slavery in Egypt and their redemption through God's power and beneficence, many Jewish vegetarians also consider the "slavery" of animals on modern factory farms. Contrary to Jewish teachings of *tza'ar ba'alei chayim* (the Torah mandate not to cause unnecessary sorrow to a living creature), animals are raised for food today under cruel conditions in crowded confined spaces, where they are denied fresh air, sunlight, a chance to exercise, and the fulfillment of their natural instincts.

In this connection, it is significant to consider that according to the Jewish tradition, Moses, Judaism's greatest leader, teacher, and prophet, was chosen to lead the Israelites out of Egypt because as a shepherd he showed great compassion to a lamb (*Exodus Rabbah* 2:2). Likewise, many Jewish vegans advocate that we commemorate the redemption of our ancestors from slavery by ending our current enslavement to harmful eating habits through the adoption of vegan diets.

Finally, Passover is the holiday of springtime, a time of nature's renewal. It also commemorates God's wise stewardship over the forces of nature. In contrast, modern intensive livestock agriculture and animal-centered diets have many negative effects on the natural environment, including climate change, air and water pollution, soil erosion, and the destruction of tropical rainforests and other habitats.

SHAVUOT

The festival of Shavuot and veganism share several themes. First, Shavuot is described as *z'man matan Torateinu* (the season of the giving of our law, the Torah). It is this Torah that has in its very first chapter God's original, strictly vegan, dietary regimen: "And God said: 'Behold, I have given you every seed bearing herb, which is upon the surface of the entire earth, and every tree that has seed bearing fruit; it will be yours for food'" (Genesis 1:29). To honor the Torah, many Jews stay up the entire first night of Shavuot to study Torah teachings. It is some of these teachings—to guard our health and our lives, treat animals with compassion, share with hungry people, protect the environment, and conserve natural resources—that are the basis for Jewish veganism.

Shavuot is also known as *Chag Hakatzir* (the Harvest Festival), since it climaxes the year's first harvest. Hence, it can remind us that many more people can be sustained on vegan diets than on animal-centered diets. Although the Torah stresses that each farmer is to leave a corner of their field and the gleanings of their harvest for the hungry, almost 70 percent of the grain grown in the United States is fed to animals destined for slaughter, as an estimated nine million people worldwide die annually because of hunger and its effects.

The talmudic sages also referred to Shavuot as *Atzeret* (the closing festival of Passover). This name not only implies that Shavuot completes the harvest begun at Passover, but also suggests that the giving of the Torah at Mount Sinai completes the physical liberation celebrated during Passover. Yet, whereas the Torah has many teachings on compassion to animals and indicates, as part of the Ten Commandments, that animals are also to be allowed to rest on the Sabbath day, most farmed animals are kept in cramped, confined spaces where they are denied exercise, fresh air, sunlight, and the fulfillment of their instinctual needs.

There are several other Torah teachings that are seriously violated by animal-based diets. For instance, the Torah mandates that people should be very careful about preserving their health and their lives (Deuteronomy 4:9, 15). However, animal-centered diets have been linked to heart disease, stroke, several forms of cancer, and other life-threatening diseases. Likewise, many Torah teachings are concerned with protecting the environment, but modern intensive animal agriculture contributes to climate change, soil erosion and depletion, extensive air and water pollution related to chemical fertilizers and pesticides, and the destruction of tropical rainforests and other habitats.

Also, the Torah mandates *bal tashchit* (Deuteronomy 20:19, 20), that we are not to waste or unnecessarily destroy anything of value. Yet, livestock agriculture requires the wasteful use of food, land, water, energy, and other resources.

Shavuot is a festival of thanksgiving to the Creator for His kindness. The full *Hallel*, psalms of praise and thanksgiving from Psalms 113 to 118, are chanted during morning synagogue services. Since one must be in good health and have a clear conscience in order to fully rejoice and be thankful, the many health benefits of vegan diets and the knowledge that such diets are not harmful to hungry people or animals are factors that can enhance thankfulness.

On Shavuot, Jews read the Book of Ruth in synagogues. One reason is that its barley-harvest setting echoes the harvest just ending as Shavuot arrives. One of Ruth's outstanding attributes was her acts of kindness. Veganism is a way of showing kindness because it helps share food with hungry people and doesn't involve the mistreatment and death of animals.

The Book of Ruth begins with Naomi, Ruth's future mother-in-law, and her family leaving Israel because of a severe famine. Today, major shortages of food in the near future are being predicted, and one major reason is that people in China, Japan, India, and other countries where affluence is on the rise are shifting to animal-centered diets that require vast amounts of grain to be fed to animals.

The Book of Ruth indicates that Naomi suffered the death of her husband and her two sons because the family fled in the time of famine rather than using their leadership to help others in need. In contrast to this selfish act, veganism not only considers personal well-being, but also encompasses broader concerns, including the global environment, climate change, the world's hungry people, animals, and the efficient use of the world's resources.

According to the Talmud, Shavuot is the day of judgment for fruit trees, and there is an obligation to pray for them. Yet, to create pasture land for cattle and to grow feed crops for farmed animals, tropical forests are being rapidly destroyed. The production of just one quarter-pound fast-food hamburger patty can require the destruction of almost fifty-five square feet of tropical rainforest, along with much animal and plant life.

Shavuot involves the highest spiritual teachings (the revelation of the Torah on Mount Sinai) and down-to-earth considerations—the wheat harvest and the offering of the first fruits in the Temple. This reminds us that ideally we should relate Heaven to Earth and translate the Divine laws to our daily lives. Veganism is an attempt to do this because it applies Torah teaching to our everyday life.

In view of these and other traditions and connections, I hope that Jews will enhance their celebrations of the beautiful and spiritually meaningful holiday of Shavuot by making it a time to begin striving even harder to live up to Judaism's highest moral values and teachings by moving toward a vegan diet.

TISHA B'AV

Tisha B'Av (the ninth day of the Hebrew month of Av) commemorates the destruction of the first and second Temples in Jerusalem. Today the entire world is threatened by destruction by a variety of environmental threats, and modern intensive livestock agriculture is a major factor behind most of these environmental threats.

In *Megilat Eichah* (Lamentations), which is read on Tisha B'Av, the prophet Jeremiah tells of the horrows of the destruction of Jerusalem due to the failure of the Jewish people to change their unjust ways. In 1992, over 1,700 of the world's most outstanding scientists signed a "World

Scientists Warning to Humanity," stating that "human beings and the natural world are on a collision course" and that "a great change in our stewardship of the earth and the life on it is required, if vast human misery is to be avoided and our global home on this planet is not to be irretrievably mutilated." Vegans join in this warning, and stress that a switch toward veganism is an essential part of the "great change" that is required.

On Tisha B'Av, Jews fast to express their sadness over the temples' destruction. So severe were the effects of starvation then that the Book of Lamentations (4:10) asserts: "More fortunate were the victims of the sword than the victims of famine, for they pine away stricken, lacking the fruits of the field." Yet, today almost 70 percent of the grain grown in the United States is fed to animals destined for slaughter, while an estimated nine million people worldwide die annually because of hunger and its effects.

During the period from Rosh Chodesh Av to Tisha B'Av known as the "nine days," Jews do not eat meat or fowl, except on the Sabbath day. After the destruction of the second Temple, some sages argued that Jews should no longer eat meat, as a sign of sorrow. However, it was felt that the Jewish people would not be willing to obey such a decree. It was also believed then that meat was necessary for proper nutrition. Hence, a compromise was reached in terms of Jews not eating meat only in the nine-day period immediately before Tisha B'Av.

The Hebrew word *eichah* ("alas! How has this befallen us?") that begins Lamentations comes from the same root as the Hebrew word *ayekah* ("Where are you?"). This is the question addressed to Adam and Eve after they had eaten the forbidden fruit in the Garden of Eden. Vegans are also asking, in effect, "Where are you?" The question asks us to account for what we are doing in response to widespread world hunger, the destruction of the environment, the brutal treatment of farmed animals, and so on. Perhaps our failure to properly hear and respond to *ayekah*, by stating *hineni* ("Here I am"), ready to carry out God's commandments so that the world will be better, causes us to eventually have to say and hear *eichah*, because of the terrible consequences of not getting involved.

The Book of Lamentations was meant to awaken the Jewish people to the need to return to God's ways. Since veganism is God's initial diet (Genesis 1:29), vegans are also hoping to respectfully alert Jews to the need to return to God's preferences with regard to our diet. As Rabbi Yochanan stated: "Jerusalem was destroyed because the residents limited their decisions to the letter of the law of the Torah, and did not perform actions that would have gone beyond the letter of the law [*lifnim meshurat hadin*] (*Baba Metzia* 30b).

In the same way, perhaps, many people state that they eat meat because Jewish law encourages or at least does not forbid it. Vegans believe that in this time of factory farming, environmental threats, widespread hunger, and epidemics of chronic degenerative diseases, Jews should go beyond the strict letter of the law and move toward veganism.

Tisha B'Av has been a time of tears and tragedy throughout Jewish history. Animal-based diets are also related to much sorrow today due to their links to hunger, diseases, cruelty to animals, and environmental destruction. However, Tisha B'Av does not only commemorate negative events. It is also the day when, according to Jewish tradition, the Messiah will be born and the days of mourning will be turned into joyous festivals. According to Rabbi Kook, the Messianic period will be vegan. He based this view on the prophecy of Isaiah: "A wolf shall live with a lamb, . . . and a lion, like cattle, shall eat straw. . . . They shall neither harm nor destroy on all My holy mount" (Isaiah 11:6–9).

The readings on Tisha B'Av help to sensitize us so that we will hear the cries of lament and change our ways. Vegans are urging people to change their diets, to reduce the cries of lament of hungry people and suffering animals. After the destruction of the second Temple, the talmudic sages indicated that Jews need not eat meat in order to rejoice during festivals. They deemed that the drinking of wine would suffice (*Pesachim* 109a).

More than a day of lamentation, Tisha B'Av is also a day of learning essential lessons about our terrible past errors so they will not be repeated. Vegans believe that if people learned the realities about the production and consumption of meat, many would change their diets so as to avoid continuing to be involved in such horrors.

After the destruction of Jerusalem, while sighing and searching frantically for food, the people regretted how they'd given away their treasures because of gluttony (Lamentations 1:11). Today, too, gluttony (excessive consumption of animal and other products) is leading to widespread hunger and destruction. Indeed, the Book of Lamentations has many very graphic descriptions of hunger. One is: "The tongue of the suckling child cleaves to his palate through thirst; the young children beg [for] bread, [but] no one breaks it for them." Today, major shortages of food in the near future are being predicted, and one major reason is that people in China, Japan, India, and other countries are growing richer and are shifting to animal-centered diets that require vast amounts of grain and soy.

The Book of Lamentations ends with *chadesh yamenu k'kedem* ("renew our days as of old"). We can help this personal renewal occur by returning to the original human diet, the vegan diet of the Garden of Eden, a diet that can help us feel renewed because of the many health benefits of plant-based diets.

In summary, Jews can and should enhance their commemoration of this solemn but spiritually meaningful holiday by making it a time to strive even harder to live up to Judaism's highest moral values and teachings. One important way to do this is by moving toward a vegan diet.

SHABBAT

Shabbat (the Sabbath day of rest) is very important in Judaism. The writer Ahad Ha'am held that "[m]ore than the Jews kept Shabbat, Shabbat kept the Jews." Yet, if deemed necessary to help save a life, one must (not may) violate the Sabbath (*Pesachim* 25a). One must not say: "Although this person is very sick and their life is threatened, I can't drive them to the hospital or call for emergency help until Shabbat is over." Better to violate the commandments on one Shabbat so that a person can live and fulfill many more commandments. The *mitzvot* were given to live by, not to die by unnecessarily. This is consistent with veganism, which has many health benefits.

The Torah mandates that animals, as well as people, must be able to rest on the Sabbath day. The *kiddush* (sanctification over wine or grape juice) recited on Sabbath mornings includes the following verse from the Ten Commandments:

> Six days you may do your work, but on the seventh day you shall rest, in order that your ox and your donkey shall rest, and your maidservant's son and the stranger shall be refreshed. (Exodus 23:12)

A similar statement is in Deuteronomy 5:12–14. Based on these Torah statements, the great Torah commentator Rashi declares that animals must be free to roam on the Sabbath day and graze freely and enjoy the beauties of nature, none of which animals can do on today's factory farms.

Jewish law does not require Jews to eat meat or fish on Shabbat. In a scholarly article in *The Journal of Halacha and Contemporary Society* (Fall 1981), Rabbi Alfred Cohen, the then editor, concludes: "If a person is more comfortable not eating meat, there would be no obligation for him to do so on the Sabbath." In a *responsum*, an answer to a question based on Jewish law, Rabbi Moshe Halevi Steinberg of Kiryat Yam, Israel, argued:

> One whose soul rebels against eating living things can without any doubt fulfill the commandment of enhancing the Sabbath and rejoicing on festivals by eating vegetarian foods. . . . Each person should delight in the Sabbath according to his own sensibility, enjoyment, and outlook.

All of the above is reinforced by the fact that there are chief rabbis— including Sha'ar Yashuv Cohen (late Chief Rabbi of Haifa)—who were vegetarians. Rabbi David Rosen, former Chief Rabbi of Ireland, is a vegan, including on Shabbat and Yom Tov.

Shabbat is a reminder of the Creation, as it is written: "And God completed on the seventh day His work that He did, and He abstained on the seventh day from all His work that He did" (Genesis 2:2). When God created the world, "God saw all that He had made, and behold it was very good" (Genesis 1:31). Everything was in harmony as God had planned: the waters were clean, the air was pure, the animals were thriving. However, modern intensive livestock agriculture is a major factor behind many environmental threats, so it is very unlikely that God would say today that conditions in the world are "very good."

Psalm 96, which is recited at the Friday night *Kabbalat Shabbat* (welcoming Shabbat) service, begins with the words: "Sing to the Lord a new song, sing to the Lord, all the earth." According to Rabbi Everett Gendler, our purpose is to join with all sentient creatures in singing praises to the Creator for all the wonders of Creation. He has stated: "To respect the life of our fellow choir members by not killing them and eating their corpses would seem an obviously desirable condition for choral collegiality."[2] Shabbat is a day of thankfulness for our blessings. On Friday night, it is traditional for fathers to bless their children. So too, veganism can be a blessing for the world because of its health, ecological, and other benefits.

The *Kitzur Shulchan Aruch* (Code of Jewish Law) states: "It is forbidden to catch any living thing on the Sabbath, even a flea, but if an insect stings a person, it may be removed and thrown off, but one is not allowed to kill it, because it is forbidden to kill on the Sabbath, anything that possesses life."[3] This mitzvah seems most consistent with veganism, which also does not involve the killing of any creature.

On Shabbat, we thank God for His mercies during the previous week. This is also most consistent with a diet that does not require the cruel treatment of animals. Furthermore, on every Shabbat (and festival) morning, Jews chant *Nishmat kol chai t'varech et shim'chah* ("the soul of all living creatures shall bless your name"). This would seem to be most consistent with enjoying Shabbat with a rich vegan meal that doesn't involve the cruel treatment of animals.

---

2   In *Rabbis and Vegetarianism: An Evolving Tradition*, Roberta Kalechofsky, ed. (Marblehead, MA: Micah Publications, 1995), 21.

3   *A Compilation of Jewish Laws and Customs* by Rabbi Solomon Ganzfried (Hyman E. Goldin, LL.B. trans.) revised edition (New York: Hebrew Publishing Company, 1961), Chapter 80, No. 52.

One of the highlights of the Shabbat morning service is the reading of the Torah. It is the Torah that contains God's original vegan regimen: "And God said: 'Behold, I have given you every seed bearing herb, which is upon the surface of the entire earth, and every tree that has seed bearing fruit; it will be yours for food'" (Genesis 1:29). The Torah also has much about all the reasons for veganism: taking care of our health, compassion for animals, protecting the environment, helping hungry people, and conserving natural resources.

Jews have sumptuous, joyous meals on Shabbat, and sing *z'mirot* (songs of praise of God and the holiness and beauty of the day). At the end of the meals, *bircat hamazon* (blessings in appreciation of God's compassionately providing enough food for everyone) is recited. Yet, today almost 70 percent of the grain grown in the United States is fed to animals destined for slaughter, as millions of people worldwide die annually because of hunger and its effects.

Shabbat is viewed in the Jewish tradition as a foretaste of the Messianic period—a time of peace, justice, and harmony. According to Rabbi Kook, chief rabbi of pre-state Israel, the Messianic period will be vegan. He based this view on the prophecy of Isaiah, "The wolf shall dwell with the lamb, . . . the lion shall eat straw like the ox, . . . and no one shall hurt nor destroy in all of [God's] holy mountain" (Isaiah 11:6–9).

Shabbat is a time of renewal. We can help personal renewal occur by returning to the original human diet, the vegan diet of *Gan Eden* (the Garden of Eden), a diet that can help us feel renewed because of the many health benefits of plant-based diets. Also, Shabbat is a time of joyful rest. A person can be truly joyful when healthy, and this is best accomplished through a vegan diet.

The manna—vegan food ("like coriander seed") provided to the Israelites in the desert after their exodus from Egypt—taught the Children of Israel several lessons, one of which is that they should refrain from labor on Shabbat. Although only enough manna was provided on other days to meet that day's needs for nourishment, a double portion was provided on Friday morning so there was no need to gather manna on the Sabbath, when none was provided. It was the vegan manna that kept the Israelites in good health for forty years in the desert. According to Yitzchak Arama, the manna was a second attempt by God to establish a vegan diet.

In view of these and other connections, I hope that Jews will enhance their celebration of the spiritually meaningful Shabbat by making it a time to begin striving even harder to live up to Judaism's highest moral values and teachings, and one important way to do this is by adopting a vegan diet.

ROSH HASHANA L'MA'ASER BEHEIMOT

Because of the wide disparities between Judaism's powerful teachings on compassion to animals and the horrible ways that animals are mistreated on factory farms and other settings, I have been working with vegan and animal rights activists to restore the ancient and largely forgotten Jewish holiday of *Rosh Hashana L'ma'aser Beheimot.*

Rosh Hashana L'ma'aser Beheimot was the New Year's Day for Tithing Animals for sacrifices, which was in effect when the first and second Jerusalem Temples stood. Our aim is to transform it into a day devoted to increase awareness of Judaism's beautiful teachings on compassion to animals and how far current realities for animals diverge from these teachings.

Many religious Jews are properly diligent in "building fences" around some *mitzvot.* For example, there is great care on the part of religious Jews to fulfill the laws related to removing *chametz* (leaven) from their homes, offices, and cars before Passover. But other *mitzvot,* including *tza'ar ba'alei chayim,* are often downplayed or ignored. Perhaps this is not surprising when one considers that with regard to animals the primary focus of Jewish religious services, Torah readings, and education is on the biblical sacrifices, animals that are kosher for eating, and laws about animal slaughter, with relatively little attention devoted to Judaism's teachings on compassion to animals. It is essential that this emphasis on the slaughter and sacrifice of animals be balanced with a greater consideration of Judaism's many compassionate teachings about animals. Restoring and transforming the ancient, long-forgotten holiday can help accomplish this important goal.

There is a precedent for the restoration and transformation of a holiday in Jewish history. *Rosh Hashanah La'ilanot*, the Jewish New Year for Trees (a day initially intended for tithing fruit trees for Temple offerings and donations for the poor), was reclaimed in the sixteenth century by Kabbalist mystics in Sefat, Israel, as a day for celebrating nature's bounty and healing the natural world. Many Jews now regard this increasingly popular holiday, *Tu Bishvat*, as an unofficial "Jewish Earth Day." It is hoped that the transformed New Year for Animals will also serve as a *tikkun* (healing or repair) for the current widespread mistreatment of animals.

Awareness about Jewish teachings regarding compassion to animals is especially important today because, as discussed in the main text of this book, animal-based diets and agriculture significantly violate at least six basic Jewish teachings and are major contributors to many life-threatening sicknesses that afflict Jewish and other communities and to climate change and other environmental threats to all life on the planet.

Rosh Hashanah LaBeheimot (a modern name in Hebrew for the transformed holiday, the New Year for Animals) occurs on *Rosh Chodesh Elul*, the first day of the Hebrew month of *Elul*, one Hebrew month before Rosh Hashanah. Since *Rosh Chodesh Elul* ushers in a monthlong period of introspection, during which Jews are to examine our deeds and consider how to improve their words and actions before the important holidays of Rosh Hashanah and Yom Kippur, this is an ideal time for Jews to consider how to apply Judaism's splendid teachings on compassion to animals, in order to reduce the current massive mistreatment of animals on factory farms and in other settings.

Restoring and properly transforming the New Year for Animals would have many additional benefits, including showing the relevance of Judaism's eternal teachings to today's critical issues; improving the image of Judaism for many people by showing its major compassionate side; and attracting disaffected Jews through reestablishing a holiday that they would find relevant and meaningful. Further information about this initiative to renew and transform this ancient holiday can be found in my four articles in a special section at JewishVeg.org/schwartz.

JEWISH DIETARY LAWS

Finally, in this appendix on the vegan Jewish year, we come to the daily practice of *kashrut*. Since Judaism is a religion that speaks to all aspects of life, it has much to say about one of life's most commonplace activities—eating. The Jewish dietary laws, also known as the laws of *kashrut* or kosher laws, are extremely important in Judaism. They regulate virtually every aspect of eating for members of the Jewish community (the only dietary law given to non-Jews is to not eat a limb from a living animal).[4]

Kashrut includes which foods may be eaten. (Although God's initial intention was that people should be vegans [Genesis 1:29], permission was later given for people to eat meat as a concession to human weakness [Genesis 9:2–5]). It defines those animals that may be eaten as those that part the hoof and are cloven-footed and chew the cud, such as cattle, sheep, and goats. Animals that do not meet both criteria, such as the pig, are forbidden. Sea creatures that have fins and scales are acceptable; most non-predatory fowl, such as chickens, most species of duck and geese, turkey, and pigeon, are permitted. Only eggs from kosher fowl may be eaten. It should be noted that all species of fruits and vegetables are kosher.

Kashrut, as we saw in the first chapter, also describes the method of slaughter (the laws of *shechitah*) by a trained religious person, known as a *shochet*. These laws do not apply to fishes or invertebrates. It determines the method of preparing meat and poultry (known as *kashering*), which primarily involves removing as much of the blood as possible, since directly after giving people permission to eat meat (Genesis 9:3), God pronounced: "Flesh with its soul, its blood, you shall not eat" (Genesis 9:4).

Kashrut establishes a prohibition against cooking or eating dairy products along with meat (fish is excluded from this prohibition), based on the biblical law prohibiting boiling a kid in the milk of its mother (repeated three times, in Exodus 23:19, 34:26; and Deuteronomy 14:21). This prohibition was extended by the rabbis so that religious Jews have

---

4   This appendix provides just a brief summary. Much more information can be found through an Internet search. Questions on *kashrut* should be addressed to an Orthodox rabbi.

separate sets of dishes, pots, and utensils for meat and dairy dishes. They also must wait a number of hours (generally three or six, depending on the tradition of the individual) after eating meat (again fish is excluded) before consuming any dairy product. Finally, certain foods are prohibited during the festival of *Pesach* (Passover).

Although not strictly part of the kosher laws, there are other laws and traditions associated with eating, including the ritual washing of hands before eating a meal that includes bread, with an associated blessing, blessings over various foods, and *bircat hamazon* (blessings of gratitude and praise recited after the meal).

Throughout history, many Jews have been dedicated to the strictest adherence to the dietary laws. Some, including a number of Marranos (Jews who had to keep their identity secret in order to avoid the Inquisition during the Middle Ages) have given their lives for it. An episode involving Syrian Greeks trying to get Jews to eat the flesh of pigs led to a revolt by the Maccabees; the Jewish holiday of Chanukah celebrates the Maccabean victory and the rededication of the Temple.

In view of the importance of the dietary laws to Judaism, some might wonder if there is a danger of Jews making a religion of veganism— becoming, in effect, more vegan than Jewish. Fortunately, we don't have an either/or situation here. Jewish vegetarians and vegans are not placing so-called vegetarian/vegan values over Torah principles. To the contrary, they are arguing that basic Jewish values and teachings (to guard our health, act with compassion to animals, share with hungry people, protect the environment, conserve natural resources, and seek and pursue peace) point strongly to veganism as the ideal Jewish diet, especially in view of the many negative effects of animal-centered diets and agriculture. Far from rejecting Judaism, they are challenging Jews to live up to Judaism's highest teachings and values.

As was suggested earlier in the book, in many ways veganism makes it easier and cheaper to observe the laws of *kashrut*, and this might attract new adherents to keeping kosher and eventually to other Jewish practices. A vegan need not be concerned with using separate dishes and other utensils for meat and dairy foods, waiting after eating meat before eating dairy products, storing sets of dishes, pots, and silverware, and many issues that the non-vegan who wishes to observe *kashrut* strictly must consider. In addition, a vegan is in no danger of eating blood, which is prohibited, or the flesh of a non-kosher animal.

Rav Kook believed that the many laws associated with the preparation and consumption of meat were an elaborate apparatus designed to keep alive a sense of reverence for life, with the aim of eventually leading people away from their meat-eating habit.[5] This belief echoes the view of Torah commentator Solomon Efraim Lunchitz, author of *K'lee Yakar*:

> What was the necessity for the entire procedure of ritual slaughter? For the sake of self-discipline. It is far more appropriate for man not to eat meat; only if he has a strong desire for meat does the Torah permit it, and even this only after the trouble and inconvenience necessary to satisfy his desire. Perhaps because of the bother and annoyance of the whole procedure, he will be restrained from such a strong and uncontrollable desire for meat.[6]

Pinchas Peli, a twentieth-century Orthodox rabbi, makes a similar point:

> Accordingly, the laws of *kashrut* come to teach us that a Jew's first preference should be a vegetarian meal. If, however, one cannot control a craving for meat, it should be kosher meat, which would serve as a reminder that the animal being eaten is a creature of God, that the death of such a creature cannot be taken lightly, that hunting for sport is forbidden, that we cannot treat any living thing callously, and that we are responsible for what happens to other beings [human or animal] even if we did not personally come into contact with them.[7]

Rabbi Shlomo Riskin, Chief Rabbi of Efrat in Israel, adds: "The dietary laws are intended to teach us compassion and lead us gently to

---

5   Rabbi Abraham Kook, "Fragments of Light," in *Abraham Isaac Kook*, Ben Zion Bokser, ed. and trans. (New York: Paulist Press, 1978), 316–21.

6   Quoted in Abraham Chill, *The Mitzvot: The Commandments and Their Rationale* (New York: Urim Publications, 2000), 400.

7   Rabbi Pinchas Peli, *Torah Today* (Washington, DC: B'nai B'rith Books, 1987), 118.

vegetarianism."[8] The three statements mentioned above might refer to veganism, rather than vegetarianism, if given today.

Some Jews reject *kashrut* because of the higher costs involved for kosher foods. They can obtain proper (generally superior) nutrition at far lower costs with a balanced, kosher vegan diet. In a letter to me, Rabbi Robert Gordis, late professor of the Bible at the Jewish Theological Seminary and former editor of *Judaism* magazine, indicated that vegetarianism, a logical consequence of Jewish teaching, would be a way of maintaining the kosher laws.

There are several examples in Jewish history when vegetarianism or veganism enabled Jews to maintain the dietary laws. Daniel and his companions avoided non-kosher food while they were held captive in the court of Nebuchadnezzar, king of Babylon, through a vegan diet (Daniel 1:8–16). The historian Josephus related how some Jewish priests on trial in Rome ate only figs and nuts in order to avoid eating non-kosher meat. As indicated above, some Maccabees, during the struggle against the Syrian Greeks, escaped to the mountains, where they lived on plant foods, since no kosher meat was available.

The Torah looks favorably on vegan foods. Flesh foods are often mentioned with distaste and are associated with lust (lack of control over one's appetite) for meat. In the Song of Songs, the divine bounty is mentioned in terms of fruits, vegetables, grapes, and nuts. There is no special *b'racha* (blessing) recited before eating meat or fish, as there is for other foods such as bread, cake, wine, fruits, and vegetables; the blessing for meat, milk, and eggs is a general one, the same as that over water or such foods as juice or soup. Also, a person being a vegan or vegetarian would not eliminate "food-oriented" *mitzvot* (commandments) from their lives, such as *kiddush* (the sanctification of Shabbat and Festivals, through the recitation of a blessing over wine or grape juice), *bircat hamazon* (blessings after meals), and Passover Seder observances.

We have already discussed that some Jews feel obligated to eat meat in order to celebrate Jewish festivals and Shabbat, and we've seen how many sources have argued that since the destruction of the Temple, Jews

---

8   Rabbi Shlomo Riskin, "A Sabbath Week—Shabbat *Ekev*," *The Jewish Week*, August 14, 1987, 21.

need not eat meat on holidays; rejoicing with wine is sufficient. Indeed, a number of modern rabbis—including Alfred Cohen, spiritual leader of the Young Israel of Canarsie and former editor of *The Journal of Halacha* [Jewish Law] *and Contemporary Society*; J. David Bleich, a highly respected Torah scholar and professor at Yeshiva University; and Rabbi Emanuel J. Schochet, author of *Animal Life in Jewish Tradition* (1984)—give many sources that indicate that Jews are not required to eat meat today, even on festivals and Sabbaths. In summary, there is no contradiction between Judaism (and its dietary laws) and veganism. In fact, veganism appears to be the diet most consistent with the highest Jewish values.[9]

---

9   If *kashrut* issues arise that Jews are uncertain about, a trusted rabbinic authority should be consulted.

Appendix D

A VEGAN VIEW OF THE BIBLICAL ANIMAL SACRIFICES

Given the emphasis I have placed on God's wish for His original humans to eat vegan diets, and the many mandates not to harm animals, a reasonable question may be asked: Why were the biblical animal sacrificial services established?

During the time of Moses, it was the general practice among all nations to worship by means of animal sacrifices.[1] There were many associated idolatrous practices. The great Jewish philosopher Maimonides concluded that God did not command the Israelites to give up and discontinue all these manners of service because "to obey such a commandment would have been contrary to the nature of man, who generally cleaves to that to which he is accustomed."[2] For this reason, God allowed Jews to make sacrifices, but, "He transferred to His service that which had previously served as a worship of created beings and of things imaginary and unreal."[3] All elements of idolatry were removed. Instead, limitations were placed on sacrifices. They were confined to one central location (instead of each family having a home altar), and the human sacrifices and other idolatrous practices of the neighboring pagan peoples were forbidden. Maimonides concluded:

---

1   Reverend A. Cohen, *The Teaching of Maimonides* (New York: Bloch Publishing Co. 1927), 178.
2   *Ibid.* Based on Maimonides' *Guide to the Perplexed* 3:32. Maimonides did believe that the Temple sacrifices would be reestablished during the Messianic period.
3   *Ibid.,* 178–79.

By this divine plan it was effected that the traces of idolatry were blotted out, and the truly great principle of our Faith, the Existence and Unity of God, was firmly established; this result was thus obtained without deterring or confusing the minds of the people by the abolition of the service to which they were accustomed and which alone was familiar to them.[4]

The Jewish philosopher Abarbanel reinforced Maimonides' argument. He cited a *midrash* (rabbinic teaching) that indicated that the Jews had become accustomed to animal sacrifices in Egypt. God tolerated the sacrifices but commanded that they be offered in one central sanctuary:[5]

Thereupon the Holy One, blessed be He, said, "Let them at all times offer their sacrifices before Me in the Tabernacle, and they will be weaned from idolatry, and thus be saved."[6]

Rabbi J. H. Hertz, the late Chief Rabbi of England, stated that if Moses had not instituted sacrifices, which were admitted by all to have been the universal expression of religious homage, his mission would have failed and Judaism would have disappeared.[7] After the destruction of the Temple, the rabbis decided that prayer and good deeds took the place of sacrifices.

The great sage Rashi indicated that God did not want the Israelites to bring sacrifices; it was their choice.[8] He based his belief on the *haphtorah* (portion from the Prophets) read on the Shabbat when the book of Leviticus, which discusses sacrifices, is read: "Neither did I overwork you with meal-offerings nor did I weary you with frankincense" (Isaiah 43:23).

Biblical commentator David Kimhi (1160–1235) also argued that the sacrifices were voluntary. He ascertained this from the words of Jeremiah (7:22–23):

---

4   *Ibid.*, 179.
5   Rabbi J. H. Hertz, *The Pentateuch and Haftorahs* (London: Soncino Press, 1958), 562.
6   *Ibid.*
7   *Ibid.*, 559.
8   Rashi's commentary on Isaiah 43:23.

For neither did I speak with your forefathers nor did I command them on the day I brought them out of the land of Egypt, concerning a burnt offering or a sacrifice. But this thing did I command them, saying: Obey Me so that I am your God and you are My people, and you walk in all the ways that I command you, so that it may be well with you.

Kimhi noted that nowhere in the Ten Commandments is there any reference to sacrifice, and even when sacrifices are first mentioned (Leviticus 1:2), the expression used is "when any man of you brings an offering," the first Hebrew word *ki* being literally "if," implying that it was a voluntary act.[9]

Many Jewish scholars, such as Rav Kook, think that animal sacrifices will not be reinstated in Messianic times, even with the reestablishment of the Temple.[10] They believe that at that time human conduct will have advanced to such high standards there will no longer be a need for animal sacrifices to atone for sins. Only non-animal sacrifices (grains, for example) to express gratitude to God would remain.

There is a *midrash* that states: "In the Messianic era, all offerings will cease except the thanksgiving offering, which will continue forever."[11] This seems consistent with the belief of Rav Kook and others, based on the prophecy of Isaiah (11:6–9), that people and animals will be vegan in that time, when "'they shall neither harm nor destroy on all My holy mount.'"

Sacrifices, especially animal sacrifices, are not the primary concern of God. As a matter of fact, they could be an abomination to Him if not carried out together with deeds of loving kindness and justice. Consider the following words of the prophets, the spokesmen of God:

For I desire loving-kindness, and not sacrifices. (Hosea 6:6)

---

9   Commentary of David Kimhi on Jeremiah 7:22–23. See Abraham Joshua Heschel, *Heavenly Torah: As Refracted through the Generations*, Gordon Tucker, ed. and trans. (New York/London: Continuum, 2006), 92.
10   *Olat Rayah*, 2:292. Rav Kook said: "In the future, the spirit of enlightenment will spread and reach even the animals. Gift offerings of vegetation will be brought to the Holy Temple, and they will be acceptable as were the animal sacrifices of old"; also see Hertz, *Pentateuch and Haftorahs*, 562.
11   *Midrash Vayikra Rabbah* 9:7; also see Hertz, *Pentateuch and Haftorahs*, 562.

"Of what use are your many sacrifices to Me?" says the Lord. "I am sated with the burnt-offerings of rams and the fat of fattened cattle; and the blood of bulls and sheep and hegoats I do not want. . . . You shall no longer bring vain meal-offerings. . . . Your New Moons and your appointed seasons My soul hates; . . . and when you spread out your hands, I will hide My eyes from you, even when you pray at length, I do not hear; your hands are full of blood." (Isaiah 1:11–16)

I hate, I reject your festivals, and I will take not smell [the sacrifices of] your assemblies. For if you offer up to Me burnt-offerings and your meal-offerings, I will not accept [them], and the peace offerings of your fattened cattle I will not regard. Take away from Me the din of your songs, and the music of your lutes I will not hear. And justice shall be revealed like water, and righteousness like a mighty stream. (Amos 5:21–24)

Deeds of compassion and kindness toward all creation are of greater significance to God than sacrifices: "Performing charity and justice is preferred by God to a sacrifice" (Proverbs 21:3).

Perhaps a different type of sacrifice is required of us today. When Rabbi Shesheth kept a fast for Yom Kippur, he used to conclude with these words:[12]

Sovereign of the Universe, You know full well that in the time of the Temple when a man sinned he used to bring a sacrifice, and though all that was offered of it was fat and blood, atonement was made for him. Now I have kept a fast and my fat and blood have diminished. May it be Your will to account my fat and blood which have been diminished as if I have offered them before You on the altar, and favor me. (*Berachot* 17a)

12   Quoted in Moshe Halbertal, *On Sacrifice* (Princeton: Princeton University Press, 2015), 40.

Reinforcing the above material are the words of Jerusalem-based Orthodox rabbi Nathan Lopes Cardozo:

> Does Judaism really need animal sacrifices? Would it not be better off without them? After all, the sacrificial cult compromises Judaism. What does a highly ethical religion have to do with the collection of blood in vessels and the burning of animal limbs on an altar?
>
> No doubt Judaism should be sacrifice-free. Yet it is not. . . . How much more beautiful the Torah would be without sacrifices.
>
> If Judaism had the chance, it would have dropped the entire institution of sacrifices in a second. Better yet, it would have had no part in it to begin with. How much more beautiful the Torah would be without sacrifices! How wonderful it would be if a good part of *Sefer Vayikra* [the portion of the Torah that refers initially to sacrifices] were removed from the biblical text, or had never been there in the first place.[13]

Echoing the words of Maimonides above, Rabbi Cardozo explains that the sacrifices are a concession to human weakness.

---

13   Nathan Lopes Cardozo, *Jewish Law as Rebellion: A Plea for Religious Authenticity and Halachic Courage* (Jerusalem: Urim Publications, 2018), 219.

Appendix E

TEFILLIN AND OTHER ANIMAL-BASED RITUAL ITEMS

An issue for Jewish religious vegans is that *tefillin* (the little boxes containing Torah verses that observant Jews wear during weekly morning prayers, except on Shabbat and certain festivals) as well as several other ritual items require the use of leather or other animal parts. I have included some thoughts on this issue that hopefully will lead to respectful dialogues and positive results for vegans, consistent with Jewish laws and traditions.[1]

Judaism considers it a *hiddur mitzvah* (an enhancement of a *mitzvah*) if the animal from which the leather came led a cruelty-free life and then died a natural death, rather than through slaughter, even ritual slaughter (*shechitah*). Unfortunately, it is not profitable for the animal industry to raise an animal just to meet these humane standards, so Jewish religious vegans so far have not been able to obtain animal-derived ritual objects that meet their ethical ideals. However, it is possible that animal sanctuaries might be willing to donate or sell at a reasonable price animals of kosher species after their natural deaths. Although they might initially be resistant, they might be convinced that use of such animals would reduce the profits of the "livestock" industry and thus be a positive step for animals. There may also be other sources of animals of kosher species that died a natural death.

Religious Jewish vegans could look into the possibility of using *tefillin* passed down in their family, received in their childhood, or obtained from a secondhand source, so that no new *tefillin* would need to be

---

1   I am grateful to Breslov chasid Rabbi David Sears for his contributions to this appendix.

purchased and therefore no additional harm to animals would occur. I am told that even today, the boxes (*battim*) of *tefillin* may be obtained from stillborn calves, as may the parchments on which the scriptural passages are written. However, the straps (*retzu'ot*) are not available except from slaughtered animals. Hence, some Jewish vegans have resorted to buying used straps and fastening them to new boxes made from stillborn calves. (*Mezuzot* are also commonly written on parchments from stillborn calves, due to the advantage of their thinness.)

Modern Orthodox rabbi Dr. Shmuly Yanklowitz, founder of *Shamayim v'Aretz*, writes the following about his use of *tefillin*:

> When I put on *Tefillin* each morning, what I'm doing is reminding myself of our life commitment to be merciful towards all, from beasts of burden and amphibians to reptiles and insects. As with all moral commitments, ritual contributes to the mindset that allows us to recharge our commitments on a regular basis. Perhaps we are binding ourselves with parts of an animal to fully commit to Godly service and to live a life with the utmost moral certitude. One of the great ethical imperatives we have is to reduce suffering for all sentient beings. Thus, paradoxically, *Tefillin* can be an animal welfare mitzvah at its core.

As I mentioned in chapter twelve, it is currently impossible to lead a life completely free of using animal products, as they pervade many aspects of life today. There are animal derivatives, and/or products that are the results of animal tests, involved in everything, from our wallboard, paints, and car tires, to the asphalt we drive on. Although billions of animals are slaughtered annually for food, no animals are slaughtered solely to make ritual objects. The fact that currently there are some animal parts used to meet Jewish ritual needs shouldn't stop us from doing all we can to end the horrible abuses of factory farming. Also, most problems related to animal-centered diets—poor human health, waste of food and other resources, and ecological threats—would not occur if animals were slaughtered only to meet Jewish ritual needs. And, as noted above, hopefully a time will soon come when the leather for *tefillin* and other ritual objects will come from animals who led cruelty-free lives and died natural deaths, or perhaps even from leather that has been developed from an animal cell. Our emphasis should be on doing a minimum amount of harm to other people, the environment, and animals.

I hope the above discussion leads to respectful dialogues that produce positive results so that Jewish religious vegans can be comfortable with both their Jewish *and* their vegan practices.

Resources

VEGAN, VEGETARIAN, AND ANIMAL RIGHTS-RELATED WEBSITES

There are literally hundreds, if not thousands, of valuable websites about vegan, vegetarian, and animal rights organizations and publications. Some are listed below. Most have links to additional important sources.

JEWISH VEGAN, VEGETARIAN, AND ANIMAL RIGHTS WEBSITES

- Alliance to End Chickens as Kapporos: endchickensaskaporos.com
- Animals Now, formerly Anonymous for Animal Rights: https:// animals-now.org/en/
- Concern for Helping Animals in Israel (CHAI): chai-online.org
- Eco-Eating: https://sites.google.com/site/eatingtheearth
- Food for Thought—and Action!: https://sites.google.com/site/ foodfood411
- The International Jewish Vegetarian Society: jvs.org.uk
- Israeli Jewish Vegetarian Society (Ginger): ginger.org.il
- Jewish Veg, formerly known as Jewish Vegetarians of North America (JVNA): JewishVeg.org
- Let the Animals Live: www.secrettelaviv.com/best/services/ let-the-animals-live
- Richard Schwartz's collection of articles: jewishveg.org/schwartz

- Shamayim V'Aretz, Jewish Animal Advocacy: shamayimvaretz.org
- The Vegetarian Mitzvah: brook.com/jveg
- Vegan Friendly: vegan-friendly.co.il
- Vegan Nation: vegannation.io

JEWISH ENVIRONMENTAL AND HUNGER WEBSITES

- Aytzim: Ecological Judaism: aytzim.org
- Canfei Nesharim (Wings of Eagles): canfeinesharim.org
- The Coalition on the Environment and Jewish Life (COEJL): coejl.org
- Hazon: hazon.org
- Mazon: mazon.org
- The Shalom Center: theshalomcenter.org
- Teva Learning Center: TevaLearningCenter.org

NON-JEWISH RELEVANT WEBSITES

- Farm Animal Rights Movement (FARM): farmusa.org
- International Vegetarian Union: ivu.org
- Mercy For Animals: mfa.org
- National Library of Medicine (NLM): nlm.nih.gov
- Physicians Committee for Responsible Medicine (PCRM): pcrm.org
- Vegetarian Resource Group: vrg.org
- VegSource: vegsource.com

ENVIRONMENTAL ORGANIZATIONS IN ISRAEL

Most Israeli websites have both a Hebrew and an English version. If a listed website first appears on your screen in Hebrew, find and click on the English icon or link for the translation.

- Arava Institute for Environmental Studies: arava.org
- EcoPeace Middle East, formerly Friends of the Earth Middle East (FoEME): foeme.org
- Green Course (*Megamah Yeruka*)

BIBLIOGRAPHY

A. Jewish Books and Articles on Vegetarianism and Veganism

Berman, Louis. *Vegetarianism and the Jewish Tradition*. New York: K'tav, 1982.

Bleich, Rabbi J. David. "Vegetarianism and Judaism," *Tradition* 23, no. 1 (Summer 1987).

Cohen, Rabbi Alfred. "Vegetarianism from a Jewish Perspective," *Journal of Halacha and Contemporary Society* I, no. II (Fall 1981).

Cohen, Noah J. *Tsa'ar Ba'alei Chayim: The Prevention of Cruelty to Animals, Its Bases, Development, and Legislation in Hebrew Literature*. New York: Feldheim, 1979.

Green, Joe. "Chalutzim of the Messiah: The Religious Vegetarian Concept as Expounded by Rabbi Kook" (text of a lecture given in Johannesburg, South Africa. Outline of some of Rabbi Kook's vegetarian/vegan teachings).

Kalechofsky, Roberta. *A Boy, A Chicken, and the Lion of Judea: How Ari Became a Vegetarian*. Marblehead, MA: Micah Publications, 1995.

———. *Haggadah for the Liberated Lamb*. Marblehead, MA: Micah Publications, 1985.

———. *Vegetarian Judaism*. Marblehead, MA: Micah Publications, 1998.

———, editor. *Judaism and Animals Rights: Classical and Contemporary Responses*. Marblehead, MA: Micah Publications,1992.

———, editor. *Rabbis and Vegetarianism: An Evolving Tradition*. Marblehead, MA: Micah Publications, 1995.

Kook, Rabbi Abraham Isaac. "Fragments of Light: A View as to the Reasons for the Commandments," in *Abraham Isaac Kook: A Collection of Rabbi Kook's works*, Ben Zion Bokser, translator and editor. New York: Paulist Press, 1978.

———. *A Vision of Vegetarianism and Peace* (Hebrew), edited by Rabbi David Cohen, the Nazeer of Jerusalem. (English translation: Jonathan Rubenstein) www.jewishveg.com/AVisionofVegetarianismandPeace.pdf (September 2013).

Labenz, Jacob Ari, and Rabbi Shmuly Yanklowitz, editors. *Jewish Veganism and Vegetarianism*. Albany: SUNY Press, 2019.

Pick, Philip, editor. *The Tree of Life: An Anthology of Articles Appearing in the Jewish Vegetarian Magazine from 1966 to 1973*. New York: A. S. Barnes, 1977.

Raisin, Jacob A. "Humanitarianism of the Laws of Israel: Kindness to Animals." Jewish Tract 06. Cincinnati, OH: Union of American Hebrew Congregations, 1939.

Roodyn, Donald Bernard. *Alternative Kashrut: Judaism, Vegetarianism and the Factory Farm*. London: Reform Synagogues of Great Britain, 1978.

Schindler, Julian S. *Animal Rights, Shechita and Vegetarianism: A Traditional Jewish Perspective*. London: Union of Jewish Students, 1987.

Schochet, Rabbi Elijah J. *Animal Life in Jewish Tradition*. New York: K'tav, 1984.

Schwartz, Richard H. *Judaism and Vegetarianism*. New York: Lantern, 2001.

Sears, David. *The Vision of Eden: Animal Welfare and Vegetarianism in Jewish Law and Mysticism*. Meorei Ohr, 2015.

Yanklowitz, Shmuly. *The Jewish Vegan*. Santa Fe Springs, CA: The Shamayim v'Aretz Institute, 2015.

———, editor. *Kashrut and Jewish Food Ethics*. Boston, MA: Academic Studies Press, 2019.

B. BOOKS ON JEWISH TEACHINGS ON VEGETARIAN- AND VEGAN-RELATED ISSUES

Amsel, Nachum. *The Jewish Encyclopedia of Moral and Ethical Issues*. Northvale, NJ: Jason Aronson, 1996.

Benstein, Jeremy. *The Way into Judaism and the Environment*. Woodstock, VT: Jewish Lights, 2006.

Bernstein, Ellen, editor. *Ecology and the Jewish Spirit: Where Nature and the Spirit Meet*. Woodstock, VT: Jewish Lights, 1998.

Cardozo, Rabbi Nathan Lopes. *Jewish Law and Rebellion: A Plea for Religious Authenticity and Halachic Courage*. Jerusalem/New York: Urim Publications, 2018.

Dorff, Elliot N. *The Way into Tikkun Olam*. Woodstock, VT: Jewish Lights, 2005.

Dresner, Rabbi Samuel H. *The Jewish Dietary Laws: Their Meaning for Our Time*. New York: Burning Bush Press, 1959.

Fisher, Adam D. *To Deal Thy Bread to the Hungry*. New York: Union of American Hebrew Congregations, 1975.

Gershom, Yonassan. *Kapporos Then and Now: Toward a More Compassionate Tradition*. Raleigh, NC: Lulu Press, 2015.

Greenberg, Rabbi Irving. *The Jewish Way: Living the Holidays*. New York: Summit Books, 1988.

Gross, Aaron S. *The Question of the Animal and Religion: Theoretical Stakes, Practical Implications*. New York: Columbia University Press, 2015.

Hirsch, Richard G. *Thy Most Precious Gift: Peace in the Jewish Tradition*. New York: Union of American Hebrew Congregations, 1974.

Hirsch, Rabbi Samson Raphael. *Horeb*, translated by Dayan Dr. I. Grunfeld. New York/London/Jerusalem: Soncino Press, 1962.

Neril, Yonatan, and Evonne Marzouk, editors. *Uplifting People and Planet: Eighteen Essential Teachings on the Environment.* Canfei Nesharim, Jewcology, and Jewish Eco Seminars, 2013.

Regenstein, Lewis. *Replenish the Earth: The Teachings of the World's Religions on Protecting Animals and the Environment.* New York: Crossroads, 1991.

Rose, Aubrey, editor. *Judaism and Ecology.* New York/London: Cassell, 1992.

Schwartz, Richard H. *Judaism and Global Survival.* New York: Lantern, 2002.

Schwartz, Richard H., with Rabbi Yonassan Gershom and Rabbi Shmuly Yanklowitz. *Who Stole My Religion: Revitalizing Judaism and Applying Jewish Values to Help Heal Our Imperiled Planet.* Jerusalem/New York: Urim Publications, 2016.

Sears, David. *Compassion for Humanity in the Jewish Tradition.* Northvale, NJ: Jason Aronson, 1998.

Seidenberg, David. *Kabbalah and Ecology: God's Image in the More-Than-Human World.* New York/Cambridge, UK: Cambridge University Press, 2015.

Slifkin, Natan. *Man and Beast: Our Relationship with Animals in Jewish Law and Thought.* Brooklyn, NY: Yashar Books, 2006.

Spiegel, Marjorie. *The Dreaded Comparison: Human and Animal Slavery* (foreword by Alice Walker). New York: Mirror Books, 1997.

C. General Books on Vegetarianism, Veganism, and Animal Advocacy

Akers, Keith. *A Vegetarian Sourcebook.* Arlington, VA: Vegetarian Press, 1985, 1993.

Berry, Rynn. *Food for the Gods: Vegetarianism and the World's Religions: Essays, Conversations, Recipes.* New York: Pythagorean, 1988.

Coats, David C. *Old McDonald's Factory Farm.* New York: Continuum, 1989.

Davis, Karen. *For the Birds: From Exploitation to Liberation.* Brooklyn, NY: Lantern, 2019.

———. *Prisoned Chickens, Poisoned Eggs.* Summertown, TN: Book Publishing Co., 1997.

Eisnitz, Gail A. *Slaughterhouse: The Shocking Story of Greed, Neglect, and Inhumane Treatment Inside the US Meat Industry.* Amherst, NY: Prometheus Books, 1997.

Foer, Jonathan Safran. *Eating Animals.* New York: Little Brown, 2009.

Godlovitch, S. R. and John Harris, editors. *Animals, Men, and Morals: An Inquiry into the Maltreatment of Non-humans.* New York: Taplinger Publishing Co., 1972.

Harrison, Ruth. *Animal Machines.* London: Vincent Street, 1964.

Lappé, Frances Moore. *Diet for a Small Planet* (20th anniversary edition). New York: Ballantine Books, 1992.

Lyman, Howard. *Mad Cowboy: Plain Truth from the Cattle Rancher Who Won't Eat Meat*. New York: Scribner, 1998.

Lymbery, Philip. *Farmageddon: The True Cost of Cheap Meat*. London: Bloomsbury, 2014.

Mason, Jim, and Peter Singer. *Animal Factories*. New York: Harmony Books, 1990.

Moran, Victoria. *Compassion: The Ultimate Ethic*. Wellingborough, UK: Thorsons, 1985.

Rifkin, Jeremy. *Beyond Beef: The Rise and Fall of the Cattle Culture*. New York: Dutton, 1992.

Robbins, John. *Diet for a New America: How Your Food Choices Affect Your Health, Happiness and the Future of Life on Earth*, 25th Anniversary Edition (Kindle, 2012).

———. *The Food Revolution: How your Diet Can Help Save Your Life and the World*. Berkeley, CA: Conari, 2001.

Rowe, Martin. *The Way of Compassion: Survival Strategies for a World in Crisis*. New York: Stealth Technologies. 1999.

Schell, Orville. *Modern Meat*. New York: Vintage Books, 1985.

Schlottmann, Christopher, and Jeff Sebo. *Food, Animals, and the Environment: An Ethical Approach*. New York: Earthscan/Routledge, 2019.

Shapiro, Paul. *Clean Meat: How Growing Meat Without Animals Will Revolutionize Dinner and the World*. New York: Simon & Schuster, 2018.

Singer, Peter. *Animal Liberation*. New York: New York Review of Books Publishers, 1990.

Tuttle, Will. *The World Peace Diet: Eating for Spiritual Health and Social Harmony*. New York: Lantern, 2005.

Walters, Kerry S., and Lisa Portress, editors. *From Pythagorus to Peter Singer*. New York: State University of New York Press: 1999.

Weis, Tony. *The Ecological Hoofprint: The Global Burden of Industrial Livestock*. London: Zed Books, 2013.

D. BOOKS ON HEALTH AND NUTRITION

American Natural Hygiene Society. *The Greatest Health Discovery*. Chicago, IL: Natural Hygiene Press, 1972.

Barnard, Neal D., MD. *The Power of Your Plate: A Plan for Better Living*. Summertown, TN: Book Publishing Company, 1990.

Campbell, T. Colin. *The China Study: The Most Comprehensive Study of Nutrition Ever Conducted and the Startling Implications for Diet, Weight Loss and Long Term Health.* Dallas: Benbella Books, 2003.

Campbell, T. Colin, and Christine Cox. *The China Project: Keys to Better Health, Discovered in Our Living Laboratory.* Ithaca, NY: New Century Nutrition, 1996.

Fuhrman, Joel, MD. *Fasting and Eating for Health: A Medical Doctor's Program for Conquering Disease.* New York: St. Martin's Press, 1995.

Greger, Michael, MD. *How Not to Die: Discover the Foods Scientifically Proven to Prevent and Reverse Disease.* New York: Macmillan, 2015.

Klaper, Michael, MD. *Vegan Nutrition: Pure and Simple.* Umatilla, FL: Gentle World, 1995.

———. *Pregnancy, Children, and the Vegan Diet.* Umatilla, FL: Gentle World, 1988.

Kradjian, Robert M., MD. *Save Yourself from Breast Cancer: Life Choices That Can Help You Reduce the Odds.* New York: Berkeley Publishing Group, 1994.

McDougall, John A., MD. *McDougall's Medicine: A Challenging Second Opinion.* Piscataway, NJ: New Century Publishers, 1985.

McDougall, John A., MD., and Mary A. McDougall. *The McDougall Plan.* Piscataway, NJ: New Century Publishers, 1983.

Messina, Mark, and Virginia Messina. *The Dietitians' Guide to Vegetarian Diets: Issues and Applications.* Wilmington, DE: Aspen Publishers, 1996.

Ornish Dean, MD. *Dr. Dean Ornish's Program for Reversing Heart Disease.* New York: Ballantine, 1990.

INDEX

Aaron (biblical figure), xxiii
Abarbanel, Isaac, 87–88, 150, 157–58, 198
Abraham (biblical figure), 33, 44, 149
Abravanel. *See* Abarbanel
Academy of Nutrition and Dietetics (American Dietetic Association), 23, 161
Achashverosh (biblical figure), 176
activism, xxii–xxxiii, 130–34, 153–62
. *See Also* vegan movement
Adam (biblical figure), 59, 114, 139, 155, 183
afikomen (dessert), 179
Africa, 50
air pollution, 55, 70, 72–73
Akedat Yitzchak (Arama), 169
Albo, Joseph, 87–88, 155
Aleph Farms, 122
alpha-linolenic acid (ALA), 94
Amar, Shlomo, 108
Amazon rainforest, 54
American Heart Association, 95
American Jewish Committee, 81
American Journal of Cardiology, 30
Amidah, 86
Amsel, Nachum, 101
Am Yisrael, 138
"Analysis of Circular Plates on Elastic Foundations under Radially Symmetrical Loadings" (Schwartz), xxviii
animal agriculture, 61–66
    climate change, affect on, 61–62, 141

crops, impact on, 77–79, 84
energy use, 64–66
erosion, affect on, 62
hunger, link to, 75–81, 89
rainforest destruction, affect on, 63–64
water use and pollution, 62–63, 65–66, 170
Animal Life in Jewish Tradition (Schochet), 195
Animal Machines (Harrison), 41–42
animal rights, 99–117, 155
    entertainment, animals as, 105–9
    experimentation on animals, 109–12
    Judaism and, 112–15
    skins, use of animal, 99–105, 168, 203–5
    . *See Also* animal welfare; factory farming; tza'ar ba'alei chayim; vegan movement
animal sacrifice, 89, 157–58, 163, 197–201
animal slaughter, 5–8, 43, 64, 88, 154–55
    shechita (ritual slaughter), 3, 6–7, 137–38, 155, 158, 191, 193, 203
    shochtim (ritual slaughterers), 7, 138, 159–60, 191
animal welfare, 33–44, 87–88
    Animal Welfare Fund, 13
    antibiotics, non-therapeutic, 27, 30, 43, 140, 150
    cattle, 37–38, 39, 63, 140, 168

ABOUT THE AUTHOR

RICHARD H. SCHWARTZ, PhD is the author of *Judaism and Vegetarianism* and *Judaism and Global Survival* among many other books and articles. President Emeritus of Jewish Veg and president of the Society of Ethical and Religious Vegetarians, he is professor emeritus at the College of Staten Island, New York. A father, grandfather, and now great-grandfather, he has since 2016 lived with his wife in Israel.

About the Publisher

LANTERN PUBLISHING & MEDIA was founded in 2020 to follow and expand on the legacy of Lantern Books—a publishing company started in 1999 on the principles of living with a greater depth and commitment to the preservation of the natural world. Like its predecessor, Lantern Publishing & Media produces books on animal advocacy, veganism, religion, social justice, and psychology and family therapy. Lantern is dedicated to printing in the United States on recycled paper and saving resources in our day-to-day operations. Our titles are also available as e-books and audiobooks.

To catch up on Lantern's publishing program, visit us at www.lanternpm.org.

 facebook.com/lanternpm
twitter.com/lanternpm
instagram.com/lanternpm